The politics of pleasure
Aesthetics and cultural theory

Ideas and Production

Over recent years the study of the humanities has changed beyond all recognition for many of us. The increasing attention given to theories of interpretation and writing has altered the intellectual circumstances and perspectives of the various disciplines which compose the group. The studies of literature, history, society, politics, gender and philosophy are increasingly finding common ground in shared assumptions about intellectual procedure and method. **Ideas and Production** addresses this common ground.

We are interested in the investigation of the particular historical circumstances which produce the culture of a period or group, and the exploration of conventionally unregarded or understudied work. We are also interested in the relationship of intellectual movements to institutions, and the technological and economic means of their production. It is through the study of the circumstances and conditions in which ideas are realised that the humanities can develop fresh approaches in a period of rapid and exciting social and intellectual change.

As thought and learning become increasingly international and older political and intellectual structures give way, **Ideas and Production** is concerned to investigate new intellectual horizons from the perspective of competing theories and methods, and through the rethinking of old or settled definitions.

Ideas and Production welcomes the potential of debate and intervention, as well as the careful study of materials. The series is aimed at the student, teacher and general reader and encourages clarity and directness in argument, language and method.

Edward J. Esche, Penelope Kenrick,
Rick Rylance, Nigel Wheale

The politics of pleasure

Aesthetics and cultural theory

Edited by Stephen Regan

Open University Press
Buckingham · Philadelphia

Ideas and Production is published by
Open University Press in collaboration with
Anglia Polytechnic University

Open University Press
Celtic Court, 22 Ballmoor
Buckingham MK18 1XW

and
1900 Frost Road, Suite 101
Bristol, PA 19007, USA

First published 1992

A catalogue record of this book is available from the British Library

Library of Congress Cataloging-in-Publication Data

The Politics of pleasure/edited by Stephen Regan.
     p.   cm. — (Ideas and production)
  ISBN 0–335–09759–6 (pb)
  1. Aesthetics.   I. Regan, Stephen.   II. Series.
  BH39.P628   1992
  111′.85 — dc20   92–19298 CIP

Typeset by Type Study, Scarborough
Printed in Great Britain by St Edmundsbury Press,
Bury St Edmunds, Suffolk

Contents

Contributors

Michèle Barrett is Professor of Sociology at City University, London. She is the author of *The Politics of Truth: From Marx to Foucault* (1991), *Women's Oppression Today* (1980/1988), co-author with Mary McIntosh of *The Anti-social Family* (1982/1991), and has written and edited other books and papers. Her most recent publication is *Destabilizing Theory: Contemporary Feminist Debates* (1992), co-edited with Anne Phillips. At City University she is Head of the Sociology Division in the Department of Social Sciences and Director of the Centre for Research on Gender, Ethnicity and Social Change.

Laurel Brake is Lecturer in Literature at the Centre for Extra-Mural Studies, Birkbeck College, London. For many years she was Editor of *The Year's Work in English Studies* and remains a contributor to the volume's Victorian literature section. She is the author of *The Special Art of the Modern World*, a study of Victorian prose, and is currently writing a biography of Walter Pater for Oxford University Press.

Steven Connor is Reader in Modern English Literature and Director of the Centre for Interdisciplinary Research in Culture and the Humanities at Birkbeck College, London. He is the author of *Charles Dickens* (1985), *Samuel Beckett: Repetition, Theory and Text* (1988), and *Postmodernist Culture* (1989). His most recent publication is *Theory and Cultural Value* (1992), a study of the ethics and aesthetics of contemporary theory.

Terry Eagleton is Warton Professor of English at Oxford University. He is the author of *Marxism and Literary Criticism* (1976),

Criticism and Ideology (1976), *Walter Benjamin* (1981), *Literary Theory: An Introduction* (1983), *The Function of Criticism* (1984) and *Against the Grain* (1986). His most recent publications include *The Ideology of the Aesthetic* (1990) and *Ideology: An Introduction* (1991).

Robin Jarvis is Senior Lecturer in Literary Studies at the University of the West of England, Bristol. He is the author of *Wordsworth, Milton and the Theory of Poetic Relations* (1991) and co-editor of *Reviewing Romanticism* (1992). He is currently working on a study of Romantic pedestrianism.

Adrian Page is a Principal Lecturer in the School of English and Communication Studies at Luton College of Higher Education. He has written several articles on literary theory and is the editor of *The Death of the Playwright? Modern British Drama and Literary Theory* (1992).

Stephen Regan is Tutor in Literature at Ruskin College, Oxford. He is Associate Editor of *The Year's Work in English Studies* and the author of a book on Philip Larkin. His introduction to the work of Raymond Williams is forthcoming.

Rebecca Stott is a Lecturer in the School of English at the University of Leeds. She is the author of *The Fabrication of the Late Victorian Femme Fatale* (1992) and articles on Thomas Hardy, George Egerton and Rider Haggard. She is currently editing a collection of essays which examine the interaction of art and literature.

Geoff Wade is a former student of Ruskin College, Oxford. He has published several articles and reviews on critical theory, post-modernism and literary studies. He has recently been teaching English in Greece.

Patricia Waugh is Lecturer in the School of English at the University of Durham. She is the author of *Metafiction: The Theory and Practice of Self-Conscious Fiction* (1984) and *Feminine Fictions: Revisiting the Postmodern* (1989). She is also co-editor (with Philip Rice) of *Modern Literary Theory: A Reader* (1989), recently published in its second edition. She is currently writing a book on modernist and postmodernist aesthetics.

Cover illustration by Adam Hoy, cover design by Will Hill.

Text illustrations

Acknowledgements

The editors acknowledge the help of the following individuals and organizations who have assisted in the production of *The Politics of Pleasure: Aesthetics and Cultural Theory*: Mike Salmon, Tom Allcock, Steve Marshall of Anglia Polytechnic University, and John Skelton and Sue Hadden of the Open University Press for their material support in establishing Ideas and Production as a Series; Ian Gordon, Head of the Department of Arts and Letters, Anglia Polytechnic University, for his consistent support for the project; Nicky Morland, Chris Coward, Christine Northrop-Clewes, Clare Langdon, and Jill Blackwell of Computer Services, Anglia Polytechnic University, Cambridge for invaluable help in the production process; Andrea Bassil, Clive Bray, John Elstone and the BTEC HND Illustration students, Department of Art and Letters, for their enthusiastic participation in production of the volume.

The editor and publishers of this volume would like to make the following additional acknowledgements:

Terry Eagleton, 'The Ideology of the Aesthetic', *Poetics Today*, 9:2. Copyright 1988, Duke University Press, Durham, NC. Reprinted by permission. Steven Connor's 'Aesthetics, Pleasure and Value' appears by permission of the author and Blackwell Publishers and is taken from *Theory and Cultural Value* (1992). Michèle Barrett's 'Max Raphael and the Question of Aesthetics' is reprinted by permission of the editors of *New Left Review*, in which it first appeared.

Stephen Regan wishes to thank the editors of the Ideas and

Production series – Ed Esche, Penelope Kenrick, Rick Rylance and Nigel Wheale – for their extensive work on the volume and for their generous encouragement, advice and support. Thanks are also due to Helen Ruth Cockin for her valuable assistance in preparing the typescript for publication.

1

Introduction: The return of the aesthetic

Stephen Regan

An article in the 1991 volume of the *Oxford Art Journal* boldly announces 'The Return of the Aesthetic'. The title is of some significance because it implicitly acknowledges the extent to which the study of aesthetics has been marginalized or simply ignored in the later twentieth century. For too long the idea of aesthetics has been synonymous in many minds with a bloodless formalism, a rarefied academic discourse of minimal social relevance and application. It was perhaps from a desire to liberate aesthetics from this narrow and specialized reserve that critics of art and literature began to use the word both loosely and indulgently. In the past twenty or thirty years, especially, 'aesthetics' has become a shorthand term for distinguishing one set of stylistic and structural principles from another. It is now common practice to talk about the aesthetics of the modern novel or the aesthetics of modern poetry, in a way that diminishes the potential range and complexity of the idea.

What 'the return of the aesthetic' signifies is a revival of interest in a more disciplined and theoretical use of the term. There is a common perception among scholars in arts and humanities subjects that the powerful new methodologies of the 1970s and 1980s, particularly those imported from psychoanalysis and deconstruction, severely challenged and displaced traditional ideals of harmony, regularity and organic unity, but failed to offer a satisfactory account of what constitutes 'value'. It is within this uncertain realm of cultural value that the aesthetic has been reactivated and redefined. The article already alluded to – 'The

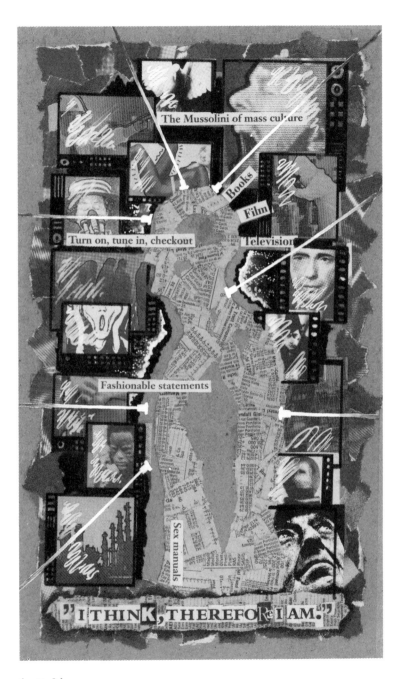

Anette Isberg

Return of the Aesthetic' – is a review of Terry Eagleton's recent book, *The Ideology of the Aesthetic*, an ambitious and inspired attempt to understand the significance of the aesthetic in relation to social and political change, but also to recover the aesthetic as a valid and valuable area of enquiry in modern culture. It is fitting that Terry Eagleton's work should be represented in this volume in an essay which argues succinctly and suggestively for a radical reappraisal of aesthetics.

In Terry Eagleton's estimation, it is precisely the versatility of the term 'aesthetics' that has allowed it to play a covert but powerful role in social and political developments. With its connotations of 'freedom', 'autonomy' and 'spontaneity', the aesthetic conveniently served the interests of the early European bourgeoisie in its struggle for political dominance. In this respect, the aesthetic came to represent an idealized form of value beyond the actual values of competitiveness, exploitation and possessiveness – a realm of order and harmony that an emerging social class could look to for its own ratification. Within this hegemonic process, the aesthetic also plays a significant role in creating a new ideal of human subjectivity and identity. Here, the aesthetic is 'no more than a name for the political unconscious', a way of ensuring social control through effective regulation of human passion, imagination and sensuality. In eighteenth-century England, for instance, debates about 'beauty' were equally debates about civilized conduct, with 'manners' serving as a hinge between aesthetics and ethics. In this opening essay, then, there is no doubt that politics and aesthetics are deeply at one.

Like Terry Eagleton, Michèle Barrett seeks to restore the aesthetic to a prominent position in critical theory and likewise insists that questions of pleasure and value are central, not marginal, to any radical cultural politics. Her remark that an interest in aesthetics is likely to be regarded not just as unfashionable but as 'politically reprehensible' is certainly evident in Tony Bennett's fiercely polemical article, 'Really Useless "Knowledge": A Political Critique of Aesthetics', first published in the journal *Literature and History* (Bennett 1987) and recently reprinted in his *Outside Literature* (1990). Taking up the question posed by Bertolt Brecht in 1927 – 'Shouldn't we abolish aesthetics?' – Bennett complains that the history of philosophical aesthetics has only served as a distraction from more committed and worthwhile endeavours and ought to have been 'written off' long ago. His article takes a dim view of what it regards as an unproductive tension between the historical, materialist impetus of Marxist thought and the ahistorical, idealist pull of aesthetics.

For Michèle Barrett, however, the challenge facing Marxist cultural theory is not to abandon 'the aesthetic' but to construct a convincing and comprehensive *materialist aesthetics*. Part one of her essay clears the ground for the essential work by confronting a range of serious political and theoretical problems, including questions of ideology, signification and representation, which have often served to inhibit or displace aesthetic considerations in recent Marxist and structuralist thinking. Part two of her essay introduces the little-known and undervalued work of the Marxist art historian, Max Raphael (1889–1952). Referring to specific art works such as Picasso's *Guernica* and the two versions of *The Last Supper* by Leonardo da Vinci and Tintoretto, the essay considers both the achievements and limitations of Raphael's methods, and concludes that we have still not satisfactorily resolved the age-old problem of relating 'form' and 'meaning'. If Cultural Studies is to advance its arguments about 'the production of meaning', it must somehow move beyond its current preoccupation with 'signification' and reconsider the role of 'the senses'.

As will be clear from the diverse approaches adopted by contributors, the purpose of this volume is not to offer its readers a single or uniform concept of 'aesthetics'. There is no attempt to define the legitimate scope of aesthetics and no attempt to propose a new definition of beauty. The essays collected here are concerned less with the science of aesthetics and its abstract terms than with the particular function and significance with which the idea of aesthetics is invested at certain moments of social and cultural change. What these essays share is an interest in the various uses of aesthetics and a preoccupation with the changing nature and meaning of aesthetic value.

The closing decades of the twentieth century have witnessed a widespread revival of interest in modernism, and there have been many attempts to distinguish modernist from postmodernist aesthetics. The essays in this book are, in part, a response to that particular critical juncture. Nevertheless, many of these essays continue to raise questions about fundamental aesthetic concepts and ask what relevance, if any, might still be attached to 'pleasure', 'emotion' and 'sensation' in modern cultural theory. Contributors have tried, whenever possible, to ground their arguments in specific cultural practices, though writing and painting are given more extensive treatment than music and film. Many different theoretical perspectives are brought to bear on the idea of aesthetics, and if this volume does not succeed in clarifying the idea it nevertheless gives ample recognition to its valency and resilience as one of the key concepts of modern culture.

An abiding concern with the related values of beauty and truth can be traced back through European Romanticism and Renaissance culture to Plato and early Greek philosophy. Most commentators, however, would agree that the word 'aesthetic', while having its root in the Greek *aisthesis* (pertaining to sense perception), does not receive extensive or systematic use until its appearance in Alexander Baumgarten's *Aesthetica*, published in Germany in 1750. The intellectual legacy of German aesthetics carried forward by Kant, Hegel, Schopenhauer and Nietzsche lends a certain neatness and continuity to histories of European philosophy, against which British aesthetics might well appear a minor and derivative current of thought. Too little attention, however, has been given to the impact of aesthetics in Britain in the eighteenth and nineteenth centuries.

A good starting point for a study of aesthetics in Britian, albeit a seemingly delayed event, is the appearance of 'Aesthetics' as an entry in the ninth edition of *Encyclopaedia Britannica* in 1875. 'Aesthetics' replaced the entry for 'Beauty' which Lord Francis Jeffrey had contributed since the sixth edition of *Encyclopaedia Britannica* in 1824. Jeffrey's theory of beauty had widely pub- licized the associationist ideas of Archibald Alison's *Essays on the Nature and Principles of Taste* (1790), proposing that 'beauty is not an inherent property or quality of objects at all, but the result of the accidental relations in which they may stand to our experi- ence of pleasures or emotions'. The new entry for 'Aesthetics' clearly shows the impact of German philosophy in Britain in the later nineteenth century, especially in the emphasis it gives to beauty as 'the supreme aim of all sensuous knowledge':

> The word aesthetic, in its original Greek form, means anything that has to do with perception by the senses, and this wider connotation was retained by Kant, who, under the title Transcendental Aesthetic, treats of the a priori principles of all sensuous knowledge. The limitation of the term to the comparatively narrow class of sensations and

perceptions occupied with the beautiful and its allied properties is due to the Germans, and primarily to Baumgarten,
who started from the supposition that, just as truth is the end
and perfection of pure knowledge or the understanding, and
good that of the will, so beauty must be the supreme aim of
all sensuous knowledge.

At the same time, however, this entry reveals a profound
dilemma in late Victorian aesthetics. The analysis of the beautiful,
it claims, has been separated into two distinct modes of interpretation: the scientific and the metaphysical. The advocates of
modern science 'no longer discuss the essence of beauty, looked
on as a transcendental conception above all experience, but seek
to determine in what the Beautiful, as a series of phenomena,
clearly and visibly consists'. In contrast, metaphysical speculation on the nature of beauty continues to be concerned with the
realization of an absolute idea.

This problem of reconciling the scientific and the metaphysical,
or the concrete and the abstract, shaped and characterized the
debate about aesthetics in the later nineteenth century, and it
appears to have presented British aestheticians with profound
difficulties. One plausible explanation of the dilemma is that
Victorian writers and critics were deeply anxious about the new
emphasis being given to 'sensuousness' in aesthetic theory.
There is a note of caution and reservation, for instance, in
Bernard Bosanquet's 1886 translation of the Introduction to
Hegel's *Philosophy of Fine Art*. Bosanquet acknowledges Hegel's
attempt to reconcile the claims of metaphysics and science, to
effect a synthesis of the idea and its sensuous medium, but seems
unduly sensitive in pointing out that what Hegel's philosophy
affords is 'a new contact with spiritual life' (Bosanquet 1886:
xiv–x). The same dilemma is evident in the work of E.S. Dallas
and D.R. Hay, both of whom contributed to the work of the
Aesthetic Society in its hapless attempt to found 'a universal
science of beauty'.

For Walter Pater and his disciples, among them Oscar Wilde,
Hegelian aesthetics helped to sustain a theory of art in which
sensuous pleasure was unashamedly promoted. Pater's famous
'Preface' to his *Studies in the History of the Renaissance* (1873) is
perhaps best understood in terms of a relatively new concern
with 'aesthetics' and a corresponding impatience with older
methods of defining beauty: 'Many attempts have been made by

writers on art and poetry to define beauty in the abstract, to express it in the most general terms, to find a universal formula for it' (Pater 1873: 15). It is here that Pater advocates the method of 'aesthetic criticism', based not on 'unprofitable' metaphysical speculation but on the careful appreciation of 'pleasurable sensations'. It is for this reason, perhaps, that Harold Bloom claims 'We owe to Pater our characteristic modern use of "aesthetic", for he emancipated the word from its bondage to philosophy' (Bloom 1974: viii).

It was undoubtedly Pater's insistence on defining beauty 'in the most concrete terms possible' that facilitated the slippage from aesthetics to aestheticism in the closing decades of the nineteenth century. Once again, the key word was 'sensuousness'. John Addington Symonds, whose notions of art and beauty had much in common with those of Walter Pater, identified the Greeks as 'an aesthetic nation', referring to their pure and undistracted contemplation of sensuous, physical beauty. In his *Studies of the Greek Poets* (1873) Symonds compared the Greek ideal of beauty with the aesthetic uncertainties of the modern age, implicitly revealing his admiration for Hellenism. Symonds complained that 'we too often attempt to import the alien elements of metaphysical dogmatism and moral prejudice into the sphere of beauty' (Symonds 1873: 416), a concern which was echoed loudly by Oscar Wilde as a fundamental precept of aestheticism. Significantly, Wilde was to refer to aestheticism as 'the new Hellenism' (Wilde 1908: 335). Wilde would also have understood the sentiments Symonds confessed in a letter of July 1892: 'I love beauty above virtue, and think that nowhere is beauty more eminent than in young men. This love is what people call aesthetic with me' (Schueller and Peters 1969: 711).

It is perhaps understandable, then, that aesthetics should have modulated into aestheticism. As Terry Eagleton argues in his contribution to this volume, the aesthetic was born as a discourse of the body and the senses. In Victorian Britain such a discourse was likely to be treated with suspicion and contempt, especially in those instances where sensuousness began to look like sensuality. John Ruskin consistently interpreted 'aesthetic' as 'sensual' rather than 'sensuous', and the manuscripts of *Modern Painters* suggest that he had originally devised a chapter on 'Sensual Beauty' to serve as a warning to his readers. In the second volume of *Modern Painters* Ruskin carefully distingushes between the theoretic and the aesthetic faculties of perception,

associating one with the 'exulting, reverent and grateful' acknowledgement of beauty, and the other with 'mere animal
consciousness' (Ruskin 1903–12: 47). When the first manifestations of aestheticism appeared in late Victorian Britain, Ruskin
chose the occasion of his 1883 edition of *Modern Painters* to
express his moral disapproval for a movement which had made
art 'at once the corruption, and the jest, of the vulgar world'
(Ruskin 1903–12: 35).

The status and function of aesthetics in the nineteenth century
were clearly unstable, and therefore subject to all kinds of
appropriation and misrepresentation. Laurel Brake's essay
shows how the aesthetic, although conventionally regarded as
the sphere of transcendental value, was perpetually and deeply
implicated in material and economic considerations. Concentrat-
ing on Walter Pater's *Appreciations* (1889), a work which in many
ways typifies the 'aesthetic criticism' of the late nineteenth
century, the essay argues that aesthetic and stylistic preferences
were frequently shaped by prevailing moral standards. To
'appreciate' the aesthetic pronouncements in Pater's work, we
need to understand their complex interaction with contemporaneous debates on censorship, national identity and sexual
politics. The techniques of cultural materialism are employed
very effectively in this essay to reveal how aesthetic value, far
from being timeless and universal, is contingent on social and
historical change.

After the trial of Oscar Wilde in 1895, the association of
aesthetics with aestheticism was handled discreetly, and it was
some time before the study of aesthetics recovered its mo-
mentum. It was with the emergence of 'modernism' as a
powerful cultural phenomenon that aesthetics came back into
play. As Rebecca Stott argues in her essay, '"Intimate Relations":
Aesthetic Revelations from Cézanne to Woolf', the unusual
convergence of the arts at the turn of the nineteenth century
helped to foster a new system of aesthetics that might promote
the shared interests of writing, sculpture and painting. The turn
is evident in those manifestoes of modern fiction – Joseph
Conrad's Preface to *Nigger of the Narcissus*, for instance, or Henry
James's essay on 'The Art of Modern Fiction' – which establish a
formal correspondence between writing and the visual arts.
Wilde had established a precedent for painterly novels in *The
Picture of Dorian Gray*, and the example is borne out in the titles of
two prominent modern novels, *The Portrait of a Lady* and *A*

Portrait of the Artist as a Young Man, both of which are intensely concerned with the consequences of an aesthetic lifestyle, of treating life in the spirit of art. In showing the young Stephen Dedalus attempting to 'fly by the nets of language, nationality and religion', Joyce's novel raises uncomfortable questions about the extent to which the artist can ever completely abrogate the demands of his place and time. Modern readings of Joyce rarely do justice to the comic and satirical dimensions of Stephen's attempt to construct an aesthetic theory which will somehow lift him free of Ireland.

It was in the work of the Bloomsbury group, however, that the most determined effort to establish a new system of aesthetics took place. Rebecca Stott argues that the aesthetic ideals of Roger Fry and Clive Bell were derived from an English tradition that included the writings of John Ruskin and Walter Pater, but were also formulated in close response to the modern experimental arts elsewhere in Europe, especially the post-impressionist paintings of Cézanne and his contemporaries. Bell's *Art* and Fry's *Vision and Design* ambitiously seek the 'Truth' of 'great art' and yet, as Rebecca Stott quietly reveals in her essay, their shared artistic project was conducted amidst the turmoil of 1914–18 and gathers its solemnity and urgency from that particular historical moment. The importance of Rebecca Stott's essay is that it reconsiders the writings of Virginia Woolf in relation to the modernist aesthetics of Bell and Fry; it avoids any simplifying account of 'influence' and concentrates instead on explaining and explicating Woolf's own frustrated preoccupation with 'vision' and 'design'.

Geoff Wade's discussion of Marxism and modernist aesthetics usefully complements Rebecca Stott's essay by looking at the reception of modernism in the Soviet Union and Eastern Europe in the middle years of the twentieth century. The central dilemma in Marxist aesthetic theory had to do with the nature and function of modern cultural practice under the debilitating conditions of monopoly capitalism. Germany once again provided some of the most subtle and engaging aesthetic concepts and the intellectual forum established by Georg Lukács, Bertolt Brecht, Theodor Adorno and Walter Benjamin occupied a powerful position from the 1930s to the 1950s. It was within this forum that writers and critics debated the problems of modern art: the meaning of 'artistic autonomy', the future of realism, the definition of 'popular culture', the impact of communications technology and the relationship between 'avant-garde' and 'commercial' art. Geoff Wade concentrates on the fierce exchange of ideas between Lukács and Adorno, highlighting Lukács's aversion to experimental modernism and Adorno's contrary belief that modernism was the most 'authentic' political art. The essay is salutary reading for anyone who might have assumed that Marxist aesthetic theory was a monolithic and homogeneous body of thought. While defending Adorno's cultural ideals, the essay shows how the debate to which he contributed retains its significance and continues to illuminate the modernist works of Franz Kafka, Samuel Beckett and others.

Within Marxist theory, 'writing' or 'literature' was one of the obvious sites of aesthetic enquiry. The years which witnessed the remarkably fertile exchanges between Lukács and Adorno, however, were also those in which 'English' was established as a discipline in colleges and universities. One of the consequences of this institutional development was the displacement of 'aesthetics' from 'literary criticism'. In English universities there was a tendency to disown the effete 'aesthetic criticism' associated with Pater and Wilde, and to accept instead the more rigorous and robust 'practical criticism' pioneered by I.A. Richards. In his *Principles of Literary Criticism* (1924) Richards dismisses the idea of 'aesthetic emotion' proposed by Roger Fry and Clive Bell on the grounds that 'aesthetic experience' cannot be abstracted as a peculiar and unique 'value' from other kinds of experience. Richards argues that attempts to analyse and define beauty are fraught with confusion and can only hinder the work of the literary critic. Rather than attempting to broaden the scope of 'aesthetics', he sends it packing with 'that paralysing apparition Beauty' (Richards 1924: 6, 12).

Like Richards, F.R. Leavis upheld the ideal of sensuous, immediate language as the object of criticism and yet distrusted aesthetics. It seems that Leavis associated aesthetics with conventional 'taste' or accepted values and was unwilling to risk any compromise with the fine immediacy of response that underpinned his theory of criticism. As Michael Bell points out, Leavis 'often remarked, in dismissive asides, that the term "aesthetic" is best avoided in criticism' (Bell 1988: 82). It is likely, too, that Leavis came to regard the word 'aesthetic' as fundamentally opposed to 'moral', and therefore of little value to his own rigorously discriminating criticism. Reviewing a new edition of *The Poems of Alexander Pope* in *Scrutiny* in 1944, Leavis remarked that '"Aesthetic" is a term the literary critic would do well to deny himself' (Leavis 1944: 75).

British 'common sense' left little space for new developments in aesthetic theory (it was, after all, a continental fashion), and when the word 'aesthetic' appeared in cultural manifestoes after 1945, it was often given a negative set of associations. Aesthetic concerns seemed antithetical to the practical needs of post-war reconstruction. Raymond Williams, taking his cue from both Marx and Leavis, attempted to understand this abstraction of 'the aesthetic' from other human activities in his formidable *Culture and Society 1780–1950* (1958), one of the most influential works of cultural theory in the post-war years. Williams identifies *aesthetic* as part of a nexus of words – *industry, democracy, class, art* and *culture* – which underwent radical redefinition in the course of the nineteenth century. In response to changes in industry and accompanying changes in social and economic relationships, the word *art* became increasingly specialized and signified not just 'skill' but 'creative' or 'imaginative' activity. In this way, art served as the embodiment of 'certain human values, capacities, energies, which the development of society towards an industrial society was felt to be threatening or even destroying' (Williams 1979: 53). The word 'aesthetics' was formulated in response to the growing specialization of 'art'. The positive consequence of these related shifts in meaning and value was that the idea of 'art' as 'a superior reality' provided an important criticism of industrialism, but the negative consequence was that art became not just specialized but isolated, and so risked losing its dynamic function. Williams clearly sees 'culture', not 'aesthetics', as the place where divisions between art and society (essentially divisions of *labour*) might be overcome.

The word 'aesthetic', however, retains its currency for Williams and is given renewed significance as the opening entry in his *Keywords: A Vocabulary of Culture and Society* (1976). Here, Williams is more pointed and explicit about the potentially negative connotations of the aesthetic, especially its association with a realm 'beyond' or 'above' the social:

> It is an element in the divided modern consciousness of art and society: a reference beyond social use and social valuation which, like one special meaning of culture, is intended to express a human dimension which the dominant version of society appears to exclude. The emphasis is

understandable but the isolation is damaging, for there is something irresistibly displaced and marginal about the now common and limiting phrase 'aesthetic considerations', especially when contrasted with practical or utilitarian considerations, which are elements of the same basic division.

(Williams 1976: 28)

In *Marxism and Literature* (1977) Williams repeats his criticism of the aesthetic as 'an isolable extra-social phenomenon', claiming that aesthetic theory has served as an instrument of evasion by removing art and the discourses of art from the social processes of which they are an essential part. Williams responds sympathetically to Jan Mukarovsky's attempt to restore the connection between aesthetics and socio-historical realities in *Aesthetic Function, Norm and Value as Social Facts* (1970), but nevertheless maintains that 'we have to reject "the aesthetic" both as a separate abstract dimension and as a separate abstract function'. In the end, Williams's argument is one about 'value': his objection to 'the aesthetic' rests largely on the belief that it invites a concentration on language and form which takes priority over 'other ways of realizing value and meaning' and assumes 'a privileged indifference to the human process as a whole' (Williams 1977: 156).

Part of Williams's concern is that literary theory has become polarized between a belief that all literature is ideology and a belief that all literature is aesthetic (one scheme of value competing with another). One of the unexpected developments in literary theory in the 1970s and 1980s, however, was that the aesthetic came to be seen not as the adversary of ideology but as its very embodiment. In the work of Paul de Man the realm of the aesthetic is to be treated with suspicion, not because it eschews political and moral concerns but because it so effectively conceals and disguises them. De Man sees aesthetic theory as having provided literary criticism with a simplified model of knowledge and communication in which language functions as the vehicle of direct sensory perception. F.R. Leavis, for instance, while avoiding the term 'aesthetics', nevertheless assumes that language is the 'sensuous enactment' of meaning and that the 'concrete' nature of literary language is a measure of its worth or value. De Man challenges this idea of compatibility between linguistic structures and ethical values.

As Christopher Norris has argued, de Man's opposition to the idea of aesthetics inevitably raises questions of 'value' since it challenges a fundamental assumption in English Studies (clearly evident in the writings of F.R. Leavis) that the value of 'literary language' resides in its 'power to communicate sensory perceptions as if by a species of phenomenal enactment' (see the Editor's Foreword to Bell 1988: xii). De Man sees this doctrine – the belief that literature can afford a special kind of sensuous knowledge – as a burden that aesthetic theory has had to carry since Kant's *Critique of Judgement*. One of the main functions of literary theory, in de Man's estimation, should be to question whether there can be any simple or natural relationship between aesthetic values and linguistic structures. In his severe dismissal of aesthetic ideology, however, de Man perhaps overlooked some of the more positive and progressive tendencies in the history of aesthetics.

In his contribution to this volume Robin Jarvis gives an intriguing and illuminating account of Paul de Man's career, explaining why de Man 'assumed an unnecessary hostile stance towards aesthetics'. De Man's earliest writings are based on a careful separation of the aesthetic from the ethical and political realms and a corresponding belief in 'the autonomy of literature'. These aesthetic arguments, however, subtly adopt the lineaments of a national culture and identity at precisely that moment when European unity is riven by German expansionism. What are presented as aesthetic issues serve to embody a complex collaborationist position in wartime Europe. The ideals of harmony, unity, reciprocity and complementarity have serious political counterparts in occupied France, which de Man (working for the Belgian newspaper *Le Soir*) could not have failed to notice. Robin Jarvis argues persuasively that the critic of aesthetics, whose principal target became 'the insidious aestheticising of politics and nationhood', was himself an early practitioner of that same 'aesthetic ideology' in his wartime writings. For de Man, 'the return of the aesthetic' was a return of a peculiarly intense and politically compromising kind.

Adrian Page offers a searching analysis of the complex set of relations between aesthetic theory and literary criticism, and considers the resulting problems of 'value'. Is it possible, he asks, to arrive at some sufficiently broad definition of 'literary art' which might simultaneously establish 'the object of study' and clarify the purpose of 'criticism'? His essay ranges widely across the dilemmas and debates that have preoccupied literary critics in the twentieth century, from T.S. Eliot to Terry Eagleton, and from F.R. Leavis to David Lodge. In trying to establish common ground between aesthetic theory and literary theory, the essay turns to modern linguistics and in particular to the concept of 'defamiliarisation'. Applying the ideas of Viktor Shklovsky and others to the poems of Craig Raine and Seamus Heaney, the essay proceeds to argue that 'defamiliarisation' can be used not just to encourage a fresh and more receptive understanding of 'literature' but to reinstate a concept of value based on social function. Notwithstanding Christopher Norris's cautionary remarks about language and sense activity, Adrian Page finds much of value in the idea of literature as a cultural practice which can radically alter 'perception'. What he proposes, then, is a socio-poetics of literature rather than an aesthetics of art in general.

Patricia Waugh's essay is a formidable contribution to the contemporary critical debate on modernism and postmodernism. While one 'ism' might be regarded as a repudiation of the other, there are clearly significant connections and continuities between them. The modern and the postmodern have together constituted a powerful critique of 'truth' and 'reason', and a continuing dissolution of traditional aesthetic ideals. At the same time, though, much of the theory of modernism and postmodernism, including new models of selfhood and subjectivity, has had a dubious relevance for feminist writers and critics. Some uncomfortable questions have to be asked. In short, is it possible for feminists to draw on the aesthetics of postmodernism without embracing its nihilistic vision and thereby fatally undermining their own emancipatory politics? As well as exploring the structural procedures of American postmodernist fiction, Patricia Waugh argues positively and optimistically that women writers are already using the formal modes of postmodern art to create an imaginative world very different from the apocalyptic vision that is often associated with postmodernism.

Steven Connor's essay forms a fitting conclusion to the volume by considering the ways in which aesthetics can continue to play a vital role in discussions of art and culture, providing a congenial space beyond the rigidities and restrictions that have often inhibited contemporary literary theory. For Steven Connor, the return of the aesthetic is very much a return of the repressed: a reappraisal of half-forgotten concepts like 'the sublime', and a new willingness and determination to confront 'the difficult problem of pleasure'. His essay looks at 'the complex exchanges between pleasure and value' in modern cultural theory, both in the early twentieth-century writings of Roger Fry and I.A. Richards and in the later psychological and linguistic explorations of Roland Barthes and Jacques Lacan. There is, throughout these theoretical texts, an interesting bifurcation between 'the disapproval of pleasure on the one hand and the assertion that pleasure is all on the other'. The essay relates this split to a more fundamental division between the hedonist view that sees pleasure and value as identical, and the moralist view that regards pleasure and value as distinct and separate. This binary approach is seen to constitute 'a ruthless logical shrinkage' in modern theory, which must be met with a more productive and fruitful account of pleasure. By drawing on a tradition of Marxist aesthetics that includes 'the pleasure industry' in the writings of Theodor Adorno and Max Horkheimer, 'the carnivalesque' in the work of Mikhail Bakhtin and theories of ideology in statements by Terry Eagleton and Fredric Jameson, Steven Connor proposes a new political awareness of pleasure that might resist the temptation to reduce the work of art to either pure pleasure or pure value. What this closing essay anticipates is a new and significant role for aesthetics. Together, the essays in this volume endorse the return of the aesthetic, not in some enfeebled academic condition but in the enlarged form of a politics of culture.

References

Bell, Michael (1988). *F.R. Leavis*. London: Routledge.

Bennett, Tony (1987). 'Really Useless "Knowledge": A Political Critique of Aesthetics', *Literature and History*, 13, 38–57.

Bloom, Harold (ed.) (1974). *Selected Writings of Walter Pater*. New York: New American Library.

Bosanquet, Bernard (1886). *The Introduction to Hegel's Philosophy of Fine Art*. London: Kegan Paul, Trench and Co.

Eagleton, Terry (1990). *The Ideology of the Aesthetic*. Oxford, Blackwell.

Leavis, F.R. (1944). Review of James Sutherland's edition of *The Poems of Alexander Pope, Scrutiny*, XII, I, 75.

Pater, Walter (1873). *Studies in the History of the Renaissance*. London, Macmillan.

Richards, I.A. (1924). *Principles of Literary Criticism*. London, Routledge and Kegan Paul.

Ruskin, John (1903–12). *Works*, Volume IV, E.T. Cook and Alexander Wedderburn (eds). London, George Allen.

Schueller, H.M. and Peters, R.L. (eds) (1969). *The Letters of John Addington Symonds*, Volume III. Detroit, Wayne State University Press.

Symonds, John Addington (1873). *Studies of the Greek Poets*. London, Smith, Elder and Co.

Wilde, Oscar (1908). *Works*, Volume VIII, (ed.) Robert Ross. London, Methuen.

Williams, Raymond (1976). *Keywords: A Vocabulary of Culture and Society*. London, Fontana.

Williams, Raymond (1977). *Marxism and Literature*. Oxford, Oxford University Press.

Williams, Raymond (1979). *Culture and Society 1780–1950*. Harmondsworth: Penguin.

2

The ideology of the aesthetic

Terry Eagleton

The concept of interpretation, as we know it today, perhaps dates back no further than the nineteenth century. This, in my view, is not going back far enough, in any discussion of the relations of criticism and power. For before 'interpretation' in its modern hermeneutical sense was brought to birth, a whole apparatus of power in the field of culture was already firmly in place and had been for about a century. This was not an apparatus which determined the power-effects of particular readings but one which determined the political meaning and function of 'culture' as such. Its name was and is aesthetics; and part of my argument in this paper will be that it is effectively synonymous with a shift in the very concept of power, which we can characterize as a transition to the notion of hegemony. 'Interpretation' might seem a broader, more generous concept than the aesthetic, traversing as it does the border between 'artistic' and other texts; but it will also be part of my argument that the 'aesthetic', at least in its original formulations, has little enough to do with art. It denotes instead a whole programme of social, psychical and political reconstruction on the part of the early European bourgeoisie, and it is to an examination of some of the elements of that programme I now want to turn.

Aesthetics is born as a discourse of the body. The vital distinction which the term signifies for its inventor, Alexander Baumgarten, is not between art and life but between the material and the immaterial: between things and thoughts, sensations and ideas, what is bound up with our creaturely life of perception as opposed to what belongs to the mind. It is as though philosophy suddenly wakes up to the fact that there is a dense,

Andrew Lambert

swarming territory beyond its own mental enclave, threatening to fall utterly outside its sway. That territory is nothing less than the whole of our sensate life – the business of affections and aversions, of how the world strikes the body on its sensory surfaces, of what takes root in the guts and the gaze and all that arises from our most banal, biological insertion into the world. The aesthetic is thus the first stirrings of a primitive, incipient materialism, politically quite indispensable: for how can everything that belongs to a society's somatic, sensational life – 'experience', in a word – be allowed to fall outside the circuit of its reason? Must the life of the body be given up on, as the sheer unthinkable other of thought, or are its mysterious ways somehow mappable by intellection in what would then prove a wholly novel science, that of sensibility itself? Doesn't Enlightenment rationality need some kind of supplement – some concrete logic at its disposal which would chart from the inside the very structures of breathing, sentient life?

For Baumgarten, aesthetic cognition mediates between the generalities of reason and the particulars of sense; the aesthetic partakes in the perfection of reason but in a 'confused' mode. Aesthetics is thus the 'sister' of logic, a kind of inferior feminine analogue of reason, at the level of material life. As a kind of concrete thought or sensuous analogue of the concept, it partakes at once of the rational and the real, suspended between the two in the manner of the Lévi-Straussian myth. Only by such a concrete logic will the ruling class be able to understand its own history; for history, like the body, is a matter of sensuous particulars, in no sense merely derivable from rational principles.

Dominion over all inferior powers, Baumgarten writes, belongs to reason; but such dominion, he warns, must never degenerate into simple tyranny. The aesthetic, in other words, marks an historic shift from what we might now, in Gramscian terms, call coercion to hegemony, ruling and informing our sensuous life from within while allowing it to thrive in all its relative autonomy. Within the dense welter of that life, with all its alarmingly amorphous flux, certain objects stand out in a kind of ideality akin to rational perfection, and this is the beautiful. The major aesthetician of the twentieth century might thus be said to be the later Edmund Husserl, whose phenomenology will seek to disclose the formal, rational structures of the *Lebenswelt* in what he calls a new 'universal science of subjectivity'. (It was not, however, new in the least.)

Schiller's project the *Aesthetic Education of Man* is similarly to soften up Kant's imperious tyranny of reason in the direction of social hegemony. For if reason is simply at war with Nature and the flesh, how is it ever to take root in the body of lived experience? How is theory to become ideology? Reason will only secure its sway in consensual rather than coercive terms: it must collude with the senses it subdues rather than ride roughshod over them. In a movement of deconstruction, the aesthetic breaks the imperious dominion of the sense-drive not by some external dictate but from within, as a fifth columnist working with the grain of what it combats. Humanity, Schiller remarks, must 'take the war against Matter into the very territory of Matter itself'.

It is easier, in other words, for reason to repress sensuous Nature if it has already been busy eroding and subliming it from the inside, and this is the task of the aesthetic. Schiller is shrewd enough to see that Kant's stark imperatives are by no means the best way of subjugating a recalcitrant material world; his Duty, like some paranoid absolutist monarch, puts too little trust in the masses' generous instincts for conformity to it. What is needed instead is what Schiller calls the 'aesthetic modulation of the psyche', which is to say a full-blooded project of fundamental ideological reconstruction.

This programme consists in the installation of what the eighteenth century calls 'manners', which provides the crucial hinge between ethics and aesthetics, virtue and beauty. Manners means that meticulous disciplining of the body which converts morality to style, aestheticizing virtue and so deconstructing the opposition between the proper and the pleasurable. In these regulated forms of civilized conduct, a pervasive aestheticizing of social practices gets under way: moral-ideological imperatives no longer impose themselves with the leaden weight of some Kantian Ought but infiltrate the very textures of lived experience as tact and know-how, intuitive good sense or inbred decorum. Ethical ideology loses its unpleasantly coercive force and re-appears as a principle of spontaneous consensus. The subject itself is accordingly aestheticized: like the work of art, the subject introjects the Law which governs it as the very principle of its free identity, and so, in Althusserian phrase, comes to work 'all by itself', without need of political constraint. That 'lawfulness without a law', which Kant will identify in the aesthetic, is first of all a question of the social *Lebenswelt*, which seems to work with all the rigorous encodement of a rational law but where such law

is never quite abstractable from the sensuously particular conduct which instantiates it. The bourgeoisie has won certain
historic victories within the political state; but the problem with
such conflicts is that, in rendering the Law perceptible as a
discourse, they threaten to denaturalize it. Once the Law is
objectified by political struggle, it becomes itself the subject of
contestation. Legal, political and economic transformations must
therefore be translated into new kinds of spontaneous social
practice, which in a kind of creative repression or amnesia can
afford to forget the very laws they obey. Structures of power must
become structures of feeling, and the name for this mediation
from property to propriety is the aesthetic. If politics and
aesthetics are deeply at one, it is because pleasurable conduct is
the true index of successful social hegemony, self-delight the
very mark of social submission. What matters in aesthetics is not
art but this whole project of reconstructing the human subject
from the inside, informing its subtlest affections and bodily
responses with this law which is not a law. The moment when
moral actions can be classified chiefly as 'agreeable' and 'dis-
agreeable' marks a certain mature point of evolution in the
history of a ruling class. Once the dust and heat of its struggles for
power have subsided, moral questions which were then necessarily cast in stridently absolutist terms may now, as it were,
crystallize spontaneously into that political unconscious we call
the aesthetic. Once new ethical habits have been installed, the
sheer quick feel or impression of an object will be enough for sure
judgement, shortcircuiting discursive labour and thus mystifying
the laws which regulate it. If the aesthetic is every bit as coercive
as the most barbaric law – for there is a right and wrong to taste
quite as absolute as the death sentence – this is not, by any
means, the way it feels. 'It has been the misfortune . . . of this
age', writes Burke in *Reflections on the Revolution in France*, 'that
everything is to be discussed, as if the constitution of our country
was to be always a subject rather of altercation, than enjoyment'
(1969: 188). The true lawfulness-without-law is the English
Constitution, at once ineluctable and unformalizable. And if one
wanted to give a name to the single most important nineteenth-
century instrument of the kind of hegemony in question, one
which never ceases to grasp universal reason in concretely
particular style, uniting within its own depth an economy of
abstract form with the effect of spontaneous experience, one
might do worse than propose the realist novel.

If beauty is a consensual power, then the sublime – that which crushes us into admiring submission – is coercive. The distinction between the beautiful and the sublime is in part one between woman and man, and partly that between what Louis Althusser has called the ideological and repressive state apparatuses. The problem for Burke is how these two are to be reconciled; for the authority we respect we do not love, and the one we love we do not respect. Only love – consent, collusion – will win us to the Law, and this will erode the Law to nothing. A Law which engages, hegemonically, our intimate affections will have the laxness of the mother; one, on the other hand, which inspires in us filial fear will tend to alienate such affection and spur us to oedipal resentment. Casting around desperately for a reconciling image, Burke feebly offers us the grandfather, authoritative yet feebly feminized by age. Authority lives in a kind of ceaseless self-undoing, as coercion and consent reinforce yet undermine one another in a cat-and-mouse game. An ennervated feminine beauty must be regularly stiffened by a masculine sublime, whose terrors must then be instantly defused in an endless rhythm of erection and detumescence. The Law is male, but hegemony is a woman, and the aesthetic would be their felicitous marriage. For Burke, the revolutionaries who seek to 'strip all the decent drapery of life' from political power, and so to de-aestheticize it, are in danger of exposing the phallus of this transvestite law, which decks itself out as a woman. Power will thus cease to be aestheticized, and what will grapple us to it will be less our affections than the gallows. The revolutionaries are protestant extremists who would believe, insanely, that men and women could look on this terrible law and still live, who would strip from it every decent mediation and consoling illusion, break every representational icon and extirp every pious practice, thus leaving the wretched citizen naked and vulnerable before the full sadistic blast of authority.

The problem with the bourgeoisie, as Charles Taylor has well argued, is that their obsession with freedom is incompatible with feeling at home in the world. Bourgeois ideology thus continually violates one of the central functions of ideology in general, which is to make the subject feel that the world is not an altogether inhospitable place. When bourgeois science contemplates the world, what it knows is an impersonal realm of causes and processes quite independent of the subject and so quite indifferent to value. But the fact that we can know the world at all, however grim the news which this cognition has to deliver, must surely entail some primordial harmony between ourselves and it. For there to be knowledge in the first place, however gloomy, our faculties must be somehow marvellously, unpredictably adjusted to material reality; and for Kant it is the contemplation of this pure form of our cognition, of its very enabling conditions, which is the aesthetic. The aesthetic is simply the state in which common knowledge, in the very act of reaching out to its object, suddenly arrests and rounds upon itself, forgetting its referent for a magical moment and attending instead, in a wondering flash of self-estrangement, to the miraculously convenient way in which its inmost structure seems somehow geared to the comprehension of the real. The aesthetic is simply cognition viewed in a different light, caught in the act, so that, in this little crisis or revelatory breakdown of our cognitive routines, not what we know but *that* we know becomes the deepest, most delightful mystery. The aesthetic, as the moment of letting the world go and clinging instead to the formal act of knowing it, promises to re-unite those poles of subject and object, value and fact, reason and nature, which bourgeois social practice has riven apart; and this is to say that for Kant the aesthetic is nothing less than, in a precise Lacanian sense, the Imaginary. The Kantian subject of taste, who misperceives as a quality of the aesthetic representation what is in fact a delightful co-ordination of its own powers and who projects onto a blind, mechanical universe a figure of idealized unity, is in effect the infantile narcissist of the Lacanian mirror phase. If human subjects are to feel themselves sufficiently centred and at home in the Kantian world of pure reason to act as moral agents, there must be somewhere in reality some image of that ethical purposiveness which, in the Kantian realm of practical reason, falls outside of representation altogether and so is not available as a sensuous, which is to say an ideological, force. That image is the aesthetic, in which a mutual mirroring of ego and world is allowed to occur – in which, uniquely, the world is for once given for the subject. This, for a bourgeois practice which continually rips humanity from Nature, thus rendering the subject sickeningly contingent at the very acme of its powers, is an essential ideological register. That it should not, for Kant, domesticate and naturalize the subject too much, thus fatally slackening its dynamic enterprise, is one of the countervailing functions of the sublime (as are the sublime's disciplinary tasks of chastening and humbling this otherwise too inertly complacent subject).

Since the Imaginary of the aesthetic is a matter of universal rather than individual subjectivity, the aesthetic provides a resolution to the tormenting question: where can one locate community in bourgeois society? The problem is that, of the two traditional answers – the state or civil society – neither is adequate. The dilemma of bourgeois civil society is that its very atomizing individualism and competitiveness threatens to destroy the ideological solidarity necessary for its political reproduction. There is, in other words, no longer any obvious way of moving from social practices to culture or, as the philosophers would say, from facts to values. If you derived your values from the market-place, you would end up with all the worst kinds of values; the non-derivability of values from facts in bourgeois society is thus a necessary structural feature of it. Values are indeed related to social practice, but precisely by their contradictory dislocation from it; it is materially necessary that ideological values should be related to social facts in such a way as to appear *non*-derivable from them. At the same time, of course, such a hiatus between practices and values is clearly ideologically disabling. You might thus turn to the state as the locus of ideal unity, as many nineteenth-century thinkers did; but the problem here is that the state is ultimately a coercive power. Solidarity thus needs a third realm, and discovers it in the universal subjectivity of the aesthetic. An intimately interpersonal *Gemeinschaft* is mapped onto a brutally egoistic, appetitive *Gesellschaft*. The aesthetic will secure the consensual hegemony which neither the coercive state nor a fragmented civil society can achieve. Paradoxically, it is in the most apparently frail, private and intangible of our feelings that we blend most harmoniously with one another – at once an astonishingly optimistic and bitterly pessimistic doctrine. On the one hand: 'How marvellous that consensual intersubjectivity can be found installed in the very inwardness of the subject!' On the other hand: 'How sickeningly precarious human unity must be if one can finally root it in nothing more resilient than the vagaries of aesthetic judgement!'

Aesthetic propositions for Kant appear to be constative, descriptions of what is the case, but conceal beneath this surface grammar their essentially performative nature as emotive utterances. In this sense, one might claim, they are the very paradigm of ideological enunciations. Like the Kantian aesthetic utterance, the ideological proposition conceals an essentially emotive (subject-oriented) content within an apparently referential form, characterizing the 'lived relation' of a speaker to the world in appearing to characterize the world. At the same time, however, such judgements, like Kantian taste, are in no sense merely 'subjective'. The rhetorical move which here converts an utterance from the emotive to the referential is a sign of the fact that certain attitudes are at once 'merely subjective' and somehow ineluctable. In this sense, Kantian aesthetics move us a little way towards a materialist conception of ideology. Given the nature of our faculties, Kant thinks, it is necessary that certain subjective judgements elicit the universal consent of others, and this is the aesthetic. Given certain material conditions, it is necessary that certain subjective responses be invested with all the force of universally valid propositions, and this is the ideological. In both the aesthetic and the ideological, subjective and universal coalesce: a viewpoint is at once mine and an utterly subjectless truth, at once constitutive of the very depths of the individual subject and yet a universal law, though a law so self-evidently inscribed in the material phenomena themselves as to be quite untheorizable. In ideology and the aesthetic we stay with the thing itself, preserved in all its concrete materiality rather than dissolved into its abstract conditions; yet this very materiality has all the compelling logic of a universal rational law, appearing as it does like a kind of incarnate maxim. The ideologico-aesthetic is that indeterminate region in which abstractions seem flushed with irreducible specificity and accidental particulars are raised to pseudo-cognitive status. Ideology constantly promises to go beyond the particular to some debatable proposition, but that proposition continually eludes formalization and disappears back into the things themselves. What is from one viewpoint an absolute rightness is from another viewpoint just something I happen to feel: but that 'happen' is *essential*. Aesthetic pleasure cannot be *compelled*; and yet somehow it is, for all that. The ethico-aesthetic subject – the subject of bourgeois hegemony – is the one who, in Kant's phrase, gives the law to itself and who thus lives its necessity as freedom. The pleasures of the aesthetic are in this sense masochistic: as with bourgeois ideology, the delight that matters is our free complicity with what subjects us, so that we can 'work all by ourselves'.

The problem with such freedom, however, at least for Kant, is that it is entirely noumenal. It cannot be *represented*, and is thus at root anti-aesthetic. This is a dilemma which dogs Hegel too. Scornful of aesthetic intuitionism as any kind of metaphysical grounding of bourgeois society, Hegel's theoretical programme signifies an heroic eleventh-hour attempt to redeem that society for theoretical reason. But any such project of rational totalization will be forced into a convoluted discursivity which threatens to limit its ideological effectiveness. The Hegelian system, as Kierkegaard complained more than once, simply cannot be lived; and Hegel is alarmingly cavalier about the necessities of aesthetic representation, in a protestant iconoclastic manner close to Kant's own. Hegel gravely underestimates the ideological force of sensuous representation. The bourgeoisie are thus caught in a cleft stick between a theoretical self-grounding too discursive for representation, and thus ideologically crippled from the outset, and an ideologically seductive aestheticization of reason (Schelling, Fichte) which spurns all rigorous conceptual totalization and leaves the bourgeois social order theoretically disarmed.

Hegel does, however, score some notable advances. For one thing, he spots the idealist feebleness of Kant's aesthetic *Gemeinschaft* and cranks the whole argument down to the institutional level of civil society. Like Gramsci after him, he thus shifts the whole concept of culture away from its aesthetic to its everyday or anthropological sense, rooting his ideal totality in the unpromising institutions of civil society itself, and so like Gramsci effecting a vital transition from *ideology* to *hegemony*. Unlike Kant, Hegel does not commit the naive error of seeking to root spiritual community in anything as hollow and slippery as disinterestedness; on the contrary, the particularism of private property, the family, abstract right and so on will become the very basis of social totality, once they have dialectically transcended their partiality into the unity of the state. The problem with this solution, on the other hand, is that it is merely unbelievable: there is no way the bourgeoisie can anchor ideological harmony in civil society, even if Hegel is right that this is what is *needed*. If political unity is to be derived from the divisions of civil society, an intricately dialectical form of rationality a good deal less blankly portentous than Schellingian intuitionism will be necessary, yet by the same token this rationality will slip through the net of sensuous representation and leave itself ideologically disarmed. Indeed the very form of Hegel's work, of cognition itself, is in a way anti-representational. It is as though the Kantian text is still struggling to handle in 'realist' or representational style that utterly unrepresentable 'thing' which will finally be encircled only by a full-blooded break to philosophical modernism – to the kind of theoretical work which, like the symbolist poem, generates itself entirely out of its own substance, has its tail in its own mouth, projects its referent out of its own formal devices and escapes in its absolute self-groundedness the lightest taint of external determination. In all this, Hegel is at one with Schelling; but unlike Schelling he refuses the supreme concretization of this mode of thought in the work of art itself, which is at least a little more ideologically persuasive than slogans such as 'the rational is the real'.

Where Hegel does marvellously succeed, however, is in reconciling the conflict between the bourgeoisie's drive for freedom and its desire for an expressive unity with the world – for, in a word, the Imaginary. The dilemma of the bourgeois subject is that its freedom and autonomy, of its very essence, put it tragically at odds with Nature, and so cut from beneath its feet any ground by which it might be validated in its being. The more full-bloodedly the subject realizes its free essence, the more alienated and contingent it accordingly becomes. Hegel solves this problem at a stroke by projecting subjectivity into the object itself: why fear to unite with a world which is itself free subjectivity? If Hegel assigns the aesthetic a lowly status, it is in part because, in uniting subject and object in this way, he has already secretly aestheticized the whole of reality.

If German rationalism, with Baumgarten, needed an aesthetic supplement to eke itself out, one might claim that British empiricism was all along too aesthetic for its own good. *Its* problem was not how to descend from the heady heights of reason in order to inform and encompass the sensuous, but how to drag itself free of the clammy embrace of the sensuously immediate to rise to something a little more conceptually dignified. How is a thought so thoroughly sensationalized to break the hold of the body over it, disentangle itself from the dense thicket of perception and launch itself out into theoretical reflection? The answer of the British 'moral sense' theorists was that there was really no need. The 'moral sense' is that spontaneous, well-nigh somatic impulse within us which links us in the very textures of our sensibility to some providential social whole. If that social whole is now frustratingly opaque to totalizing theory, we can find its trace on the body itself and its spontaneous affections and aversions. In one sense, this is a clear confession of ideological defeat: incapable of extrapolating its desired harmony from the anarchy of the market-place, the bourgeoisie is forced to root it instead in the stubborn self-evidence of the gut. In another sense, it provides a powerful *ideological* riposte to an arid Enlightenment rationality; if a social order *needs* rational justification, then the Fall has already happened. The aesthetic for a Shaftesbury or Hutcheson is no more than a name for the political unconscious: it is simply the way social harmony registers itself ineluctably on our senses. The beautiful is just political order lived on the body, the way it strikes the eye and stirs the heart. But to assimilate moral judgement to spontaneous feeling in this way is to risk aestheticizing it, thus opening the floodgates to an ethical relativism which is ideologically dangerous. The 'moral sense' theorists see shrewdly that the rationalists wantonly elide the whole medium of senses and sentiments – call it the aesthetic – through which abstract ethical imperatives can alone take political flesh in human lives. But virtue, so their rationalist opponents claim, is thereby reduced to a matter of taste and ethical ideology accordingly subverted. The bourgeoisie, once again, is divided between a rationally grounded ethics which proves ideologically ineffectual, and an ideologically forceful theory which rests itself on nothing more respectable than the gut. In seeking to anchor one's political power more deeply in the subject – the project of aesthetics or political hegemony – you risk ending up undermining it.

There is a greater risk still, however. The aesthetic begins as a supplement to reason; but we have learned from Derrida that it is in the manner of such lowly supplements to supplant what they are meant to subserve. What if it were the case that not only morality but cognition itself were somehow 'aesthetic'? That sensation and intuition, far from figuring as reason's antithesis, were in truth its very basis? The name for this subversive claim in Britain is David Hume, who, not content with reducing morality to a species of sentiment, threatens to collapse knowledge to fictional hypothesis, belief to intensified feeling, the continuity of the subject to a fiction, causality to an imaginative construct and history to a kind of infinite intertextuality. For good measure, he also argues that private property – the very basis of the bourgeois order – rests simply on our imaginative habits, and that political order – the state – arises from the *weakness* of our imagination.

We seem, then, to have traced a kind of circle. Reason, having spun off the subaltern discourse of aesthetics, now finds itself threatened with being swallowed up by it. The rational and the sensuous, far from obediently reproducing one another's inmost structure à la Baumgarten, have ended up in Hume wholly at odds. What, after all, to paraphrase Nietzsche, if experience were a woman? What if it were that slippery, tantalizing, elusive thing which plays fast and loose with the concept, the eternally labile which is gone as soon as grasped? At once intimate and unreliable, precious and precarious, indubitable and indeterminate, the very realm the aesthetic addresses itself to would seem to have all the duplicity of the eternal female. If this is the case, then the only possibility would seem to be to go back to where you started and think everything through again, this time from the basis of the body. It is exactly this which the two greatest aestheticians, Marx and Freud, will try to do: Marx with the labouring body, Freud with the desiring one. To think everything through again in terms of the body: this, surely, will have to be the logical next stage of the aesthetic and the one which carries its earliest proto-materialist impulses to their logical conclusions.

There is more than this, however, to be rescued from this otherwise somewhat discreditable current of bourgeois thought, which far from being centrally about art is in effect about how best to subdue the people. (It is not for nothing that Kant refers at one point to the senses as the 'rabble'.) Aesthetics are not only incipiently materialist; they also provide, at the very heart of the Enlightenment, the most powerful available critique of bourgeois possessive individualism and appetitive egoism. Before we have even begun to reason, there is, for the British moral-sense theorists, that nameless faculty within us which makes us feel the sufferings of others as keenly as a wound, spurs us to luxuriate in another's joy with no thought of self-advantage, pricks us to detest cruelty and oppression like a hideous deformity. The body has its reasons, of which the mind knows little or nothing. Speaking from the Gaelic margins, from Scotland and Ireland, these men denounce bourgeois utility and speak up bravely for sympathy and compassion. Disinterestedness, against which modern radicals have learned to react with Pavlovian precision, means indifference in the first place not to the interests of others but to one's own. To judge aesthetically, for Kant or Hume, means to bracket one's own sectarian interests and possessive desires in the name of a common general humanity, a radical decentering of the subject. The aesthetic may be the language of political hegemony and an imaginary consolation for a bourgeoisie bereft of a home, but it is also, in however idealist a vein, the discourse of utopian critique of the bourgeois social order.

What happens in the early development of the bourgeoisie is that its own secularizing material activities bring into increasing question the very metaphysical values it urgently needs to validate its own political order. The birth of the aesthetic is in part a consequence of this contradiction. If value is now increasingly difficult to derive from a metaphysical foundation, from the way the world is or from the way it might feasibly become, then it can only be derived in the end from itself. Value, as with Kant, is what is radically autotelic, bearing its own conditions of possibility, like the Almighty Himself, within itself. Alasdair MacIntyre has well shown, in his *Short History of Ethics*, how this idealist self-referentiality of moral discourse is a result of that great historical transition in which moral rights and responsibilities, in the growing anomy of bourgeois society, can no longer be derived from one's actual social role and practice. The only alternatives are then to see value as self-grounded – for which the model is the aesthetic – or to ground them in feelings – for which the model is also the aesthetic. But if this signals a certain ideological crisis from which we have never recovered, it also releases an opportunity. The aesthetic is at once eloquent testimony to the enigmatic origins of morality in a society which everywhere violates it, and a generous utopian glimpse of an alternative to this sorry condition. For what the aesthetic imitates in its very glorious futility, in its pointless self-referentiality, in all its full-blooded formalism, is nothing less than human existence itself, which needs no rationale beyond its own self-delight, which is an end in itself and which will stoop to no external determination. For the Marx of *The Eighteenth Brumaire*, the true sublime is that infinite, inexhaustible hetero-geneity of use-value – of sensuous, non-functional delight in concrete particularity – which will follow from the dismantling of abstract rational exchange. When Marx complained that he wished to be free of the 'economic crap' of *Capital* to get down to his big book on literature, he did not realize that an aesthetician was what he had been, precisely, all along.

References

Baumgarten, Alexander (1750). *Aesthetica*. Hildesheim, Georg Olms. (1961)

Burke, Edmund (1790). *Reflections on the Revolution in France*, edited by Conor Cruise O'Brien. Harmondsworth, Penguin. (1969)

Kant, Immanuel (1790). *The Critique of Judgement*, translated by James Creed Meredith. Oxford, Clarendon Press. (1952)

MacIntyre, Alasdair (1966). *A Short History of Ethics*. New York, Macmillan.

Marx, Karl (1852). *The Eighteenth Brumaire of Louis Bonaparte*, translated by Eden and Cedar Paul. London, George Allen & Unwin. (1926)

Schiller, Friedrich von (1795, 1801) *On the Aesthetic Education of Man: In a Series of Letters*, translated by Reginald Snell. New York, Frederick Ungar. (1965)

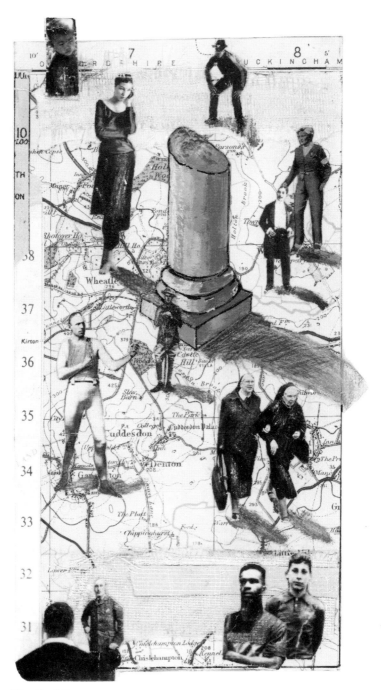

Dino Squillino

3

Max Raphael and the question of aesthetics

Michèle Barrett

Questions of aesthetics, never unduly prominent in Marxist approaches to culture, have recently become relegated to an extremely marginal position in theoretical and critical debates. It is not that Marxism has failed to develop a tradition of work on aesthetics – for in the past it has – but that such concerns are currently out of fashion and, indeed, seen as politically reprehensible. Insofar as this generalization is right, it poses major theoretical and political problems, suggesting in particular that Marxists are unable to engage with bourgeois criticism, dominant educational practices, or popular beliefs. Evasion of the question of aesthetic pleasure and value has left not only Marxist criticism but also radical cultural intervention in a relatively weak position. For this reason I shall argue that it would be useful to re-open the question of materialist aesthetics. Later sections will critically consider the analysis of the art critic Max Raphael, whose work illuminates both the points of interest and the dangers inherent in such a project.

I The importance of the aesthetic

'Aesthetic' is commonly defined (see, for example, the *Oxford English Dictionary*) as having three meanings: (a) received by the senses; (b) referring to beauty; and (c) of superior taste. The last need not detain us, since sociological approaches have truly demonstrated the historical variability and vulnerability of 'taste' (Wolff 1983: 18–19). The other two meanings we can usefully translate into the questions of pleasure and value. When someone says a piece of music or a poem makes their hair stand on end, when Cézanne records in his diary that he feels his eyes bleeding as he looks at what he is painting, they refer to sensations which might be called an aesthetic mode of feeling. A possible equivalent to these heightened sensory perceptions is sexual pleasure, and indeed certain 'pleasurable' features of art (abundance, extravagance of expression, the tension and resolution characteristic of much Western classical music for example) can readily be interpreted in more directly sexual analogies. In general, however, the advocates of an aesthetic mode of sensation see it as a separate faculty. The object of this mode of perception may not be seen as identical to 'beauty', since it could be recognized that a work of art was 'of great value' without being tied to a particular definition of beauty.

The questions raised by the term 'aesthetic' may be summarized as follows: (1) Can we say that there is a distinctive faculty or mode of perception called 'aesthetic' and what would be the nature of the pleasure afforded? (2) Can we identify objects or works to which universal aesthetic value adheres? These questions are difficult to formulate in a non-circular way and the history of attempts to get to grips with them is, perhaps surprisingly, very sparse. Aesthetics constitutes a minor subfield of philosophy in which the questions are considered in the abstract (what is beauty? and so on) rather than in respect to the claims of particular instances. Art history, the subject where one would expect to see aesthetic matters considered, is strikingly silent, tending professionally towards tracing the influence of X on Y and delighting in the niceties of obscure attributions. Art criticism tends to emphasize formal properties of a work rather than relating these to aesthetic pleasure and value. This situation seems curious, since art and literary history and criticism do not suffer from any reticence in assessing and grading their objects of study. However, in a remarkable number of instances the works are ranked on a range of criteria that are not *aesthetic*: a work is stoical, uplifting, cathartic, illuminating or whatever. What is often *not shown* is how and why formal properties of the work (situated in an understanding of the different dimensions of particular art forms) might account for the value assigned.

The question might be looked at another way by asking if the aesthetic properties of a work can be differentiated from its meaning. This is highly problematic. Poetry, for instance, is characterized by condensation of language (in a non-Freudian sense) – a multiplicity of meanings arise from one signifier. This surplus of meaning could be regarded as distinctively aesthetic. Yet the reverse is also held – that the aesthetic is precisely constituted in the excess of the signifier over the signified. As Terry Eagleton puts it: 'if you approach me at a bus stop and murmur "thou still unravished bride of quietness", then I am instantly aware that I am in the presence of the literary. I know this because the texture, rhythm and resonance of your words are in excess of their abstractable meaning . . .' (Eagleton 1983: 2). Formulations of this kind are inconclusive since they apply equally well to situations where no question of the aesthetic arises. Many an Oscar Wilde epigram can be said to generate surplus meaning without being regarded as an instantiation of 'the literary' or of aesthetic value. Many academic papers flaunt a 'texture, rhythm and resonance of language' clearly in excess of any abstractable meaning, but they are not, by this token, deemed works of 'literature'. The unresolved relationship between the categories of meaning and the aesthetic underlies the vexed position of the latter in Marxist (and in sociological) criticism today.

Ideological contestation

One major historical barrier to serious consideration of aesthetic questions has been the dominant influence of the concept of ideology in critical studies. The ghost of Lukács has yet to be laid in a critical tradition that may long since have rejected class-reductionism but has been content to argue the toss over whether a given work is *'really about'* class conflict or gender difference for instance. Criticism of many classic texts often takes the form of an unending procession of 'readings' that claim to have uncovered the essential ideological message of the text. That such readings, by Marxists as well as bourgeois critics, are children of their time is demonstrated in R. Frankenberg's history of Marxist critics on *Wuthering Heights*.

In the general area of cultural studies, and in radical criticism in the humanities, texts of varying kinds are now consensually regarded as sites of ideological contestation. This is an important improvement on the reflectionist models of culture that were hegemonic in these fields until, roughly, the moment of Althusserian influence that deposed them. But the insertion of struggle, silence, resistance, subversion and rupture into the vocabulary of the interpreter is a modification to, rather than a rejection of, the view that texts are primarily to be understood in ideological terms. It is to see texts as encoding ideological conflict rather than as reflecting ideological certainty. Clearly this is right, but it is often limited in its purchase on the general significance of the works in question. Of course works of art do encode such ideological material, but it would be rash to think that a decoding exercise will yield an exhaustive account of their significance. It cannot explain, for example, how works sharing comparable ideological ground can vary sharply in their consumption and reception over time. Nor does it make much headway in developing a sophisticated understanding of the experiential dimension of this consumption.

The roots of this view of art lie solidly within the dominant tradition of Marxist approaches to art and literature – in the work of Georg Lukács and Theodor Adorno in particular. It is a view characterized by seeing art in terms of a cognitive axis between knowledge on the one hand and ideology on the other. Although Adorno is usually seen as the theorist who most keenly argued for specifically aesthetic considerations to be taken into account, for example differentiating between 'autonomous' (authentic) and heteronomous (art as entertainment, for example) art, he too is locked in the 'cognitive' model. In passing he says 'Granted, art implies reality because it is a form of knowledge', in the course of elaborating his view that the 'truth content' of art must be immanent to the work rather than implanted from outside (Adorno 1984: 366–7). In this Adorno shares the view associated with the whole German post-Hegelian tradition that art is a privileged bearer of social-historical 'truth'. (As the poet said, 'beauty is truth, truth beauty'.) This conceptual alliance of art with the knowledge/ideology axis is now so much part of Western culture that a separation is difficult. Within the Marxist tradition it has frequently taken the form of an insistence that aesthetic value can or should be tied to historical-political 'truth' or progressiveness. Although this argument obviously resolves the problem of universal aesthetic value by defining value in relative political terms, it is itself problematic. The principal difficulty is that addressed in Terry Lovell's *Pictures of Reality*, where she argues that the knowledge/ideology axis should be seen as the secondary, not the primary, dimension in works of the imagination. Lovell does not engage with aesthetic value as such (although she does offer some fresh thoughts on aesthetic pleasure). Yet her perspective is interesting as a radical rejection of the view that the 'truth' content of art is inseparable from its value. By far the most dominant view on the left, however, is the politicization of aesthetic value that has gone hand in hand with the reduction of cultural forms to a reading of their ideological content.

Representation and signification

The second major tendency I want to mention is the very broad influence of structuralism, poststructuralism and deconstructionism. The break with classical theories of representation has rightly led to a reconsideration of the means of representation rather than an exclusive concern with a pre-given signified. A theory of signification that emphasizes the text's internal powers of meaning-construction, and stresses the multiplicity of readings available in consumption, has both strengths and weaknesses. One major strength is that it enables us to transcend the boundaries of bourgeois categories – high art and mass culture, literature and popular fiction, the various academic disciplines. It is, of course, deconstructive of the categories of 'Art' and 'Literature' to subject their objects and texts to the same processes of examination as are applied to those formerly relegated to the sphere of 'popular culture'. This basic egalitarianism, this refusal to categorize according to a supposed attribute of aesthetic status, gives structuralist approaches such subversiveness as they have. The point I want to make here, however, is that this radical and democratizing challenge to the definition of what is art necessarily has certain limiting consequences. If we apply the same conceptual tools to a cartoon or postcard as to a Picasso, we concentrate by definition on the common features (those that our concepts *can* address) rather than on what divides them. Although this is in itself iconoclastic, it inevitably leaves a range of important questions connected with cultural and aesthetic *experience* to the unchallenged pronouncements of bourgeois cultural pundits and critics.

Structuralism's rejection of the salience of aesthetic value is an integral part of its project, and the political thrust has been to deconstruct the pretensions of 'the aesthetic' as a separate realm. Alongside this, however, there is another reason for rejection of the question of aesthetics. This is the intransigent anti-humanism of structuralist discourse. The idea of a human aesthetic faculty, or mode of sensation, has historically proved to be more problematic for a structuralist perspective than the question of aesthetic value itself. This can be seen by looking at the respective fortunes of the notions of aesthetic value and pleasure in contemporary cultural studies and Marxist criticism. Value may be beyond the pale, but pleasure has for some while been definitely in the foreground. What is being attempted is, precisely, an anti-humanist discourse of pleasure such as Roland Barthes tried to construct in *The Pleasure of the Text*. The deconstruction of the human subject underlies the reconstruction of the text as subject: 'The text you write must prove to me *that it desires me*' (Barthes 1976: 6). This notion of the desiring text is built on a rejection of the subjectivism – seen in this discourse as the product of an essentialist theory of the subject – which is characteristic of most accounts of the experience of aesthetic pleasure. The desire to evade formulations that smack of vulgar humanism leads to the extraordinarily cerebral and skeletal character of 'the body' in some of these new theories of pleasure. Fredric Jameson, for instance, defines pleasure in the following terms: 'Pleasure is finally the consent of life in the body, the reconciliation – momentary as it may be – with the necessity of physical existence in a physical world.' (Jameson 1983: 10). This is a curiously grudging description (consent, reconciliation, necessity) that makes one wonder what would constitute unpleasure.

Semiotics and psychoanalysis

Claire Pajaczkowska, in an article on semiotic and psychoanalytic theories of art, argues that the psychoanalytic development of linguistic theory facilitates a consideration of the text in its relation to the reader. Although much of what Pajaczkowska has to say concerns visual forms and the analysis of colour, her conclusion makes clear that art must be understood in psychic rather than aesthetic terms. The following passage clarifies the necessary marginality of pleasure to a deconstructionist theory of the subject:

> Or in other words the function of the work of art is to represent the dialectic of the subject, split and triangulated through the exigencies of the incest taboo, to represent and contain this splitting; to represent it as a doubling which is the process of negotiating an imaginary identity, the ego. This process of identification requires the negotiation of sexual difference, it is perhaps its most important function,

and *pleasure and meaning (the two tenets of bourgeois concepts of art) are simply by-products* of this socially prescribed and biologically inscribed process of the organization of energy.

(Pajaczkowska 1983: 13)

This conception of art and its 'functions' is less mystifying than the notion that a text has its own subjectivity. This particular psychoanalytic account is methodologically analogous to the old sociologically reductionist readings of art that excluded anything that might muddy the waters of a purely social view of the determination of a work of art. And just as those sociological accounts were more plausible when attached to representations of manifestly 'social' themes and content, so this approach seems strongest when dealing with subject matter of obvious psychic interest – the madonna and child image, for instance. It seems likely that any psychoanalytic interpretation of art would lean towards 'psychic reductionism', and certainly it is also true of the readings of art-works that Peter Fuller has offered from a Kleinian point of view. Whether or not Adorno is right that a psychoanalytic reading of art 'mistakes works of art for documents, lodged in the dreaming person's head', it is certainly true that the explanatory exclusivity of the psychoanalytic approach is not readily reconciled with any competing claims (Adorno 1984: 12).

Contemporary poststructuralist work in the area of the humanities has often tended to tie together a broadly semiotic analysis with an argument that sees psychoanalytic theory (particularly the Lacanian approach) as the most fruitful system for exploring subjectivity in a critical way. Linked to this has been an overt and systematic critique of the 'bourgeois subject' assumed in classic liberal-humanist discourse and reproduced by default in Marxist theory. Yet a number of questions in this triangulated theoretical perspective remain unresolved, not the least being the issue of whether semiotics, psychoanalysis and anti-humanism are an integrated package or a contingent theoretical alliance.

I mention these questions simply to draw attention to the way in which questions about aesthetic sensation, experience, pleasure and value, have been defined – often by a process of shorthand or guilt by association – as irretrievably contaminated by 'bourgeois humanism'. (This purely negative construction of humanism is, of course, a travesty of the history of a philosophical secularism that might be thought to deserve better from modern progressives.) Although the left, particularly through the influence of feminism, has attempted to take up questions of pleasure and fantasy, this has proved peculiarly difficult to do in terms that equal the resonance of the traditional 'humanist' discourses on these topics. Yet the question of separating humanism from 'bourgeois-humanism' has been begged in modern theory. It is an important project, partly for reasons of political persuasion. There is a widely held popular assumption that the dividing line between animals and human beings is marked by 'civilization', by considerations beyond those of mere survival, by appreciation of the realm of the aesthetic. It may well be that such beliefs are historically explicable and/or wrong, but their prevalence cannot be doubted. So at the least we can expect some sort of engagement with them, rather than a distanced dismissal of the problem.

It seems to me that what is known as 'cultural studies', and much of what is known as Marxist or radical criticism, operates within the two parameters I have sketched out. The major legacy from Marxism is the concept of ideology and the major legacy from structuralism is the rejection of the subject. These two traditions, incompatible as they undoubtedly are in some respects, have been immensely influential in contemporary work in the general field of culture. Singly and jointly they account for the marginalization of aesthetic questions in the interpretation of culture. In fact, this rejection is one that criticism shares with many practitioners and art educators. The notion of serving an apprenticeship in order to acquire skill in an art-form has been abandoned in favour of criteria that are by and large non-aesthetic. For instance, the judges in a recent poetry competition, filmed as they worked, articulated the notion of 'truth to experience' as the main criterion for the winning poem. 'Social relevance' is an equally influential basis of judgment. The lack of interest in aesthetic training is surprisingly marked among professionals, and the assessment criteria they use, in public examinations for instance, are reduced to vague formulations about relevance and conviction. And if radical critiques of bourgeois criticism have taught us something, it is that criticism, however 'formal' its modality, is frequently social and ideological in its essence.

Relativism

It should be emphasized that we are talking of a rejection, not just an evasion, of aesthetic questions. Principled relativism on the aesthetic is an often argued, and indeed now hegemonic, stance on the left. My concern here, whilst taking for granted the reasons why this relativism developed, and fully accepting the spirit of the critique of bourgeois criticism, is that it brings in its train serious political and theoretical problems. First, this relativism is simply unconvincing, and leaves the more plausible position – that we can say a Rembrandt is 'better' than an Angelica Kaufmann – to popular and reactionary ideologues. Although we protest at the (undoubted) class, race and gender bias of much criticism, and the definition of whose work shall be studied and on what assumptions, this does not close the matter. Is it really only because of male dominance in art history that we consider Rembrandt the better painter? Is the limerick I compose on the back of my cigarette packet indistinguishable from a Shakespeare play in terms of value? We need to engage with the widely held beliefs that one work is 'better' than another and produce convincing arguments either way about why this is not so or about what it is based on.

Secondly, the denial of the aesthetic ignores the fact that the works analysed in radical criticism are works of the imagination, or fictional. I do not suggest that this gives them any form of historical or social transcendence, but it does at least mean that they do not reflect, mediate or encode in any direct way the content and position frequently attributed. This makes the conflation of author and ideology, so common in the content-analysis type of radical literary criticism, particularly fraught. This is important, since it leads to a third problem – that this imaginative element, and the ambiguity of aesthetic codes, allow considerable play in the meaning of the work. Meaning is not immanent, it is constructed in the consumption of the work. Hence no text can be inherently progressive or reactionary – it becomes so in the act of consumption. There may be an authorial 'preferred reading' but the effects may be different, opposite even, to those intended. The important point is that, whatever the formal properties of a work, its ideological content, its 'political implications' are not *given*. They depend upon the construction that takes place at the level of consumption.

Thirdly, and perhaps most important, to ignore questions of aesthetic pleasure and value gives away ground to a mystificatory view of art. It is precisely part of the mystique of art, of the separation between art and work in our society, that we abandon the rational criteria we apply to all other forms of social production. In this we reproduce the traditional bourgeois ideology of art. In what other work would we deny or evade the question of skill? These attitudes are part and parcel of a highly romanticized view of art. Max Raphael says,

> I might also point out that inspiration is nothing but an illusion on the part of the most barren class in modern society, an illusion which rests upon the distinction that arose in the nineteenth century between socially mechanized production of material goods and individual craft production of spiritual goods. It is a petty-bourgeois fiction which has degraded art to a substitute for religion.
>
> (Raphael 1968: 207)

Paradoxically, it is through a consideration of skill, technique and formal properties of art that we can escape romantic and mystificatory assumptions about art and move towards a different understanding. In this context an emphasis on aesthetic skills is in fact democratizing rather than elitist – for skills may be *acquired*, whereas the notion of an artistic 'genius' forbids the aspirations of anyone outside the small and specialized group. This is true even if we accept different degrees of individual aptitude.

Few critics, Marxist or otherwise, have attended closely to detailed formal and technical issues in the development of their interpretations of works of art. By and large a gulf has been created between those who interpret a work in terms of its 'background', 'life' of creator, or 'conditions of production' and those who stick to close textual analysis. The latter tend to argue, as does for instance the doyen of 'internal' analysis of art-works, Heinrich Wölfflin, that external considerations are irrelevant. Sociologists and Marxists have recently been in the camp that rejects the internal approach, always seeing the ideological character of a work as socially and historically situated. Or, in the case of Marxist structuralist criticism, they have tended to analyse the text to the exclusion of the consumer. It could be said, however, that a distinctive tradition exists in European Marxist cultural thought, represented in Adorno's work on music, Della Volpe's on poetry and that of Max Raphael on art. Raphael's work in my view shows us clearly the strengths and difficulties of attempting to combine detailed analysis of the composition of specific works with a broader Marxist interpretation.

II Max Raphael's theoretical contribution

Max Raphael was born in Prussia in 1889 and educated in Germany. He lived in various cities, including Paris, and in 1941 he settled in New York, dying there in 1952. Much of his work was published posthumously and some of it is still not available in English translation. *Proudhon, Marx, Picasso: Three Studies in the Sociology of Art* (1980) contains a 20-page bibliography of Raphael's published and unpublished work, compiled by John Tagg. The exposition I give in this paper is drawn largely from *The Demands of Art*, which deals principally with aesthetic questions. *Proudhon, Marx, Picasso* is more theoretical and sociological in its focus. Before looking at his specific analysis of paintings I want to recapitulate some central points from its approach. These concern his attempt to apprehend art works as aesthetic compositions, and I discuss them under the headings of definitions, method, concept of aesthetic value and theory of viewing.

Definitions of the aesthetic

Raphael is bold enough to define and elaborate on the aesthetic as a human faculty, the work of art and the criteria of artistic excellence. *Aesthetic feeling* is regarded by Raphael as a process in which individual sense perceptions are exteriorized. Feeling becomes relatively independent of individual emotional experience and is assimilated to more universal categories through which the world is appropriated. Art is thus produced by a union of faculties, rather than one faculty. Raphael sees the aesthetic *attitude* as more general than specific aesthetic feelings:

> It is not important how the particular part of the world looks that releases our aesthetic vision. What is important is to see it whole, in such a way that we extinguish all our momentary, individual concerns as well as the facticity of things outside us. We may find ourselves in harmony or disharmony with the world, we may feel the sublimity of the cosmos in relation to our tragic finitude or the ridiculous pettiness of our individual selves. Such an experience gratifies and purges us because in it our conflicts, whether with ourselves or with the world, are resolved.
>
> (Raphael 1968: 190)

Within this framework of aesthetic perception Raphael argues that aesthetic feeling has a historical and normative aspect, particularly in that the ways in which people constitute a relationship to the world will depend, for instance, on epochs of religious belief or romantic humanism. In this insistence on the historical character of aesthetic feeling Raphael concurs with his former teacher, Wölfflin, who writes that 'beholding is not just a mirror which always remains the same, but a living power of apprehension which has its own inward history and has passed through many stages' (Wölfflin 1950: 226).

The work of art is defined by Raphael as that which connects a sensual appropriation of the world to an ideational or cognitive mode of apprehension: '. . . the work of art is reality enhanced, which engages the senses both as a whole and in every one of its details and is yet a symbol of non-sensory meanings which extend down to still deeper layers without ever ceasing to appeal to our senses' (Raphael 1968: 191). *Artistic excellence* is characterized by, on the one hand, an engagement of the senses and the intellect and, on the other, a fusion of materials and imagination. Raphael illustrates the first in saying, 'The place in history of such unities as the Gothic cathedral or Doric temple proves that the richest artistic sensibility was achieved not in periods of pure sensualism, but in periods in which sense perceptions were most readily combined with the other human faculties of cognition – the body, the intellect, and Reason.' Quoting Goethe's view that 'that artist will be the most excellent in his genre whose inventiveness and imagination are, so to speak, directly fused with the material in which he has to work', Raphael also emphasizes that artistic materials are not contingent or extraneous but are the necessary condition of artistic existence (Raphael 1968: 215–16).

Moving from artistic excellence to the purpose of art history, Raphael argued for a historical, and relativist, understanding of judgments of taste. He thought that the task of art history was to show the extent to which assignations of artistic value, and the normative status attributed to particular works, are historically bounded. With characteristic confidence he declares, 'Norms of this type are simply the mistakes an epoch makes about itself, inasmuch as relative, period factors are usually absolutized along with others. Art history demonstrates this by showing to what extent such predilections vary, and the sociology of art, which shows the economic and social causes that account for each given selection, confirms it' (Raphael 1980: 83). Raphael's insistence on a historical approach leads him to argue that Marx's thesis on art –

as ultimately (though not solely) determined by economic factors – is fruitful not as a universal thesis but in given historical contexts: 'It is disclosed only in the course of a specific analysis' (Raphael 1980: 77). This leads Raphael to re-pose Marx's famous question about Greek art – Why do we still like it when its foundations are a dead mode of production? He says Marx's question cannot be answered as it is too general: 'Let us formulate the problem concretely: Why could Greek art repeatedly take a normative significance at various epochs of Christian art?' (Raphael 1980: 105).

Raphael's method

Raphael's method is encapsulated in the remark he quotes from Rodin:

> If you want to write a good book about me, just study one of my sculptures. All that matters is my method. A work that never came off will suit your purpose better than a good one, for it will show the limitations of my method. Should you be unable to discover my method from study of a single work, then you'll never write a decent book either about me or about art. Of course, art critics write about everything under the sun except art.
>
> (Raphael 1968: 22)

Raphael believed in the closest possible examination of the selected work in order to arrive, first and simply, at a description of it. Such a description is, Raphael argues, a *conceptual reconstitution* of the work and involves the following considerations: (1) The constitution of the individual form in terms of material and space. (2) The constitution of the work as a whole externally (format, immanent structural lines, lines of orientation) and internally (mode of reality, individual idea, aesthetic feeling, motif, etc.). (3) The constitution of the relations between individual forms within the work (internal and external composition, logic of the structure, etc.). (4) The realization of the individual forms as well as of the configuration as a whole. Each of the four stages represents the artistic method as concrete phenomenon (Raphael 1968: 198).

It is in relation to (1), the constitution of individual form, that Raphael is most clear. *Materials* (paint, wood, and so on) are translated into *the means of representation* (in the visual arts colour, light, shadow, line), which in turn are transformed into *means of figuration* through the unique way in which they are blended or contrasted. In addition to a consideration of means of representation, Raphael's 'reconstructive description' also explores the artistic form as a spatial structure, examining the number of planes, and the tensions generated between them. Raphael's discussion of composition and realization becomes more diffuse and less clear than his elaboration of the earlier stages of artistic production. This is because he is concerned now with *meaning*: his concepts here are those of expressive value, psychic content, world view, mode of reality, mode of life. It is here, in the reconciliation of formal and historico-ideological considerations, that his theory of aesthetic value begins.

Aesthetic value

Although Raphael sought to banish mystificatory views of art as inspiration, he developed a view of artistic originality (which he saw etymologically – getting to the root) and argued a claim towards universal aesthetic value. In brief, he believed that value lay in the artist's ability to create a form appropriate to the content – to express a reality in the only possible representational form. Two major elements of this are noted as important – that the work be *organic* and that it be *dialectical*. By organic Raphael means that the configuration could not be constructed differently:

> We speak of an organic or quasi-organic configuration when every individual form is determined by all the others and serves a specific purpose in relation to the whole (Poussin, Leonardo, Houdon, etc.). Such a configuration is self-contained, self-sufficient, speaks for itself – in order to understand it we need not refer to nature or to the artist's personal experiences. It is autonomous, more accurately, has become autonomous as a result of the process of artistic creation.
>
> (Raphael 1968: 232)

The dialectical dimension of great works of art can be approached in terms of their ambiguity. 'Art frees us from enslavement to words, concepts and false moral values by showing us that life knows differentiations that cannot be reduced to concepts as well as situations which cannot be judged by accepted moral standards.' (Raphael 1968: 201). This 'dialectical' aspect is crystallized in art's ability to 'enhance reality' and extend its meaning. The world of things must be undone and a new world constituted through the construction of the world of values, and the more the artist can accomplish this – the more symbolic the work – the greater it is. Value lies, therefore, in the work that can encompass: polarization and harmony; determination and playfulness; diversity and unity; tension within a logical structure. Hence Raphael posits a scale on which relative values can be assigned, without placing absolute (perfect) value on the agenda at all (Raphael 1968: 196–7). In practice, he is quite sweeping in his own judgments and argues that these desiderata enable us to distinguish between 'factitious and true works of art' (Raphael 1980: 84). Before we take up these contentious claims, however, let us briefly consider Raphael's theory of the artist-viewer relation and look at some illustrations of his method.

The active viewer

It is here, and in the connection of this theory to his formal analysis, that Raphael's greatest contribution to Marxist aesthetics lies. He instantiates my earlier point on the paradoxically democratizing effect of an emphasis on artistic skill. Raphael argues that, through the *reconstitutive description* articulated by the art critic but also experienced by any viewer of the painting, the energy in the work is released. Hence the viewer shares the work of the artist insofar as he or she reconstructs the work. This is why Raphael emphasizes that art leads from the work to the process of creation:

> We see how form is constituted by a specific artistic method and how form follows necessarily upon form. That is what I meant when I said that art leads us from the work to the process of creation. The icy crust of mere presence has melted away and we experience the creative process itself in the new, enhanced reality which both appeals to our senses and suggests an infinite wealth of meanings.
>
> (Raphael 1968: 191)

In this way, the artist is obliged to proceed by compelling the viewer to recreate the process by which the form of the work was made effective. If not, the viewer passes over the work:

> The extent of the viewer's participation in the work varies. In the case of works that do achieve effective form, we are

impelled to view them over and over, re-creating them each time; the process may go on indefinitely. In the case of an inferior work, we feel no such urge. This is how the artist gives a finished work the quality of continuing life: he gives the finite the character of infinity, activating the viewer's own infinite aspirations, awakening them and keeping them awake by certain features present in the actual form itself: tensions between opposites and their resolution.

(Raphael 1968: 224)

Hence, according to Raphael, artistic energy is locked in the work only to be released by this reconstitution in consumption. His position here is not only that of espousing a theory of the active viewer (hence reconciling aesthetic production and consumption) but of rejecting a reflectionist theory of art in favour of a more active, somewhat Brechtian view:

Whatever the deficiencies of Marx's theoretical attitude toward art may have been, he was perfectly aware that after the economic, social and political revolution the most difficult revolution would still remain to be made – the cultural one. Nowhere did he ever exclude art, as he excluded religion, on the ground that there would be no place for it in a classless society. The pseudo-Marxists who put art on the same footing with religion do not see that religion sets limits to man's creative capacities, diverts him from the things of this world, and reconciles class antagonisms by obviously imaginary and frequently hypocritical theories of love, whereas art is an ever-renewed creative act, the active dialogue between spirit and matter; the work of art holds man's creative powers in a crystalline suspension from which it can again be transformed into living energies. Consequently art by its very nature is no opiate; it is a weapon. Art may have narcotic effects, but only if used for specific reactionary purposes; and from this we may infer only that attempts are made to blunt it for the very reason that it is feared as a weapon.

(Raphael 1968: 187)

On this one passage might be said to rest Raphael's position as a Marxist aesthetician. It is, though, in his substantive analyses that we must examine critically the validity of his method.

Analyses of specific works

The kind of approach that Raphael developed can initially be illustrated by looking at his comparison of how *The Last Supper* is treated by Leonardo da Vinci and Tintoretto. He shows that the two artists differed in their ideas as to the meaning of the subject and in their representation of it. What they share, however, is that each found a visual form that in itself expressed the meaning the subject had for him. Hence, says Raphael, Leonardo da Vinci expresses degradation, betrayal and collapse in a 'dropping' of the long table below the line of vision and in the clustering of the apostles in confused groups. Raphael notes that for Tintoretto the dominant meaning of the subject was not that of betrayal but the doctrine of transubstantiation that emerges from the last supper. To express this movement between the terrestrial and other-worldly spheres, Tintoretto represented a table placed along a wall stretching into infinity, with light and shadow playing along its length. Tintoretto's discovery of this most appropriate artistic form is all the more striking in that, as Raphael shows, he spent fifty years painting the subject in different ways before finding the particular form that matched his understanding of the theme. Raphael's basic point is that in two different ways these artists use figuration (including means of representation) to render their particular idea in a material form.

The Demands of Art consists in large part of detailed analyses of individual paintings, and although these cannot be done justice here, it is possible to sketch in some examples of how Raphael 'reconstitutes' works of art. We can take first a painting for which Raphael expresses very great admiration, Cézanne's *Mont Sainte-Victoire* of 1904–6. According to Raphael, this version is the only one of the seven treatments of this subject by Cézanne that balances tension and arrives at a truly great work. He stresses the radical rejection in the painting of the conventions of perspective: instead of representing empty space receding to infinite depth, Cézanne gives us filled space. The back of the picture is tightly closed, with the mountain in the plane at the top tilting forward into the picture. Raphael sees the painting primarily in terms of the use of planes – the back/top plane pushing forward and inward and the bottom/front plane pushing outward to the back of the picture, with the tension balanced and held in check by the middle plane. Raphael explains in some detail how the use and juxtaposition of colour contributes to this division of the picture into planes.

Although it is widely known that Cézanne's theme is taken from the countryside around Aix-en-Provence (and indeed people visit Mont Sainte-Victoire to 'see the original'), the picture is not based on any one viewpoint. No photograph can correspond to what is shown in the painting, since (in Raphael's words) Cézanne has subordinated visual perception to pictorial figuration. This, according to Raphael, is Cézanne's great achievement: he uses some aspects of natural appearance but not others. So the painting is not a landscape, but nature has provided a model. Cézanne has 'refashioned the classical and given nature a classical solidity'.

Raphael's analysis of Picasso's *Guernica* concludes that the primary effect of the painting is shock and that it conveys the 'destructiveness of a disintegrating society with a power no other artist has equalled'. He describes the painting by saying that the figuration is constituted by the use of black and white, rather than colour, and by line. He sees the former as expressive of the most ultimate and general and the latter as exemplifying individual emotion. But, he insists, the real world is composed of objects, nature, society and history; it does not operate with these extremes of abstraction on the one side and individuality on the other. Picasso's exclusive reliance on black and white and on line restrict the painting to the category of private allegory, and hence the understandable confusion among critics as to what, for example, the bull in the painting stands for. Raphael points out that the pictorial vocabulary is limited and that the codes used (for example, triangles and angles referring back to earlier representational conventions) are not accessible to all.

Raphael argues that the content of the painting – a world without hope, mankind reduced to a scream – is not expressed or achieved *in* the figuration but is a private intellectual and emotional motivation of the painter that can be seen *through* the figuration. There is, therefore, an arbitrary rather than a necessary relation between form and content in this work. *Guernica*, according to Raphael, offers no progression, development or resolution and has no reference point in its ordering of space. Hence, although Raphael recognizes the power of the painting in terms of *shock*, he concludes that it is an outright failure as a picture since Picasso could find no figuration suited to his idea and so resorted to allegory.

Raphael's view that formal characteristics of a painting can be linked to social or sociological considerations is taken a step further in his discussion of a painting with a more straight-forward social content, *The Peasant Family* by the seventeenth-century painter Le Nain. This, argues Raphael, is a 'materialist text' in that it views the ruled class from its own point of view, doing so by representation of both oppression and resistance. John Tagg's summary of Raphael's interpretation conveys most clearly this dialectical dimension of the painting: 'Yet the picture Le Nain gives of the plight of the peasants is not one-sided. In their very abject state, one sees the peasants' strength and their struggle for existence. One sees, too, that the formal and sensory means by which this strength is expressed are closely linked with the means used to convey their poverty. Whereas the viewer's line of sight depresses them, each of the figures seems to rise up from the hips, as if protesting against its repression. Each individual is constituted by a double and conflicting force: a sinking down and a rising up which embodies that unity of poverty and strength, exploitation and will for freedom which no present-day work has been able to show. "Only by expressing this unity", Raphael declares, "is it possible to avoid the one-sidedness of sentimental pictures about the poor on the one hand, and of falsely heroic, hero-worshipping pictures about workers on the other"' (Tagg 1980: 5). As this example shows, Raphael's primary concern is with the ways in which an artist finds a pictorial form that inherently and inevitably expresses the idea or content of the work. For Raphael this integral relation of form and meaning is the necessary condition of artistic excellence and aesthetic value.

III   A critical assessment

Raphael claimed that his method amounted to a science of art, in which laws could be expressed. The Appendix to *The Demands of Art* starts with a bold declaration: 'This work sets itself the task of making art an object of scientific cognition.' His theory he describes as 'empirical', since based on a study of works from all periods and nations. He goes so far as to make the extraordinary statement that 'I am convinced that mathematics, which has travelled a long way since Euclid, will someday provide us with the means of formulating the results of such a study in mathemat-ical terms' (Raphael 1968: 207). Yet, as with so many art critics, many of his *interpretative* comments are entirely devoid of qualitative justification let alone scientifically validated. Many of the examples he uses, particularly when illustrating passing points, are ideological readings rather than formal analyses, and indeed it is part of his method that slippage occurs. There is a difference between uncontentious observations such as that line is dominant in *Guernica*, or that *Mont Sainte-Victoire* is composed of more than one plane, and idiosyncratic statements such as the following: 'In *The Virgin and Child with St. Anne* Leonardo da Vinci embodies an idealistic conception of Reason in sensory qualities, which are most fully expressed in the shoulder line' (Raphael 1968: 217). Indeed, it is not self-evident that Leonardo's dropping of the table in *The Last Supper* necessarily expresses collapse or degradation, or that the raising of the line of vision in Le Nain's *The Peasant Family* inevitably conveys poverty. Such judgments veer perilously towards the reefs on which much bourgeois art history and criticism often founder – such and such a feature is held inherently to express stability or resignation or whatever the critic reads into it.

Raphael insists that these judgments, based in the first instance on technical observation, must be neutral and impersonal. The question of *value*, he argues, should only be considered at the *end* of the analysis. In fact, however, he does not himself accomplish this desirable state of affairs. The underlying reason for Raphael's weakness here is that his theoretical framework reveals an unresolved conflict between an emphasis on artistic *production* (in the spirit of Walter Benjamin) and a profoundly Lukácsian subsumption of art to the category of ideology. Raphael was an early exponent of the 'relative autonomy' approach to art. He at times categorizes art as a subset *within* ideology and sees types of artistic work (expressive, dogmatic, sceptical and so on) as ideological. By and large he regards art as a battleground of ideological struggle, although he tries to insist that (to put it crudely) the ideological content is less important than the question of whether the artist can find an appropriate form in which to express it. 'What matters in a work of art is not this specific "something" contributed by the subject-matter but the intensity with which the overall meaning is conveyed by the figuration and for the sake of which whatever might create discrepancy between meaning and content is eliminated' (Raphael 1968: 196).

Raphael's position on the classic problem of economic determination of the cultural is somewhat unclear and contradictory.

Although, as quoted earlier, he describes cultural revolution as the most difficult of revolutions, he concludes *The Demands of Art* with the following rather orthodox view:

> Creative instinct manifests itself with greater freedom in art than in any other domain. A creative, active study of art is therefore indispensable to awaken creative powers, to assert them against the dead weight of tradition, and to mobilize them in the struggle for a social order in which everyone will have the fullest opportunity to develop his creative capacities. The details of this social order cannot be anticipated without falling into utopian dreams. We can and we must be satisfied with the awareness that art helps us to achieve the truly just order. The decisive battles, however, will be fought at another level.
>
> (Raphael 1968: 204)

In addition to this general orientation Raphael's interpretations are based on specific Lukácsian concepts, of which the most important is *totality*. Raphael's understanding of dialectic is rooted in the Lukácsian balance between particularity and totality and in the notion of the historically-typical individual. ('I believe that it would not destroy but enlarge scientific method in the domain of art to pair the concept of particularity with the concept of totality – a totality which combines the same factors of form, content and method at a higher level.') (Raphael 1968: 208). We may query whether Raphael's judgments of aesthetic value really do wait, as he demanded, for the end of the analysis. In fact, although I have glossed his specific analyses in such a way as to minimize it, much of his interpretation is grounded in the familiar and tedious rhetoric of support for realism and hostility to modernism that vitiates so much of Lukács' own work. To illustrate this, let us turn to the 'value' element of Raphael's analysis of Cézanne and Picasso.

Content and form

It is entirely characteristic of Raphael's originality that, although a Marxist aesthetician, he can regard a Cézanne landscape as one of the greatest art works ever produced and castigate *Guernica*, for decades a symbol of anti-fascism, as 'ineffective propaganda'. The substance of Raphael's case is that allegorical painting (of which *Guernica* is an example) must always be inferior to painting in which the content is realized in the form (Raphael 1968: 153). As will readily be seen, this demand is tied closely to a realistic aesthetics such as Lukács elaborated. Raphael's strictures on Monet's paintings echo, often in detail, those of Lukács on writers such as Joyce or Eliot. Raphael writes that, 'for all their lyricism they remain bound up with the description of a localized atmosphere. In their contents the here-and-now takes precedence over the universal, the monetary over the enduring. Reason and the human body are alike eliminated as cognitive faculties; the intellect serves only to analyse and differentiate sharpened sense perception, and the feeling accompanying it is vague' (Raphael 1968: 232).

Raphael's unstinting praise for Cézanne and unswerving criticism of Picasso is at times difficult to comprehend when some of the very features under discussion are shared. Both, Raphael agrees, reject the conventions of perspective, rendering space as filled rather than empty. But he is too critical of Picasso's rejection of pictorial coherence to tackle the argument that Cézanne and Picasso were engaged in comparable challenges to representational conventions (see Ehrenzweig 1965). The class position of any realist aesthetics is that the means of representation must be concealed, and the Brechtian and modernist challenge to realism was principally concerned with the rejection of this desideratum. Raphael's insistence that meaning must be realized in form goes hand in hand with the orthodox realist view. His approval of the Le Nain painting mentioned earlier rests partly on the fact that the composition of the work is 'concealed and made as far as possible invisible, so as not to interfere with an impression of easy and accidental naturalness' (Tagg 1980: 6).

Insofar as these fundamental realist precepts inform Raphael's reconstitution of the work as well as his final evaluation we can see that he attempts to elevate a particular aesthetic to universal status. Many Marxist aestheticians have claimed realism as the natural companion to historical materialism but the case is very far from made or accepted (see Lovell 1980). Raphael, for all his insistence that the work of art be apprehended in aesthetic terms, tends to concur with Lukács that 'great art' is art that embodies the truths of historical materialism. His objection to *Guernica* is that it only *shocks* and does not point to any resolution. Yet Marxism is not a theory that resembles the eighteenth-century ideal of balance, stability and the inevitably resolved chord. Nor is it the politics of the 'realist' happy ending – waiting for history to make a revolution. Insofar as Marxism is an active theory and politics, calling upon us to make our own struggle, it requires a less dogmatic and complacent aesthetic.

However unsatisfactory Raphael's interpretations of particular works may be, his method exposes some issues that I think we need to confront. His precept, drawn from Rodin, of 'study the work' and the theory he elaborated of the 'active' viewer's role in the reconstitution of the work are useful but limited. They are limited by the degree to which they exclude social and historical considerations. Raphael does not recognize that meaning is, at least partially, constructed in the history of a work's reception; we cannot view a Rodin sculpture with an eye that is innocent of all knowledge of Rodin's place in a 'canon' of works. And just as the work is located in a cultural-historical context so our modes of apprehension are specific to the concerns of a particular con- juncture. Although Raphael recognizes the fact of 'vision having a history', he tends to relate it to epochal characteristics such as religious belief and to ignore its more local purchase. So Raphael does not really acknowledge the social constitution of the body of work he scrutinizes; does not add to his detailed visual descrip- tions an adequate account of the social factors that structure the status of the works he chooses to study. Raphael's interpretations show the weaknesses of ignoring the social dimensions of reception. He rules by fiat that *Guernica* is ineffective propaganda when as a matter of fact the absence of an allegorical key to the painting has not hindered the polemical manipulation of this powerful work in a propaganda campaign against fascism. Indeed many would argue that the subject of *Guernica* is treated more effectively through ambiguous and allegorical means than it ever could have been in a realist mode.

The main difficulty with Raphael is that he tries to tie form and meaning too closely together. We do not have to espouse a totally relativist position on meaning (which would be to say that any given work was completely open to the construction of an infinite range of meanings) to argue that the meaning of a work cannot be contained by simple formulae such as that meaning should be realized in form, or that reconciliation and synthesis are an essential element of aesthetic value. Raphael's theory of the active viewer tends to see the only possible appropriation of the work as a recreation of the author's work and ties meaning too closely to the question of authorial intention and imagination.

Raphael's work has, to us now, a certain methodological

innocence. He fails to see that definitions of beauty and aesthetic value, such as his own, are constructed from theoretical tools that have a history just as vision and mode of aesthetic apprehension have histories. Of itself, however, this does not render his work of no interest. By and large the concepts we use and the subjects we scrutinize are all historically constituted and we need to beware of the assumption that our own methodologies are somehow purer than the old ones. 'The very analytic instruments we deploy are in this sense ideologically guilty' (Eagleton 1983b: 64). We should avoid the assumption that there are reactionary, bourgeois, historically-specific categories such as the aesthetic and that our new categories of 'signification' or 'pleasure' are in some way purged of these limitations.

We have to ask, too, what is at stake in the recognition that 'vision has a history'. The relativist arguments about art are easy to make and impossible to refute; there is no consensus, even, on what objects might come into the category of art, and it is fundamentally true that art is what is successfully defined as art. Perhaps more importantly, the concept of art as the product of an individual artist (with all the associated ideological constructions of romantic genius and the transcendent possibilities of art) is historically specific to modern Western capitalism. This sense of art as a historically specific social institution has recently been stressed in Peter Bürger's important book, *Theory of the Avant-Garde*, but it forms part of a debate about the historical emergence of the modern conception of art that has been going on for some while now (see Woolf 1981, 1983). Yet to understand the historical nature of art, of subjective aesthetic experience, of visual apprehension or of the role of the artist in society is not to sink into the complete relativism of thinking that this area of experience is therefore in some way 'not real'. This would be the equivalent of thinking that 'work' under capitalism was – because historically a product of alienated labour – not a 'real' object of thought and analysis.

Raphael's usefulness lies in the fact that he tried to explore the ways in which meaning is connected on one hand to aesthetic form and on the other to the senses. This project is difficult, and few writers have addressed it in any detail. As I argued earlier, it is not currently considered as very important. It would, perhaps, be fair to comment that the dominant interest in cultural studies at the moment is in a conception of meaning that has been stripped of traditional aesthetic questions and does not engage with the issue of the senses. Hence the very definition of culture current in 'cultural studies' tends to be exclusively concerned with meaning. It is illustrative of this that signification theory – analysis of the meanings constructed in systems of signs – is now a consensual position in the debate on the definition of the term culture. The insistence that culture is a field of production, and that its product is meaning, was radical at a time when we were trying to wrest the definition of culture from the grip of reflection theory. That battle, however, is now over and I think the exclusive emphasis on meaning in the analysis of culture needs further thought. Insofar as Raphael tried to explore the connections between meaning and the senses, and between meaning and aesthetic form, his work is of some current interest. If we are to pursue the work of trying to understand cultural experience as well as signifying practice we shall need to question the current exclusive association of culture with meaning.

References

Adorno, Theodor (1984). *Aesthetic Theory*. London, Routledge.

Barthes, Roland (1976). *The Pleasure of the Text*. London, Cape.

Eagleton, Terry (1983). *Literary Theory*. Oxford, Blackwell.

—— (1983b). 'Poetry, Pleasure and Politics', *Formations of Pleasure*. London, Routledge & Kegan Paul.

Ehrenzweig, Anton (1965). *The Psycho-analysis of Artistic Vision and Hearing*. New York, Braziller.

Frankenberg, Ronald (1978). 'Styles of Marxism: Styles of Criticism. *Wuthering Heights*: A Case Study', *Sociological Review Monograph* 26. Keele, University of Keele.

Fuller, Peter (1980). *Art and Psychoanalysis*. London, Writers and Readers Publishing Cooperative.

Jameson, Fredric (1983). 'Pleasure: a Political Issue', *Formations of Pleasure*. London, Routledge & Kegan Paul.

Lovell, Terry (1980). *Pictures of Reality: Aesthetics, Politics, Pleasure*. London, British Film Institute.

Lukács, Georg (1963). *The Meaning of Contemporary Realism*. London, Merlin Press.

Pajaczkowska, Claire (1983). 'Structure and Pleasure', *Block*, 9: 4–13.

Raphael, Max (1968). *The Demands of Art*. London, Routledge & Kegan Paul.

—— (1980). *Proudhon, Marx, Picasso: Three Studies in the Sociology of Art*. London, Lawrence & Wishart.

Tagg, John (1980). 'The Method of Criticism and its Objects in Max Raphael's Theory of Art', *Block*, 2: 2–14.

Wolff, Janet (1981). The Social Production of Art. London, Macmillan.

—— (1983). *Aesthetics and the Sociology of Art*. London, Allen & Unwin.

Wölfflin, Heinrich (1950). *Principles of Art History*. New York, Dover Publications.

—— (1980). *Classic Art*. Oxford, Phaidon.

4

Aesthetics in the affray: Pater's *Appreciations, with an Essay on Style*

Laurel Brake

Even imagination is the slave of stolid circumstance.
(Hardy 1890: 15)

The procedure of this essay and the 'Affray' of its title offer a critique of aesthetics, insofar as aesthetics is defined as a discourse which treats universal and metaphysical categories of beauty. Here aesthetics is treated materially and historically; the definition of the subject – beauty itself – is seen as a subject of the history of knowledge, historically contingent, and part of the establishment of the ground of high culture rendered fit for philosophical inquiry.

The year is 1889, and Walter Pater, at the age of 50, publishes his first and only book of 'literary' criticism. Culled from writings of twenty years, *Appreciations* is Pater's first critical book since *The Renaissance* (1873), and represents a project deferred; resonant with debates of the recent past it recontextualises and re-views them in the present. Appearing just after Matthew Arnold's death and the publication of *Essays in Criticism: Second Series* in 1888, and in the midst of debate about English as a degree subject, *Appreciations* is a responsive collection, addressing itself to English literature and the romantic tradition. Other indicators of its historicity may be read in its presentation of gender as connected with scholarship, authorship and readers, and with

Darren Butcher

its own writing practice and critical discourse. Looking backward, *Appreciations* undermines Arnold's effort to establish English on the bedrock of C/classicism; looking forward, it is liberated by the presence of the steady circulation of gay discourse as well as by Arnold's death.

In compiling *Appreciations* Pater is adopting the model of collecting essays from periodicals into book form which was pioneered by Francis Jeffrey (who first published his anonymous pieces from the *Edinburgh Review* in 1861) and quickly echoed by Arnold in 1865 in *Essays in Criticism*. Constructed of articles and fragments from diverse periodicals published between 1866 and 1888, *Appreciations* is visibly discontinuous; its paste-up character is signalled in the jarring dates appended to each article, though the periodical origins are nowhere mentioned. Unity is not attempted through chronological ordering of authors. But if *Appreciations* is eclectic, it is also laboriously structured, with sequence, balance, weight and deselection palpable elements of the signifying practice. It begins and ends with essays on the theoretical problems in the foreground of the book, those of style and R/romanticism, with 'Style' written for the book in 1888 and 'Romanticism' (1876) functionally renamed 'Postscript' to end the volume.

Following the first essay and preceding the last are pairs of reviews of named poets – Wordsworth and Coleridge, and Morris and Rossetti – with the review element of the originals obscured, in a variety of ways. Although the word 'Romanticism' is suppressed by the word 'Postscript', the concept of romanticism is repeatedly trailed and explored in that essay and in the volume, and it is into that category that the pieces on the Lake School poets, and Morris and Rossetti, are swept. In a reverse move, the volume displaces Morris's name to introduce prominently the concept of 'Aesthetic Poetry'. The volume thus treats both work from the historical English Romantic movement and from the aesthetic movement, a particular form of contemporary romantic writing which produces the volume's pervasive writing practice of 'aesthetic criticism'. This double valence of R/romanticism is one argument of the book's 'Postscript', and the text of *Appreciations* inscribes it. Between these wedges of nineteenth-century English romanticism is found a slab of essays on earlier English literature which move chronologically backwards to form a core in three essays on Shakespearean drama. Less predictable are the other earlier texts, by two authors of non-fictional prose, Charles Lamb and Sir Thomas Browne. An interest in prose as a genre is announced in the introductory essay on 'Style', and these essays find a place in this volume as much out of a commitment to prose as out of the Englishness of their subjects and their ripeness for reprinting.

'Prose' and censorship

As significant as the presence of these essays on prose is the absence of any essays on prose fiction. However, *Appreciations* is not anomalous in this respect, for the English novel was struggling for its freedom from crippling constraints and for recognition as a serious literary genre as late as 1889, although the finished work of George Eliot, Dickens and Thackeray was in circulation. Thomas Hardy argues that the cultural formations, the very institutions of literary production, are implicated: 'The magazine in particular and the circulating library in general do not foster the growth of the novel which reflects and reveals life. They directly tend to exterminate it by monopolising all literary space' (1890: 17). The ways that *Appreciations* negotiates the thorny and topical question of the current status of fiction in Britain show that question to be at once one of the principal subjects of the volume, and one of the conditions which produces a volume which obscures this subject.

Hardy was writing in a forum on 'Candour in English Fiction' in the January 1890 number of the *New Review* which articulates that debate six weeks after the publication of *Appreciations* on November 15. The three contributors unanimously state outright what is implicit in 'Style' in particular: that the recent constraints on English fiction (and even on fiction in English) have produced and circulated inferior fiction in which ' "la dignité de la pensée" ' (Hardy 1890: 21) is suppressed through censorship. The same author writes of ' "the fearful price" that he [the true artist] has to pay for the privilege of writing in the English language – no less a price than the complete extinction, in the mind of every mature and penetrating reader, of sympathetic belief in his personages' (1890:19). It is the similarity of the elements of the analysis of this problem in the *New Review* with the preoccupations of *Appreciations* which reveals the framework in which Pater's discussions of prose, fiction, the status of literature, and romanticism take place.

It is perhaps astonishing to late twentieth-century readers, to whom the novel is a dominant if not the dominant form in literature, that a critic like Pater, an author of fiction and writing regularly for the periodicals from 1866, reviewed only two English novels in his lifetime, *Robert Elsmere* in 1888 and *The Picture of Dorian Gray* in 1891.[1] Both of the authors of these books were personally known to him, and both reviews constituted a form of puffing: the Ward review was anonymous and the Wilde review, though signed, seems to have been very reluctantly undertaken as repayment for a favourable review of *Appreciations* by Wilde. A relatively small number of well-known mid-century English critics regularly reviewed English fiction, with E.S. Dallas, R.H. Hutton, Geraldine Jewsbury, George Henry Lewes and Margaret Oliphant the most prominent among them. Pater's bleak record is not atypical, and although he, like his peers, clearly reads English novels, his silence on English fiction, as a critic, is pronounced.[2]

A second forum, on 'The Science of Criticism', which appeared in the *New Review* eighteen months after *Appreciations*, in May 1891, indicates two factors that help to produce this silence: the low status of fiction and the status of the activity of reviewing itself. All of the critics – Henry James, Andrew Lang and Edmund Gosse – construct criticism as qualitatively divided, but the terms of James's division are 'reviewing' versus 'criticism', with reviewing an object of contempt. Lang, in an evaluation of the usefulness of criticism, places the novel review at the bottom of his pyramid of cultural value:

> Occasionally modern reviews are essays worth reading. If the reviewer be a student and competent, he can hang a charming article on the revival of an old play or the success or failure of a new play. Even the review of a novel may show good manners, wit, knowledge, a happy knack of bringing ideas together, and of elucidating the grounds of liking and disliking.
>
> (Lang 1891: 406)

This notion of the commonness of the novel – how it is distinct from art – points to its perceived alliance with the market, the audience of mass journalism, and paid work. In June 1888 another periodical put this more positively: 'The writing of novels is in England more nearly a profession than any other work in literature'. R.R. Bowker's terms of praise for the English novel in *Harper's*, an American periodical (1888: 3), may have impressed

American readers, but in late nineteenth-century Britain pro-
fessionalism was still too close to 'trade' for the association to
escape altogether a pejorative reading.

When Hardy wrote of 'the fearful price of writing in the English
language' (1890: 19), he was alluding to the tantalising proximity
of French fiction which was more free to include naturalistic
detail. In the same forum, Besant's blustering 'The modern
Elephantis may continue to write in French' (1890: 9) is more
explicit. In a long disquisition in 'The Science of Criticism' a year
later, Henry James also registers the immanence of French
literature at the time, arguing that French criticism is finer: 'The
custom of rough and ready reviewing is, among the French,
much less rooted than with us, and the dignity of criticism is, to
my perception, in consequence much higher' (1891: 400). So, it is
not altogether surprising that most of the fiction which Pater does
review is French. In *Appreciations* French literature is a pervasive,
if uneasy, presence, and for the second edition, some six months
after the first, it actually invades this book on English literature. It
would seem that Pater saw the irony of the vociferous defence of
'imaginative prose' with which *Appreciations* begins, and the
absence of any subsequent essay in the volume on prose fiction:
when 'Aesthetic Poetry' is rapidly removed for the second edition
in May 1890, it is replaced with a previously published review of a
novel: Feuillet's *La Morte*. That Pater introduces in 1890 an essay
on a French novel into his otherwise 'English' volume is
indicative of the current status of the French novel, of English
fiction – fit only for the nursery and women according to the
critics in the *New Review* – and of his dearth of choice (he had
published only one review of English fiction to date).

But the 'Englishness' of the 1889 volume was already defensive
and precarious, achieved in part by suppression of the origins of
'Style' in reviews of Flaubert's correspondence, and the re-
fashioning of the subject from characteristics of French fiction to
that of English style. While Matthew Arnold, and later George
Moore and Arthur Symons, publicly extolled French culture and
authors, many Victorian readers, of French fiction in particular,
shared Pater's wish to hide this taste from full view. Strategies
vary, depending on gender, class and situation: from the
proverbial woman reader stuffing the novel under a cushion
when visitors call, to unsigned reviews by authors of both
genders. French literature seems to command widespread intellectual respectability and general social disapproval. E. Lynn

Linton in the *New Review* makes this point clear when she praises Balzac as 'the greatest master of analytical fiction and the boldest handler of themes' (1890: 13), and then observes:

> But an English Balzac would be hunted out of social life as well as out of literary existence, and his success would be only of the surreptitious hole-and-corner kind which includes shame as well as secrecy – shame to both author and reader alike. The thousand and one life-like touches which make Balzac's portraits real would be impossible in an English novel.
>
> (1890: 13)

That 'literary existence' is the province of the adult male, and the 'social life' that of women and children are allegations which make this paradox intelligible. In *Blackwood's*, renowned for its fiction, its consequent female readership, and its high Tory moral ground, their reviewer of *Appreciations* disapprovingly unmasks the book's affinities with French literature: 'his models of style are all French. That is, we think a great mistake' (Oliphant 1890: 14). The *Spectator*, noting with approval that the criticism in *Appreciations* is, on the whole, self-restrained and 'more manly', nevertheless judges that Pater's 'effort to acclimatise a Gallicism' in the book's title 'smacks of affectation' ([Graves] 1889: 888). Arthur Symons, male, and a connoisseur of French writing, in the more gentlemanly *Athenaeum*, was able to savour the French connotation of the volume's title: 'a word occurring very often in the essays, and used, evidently, in the sense of the French appreciation, a weighing, a valuing, more even than in the general English sense of valuing highly' ([Symons] 1889: 813). So did another man, a friend of Pater's and a poet, writing in an avant-garde little magazine, *The Century Guild Hobby Horse*, one of the sumptuous periodicals associated with the aesthetic and decadent literature and art of the late 1880s and 1890s. Edited by Herbert Horne, its exotic content and its consequently largely male readership overlapped with that of the *Yellow Book*. Addressing his particular readers, Lionel Johnson constructs an aesthetic provenance for the French word, and identifies Pater and the volume with the introduction of this French word into English:

> In the French tongue of our day, that word has come to mean no more than Essays or Studies; critical estimates. But to our English the word, I think, is new: and we may fancy in it a

> meaning something more delicate and subtile; it would seem
> to promise a quality of reserve, a judgment very personal, a
> fine tolerance towards the reader.
>
> (Johnson 1890: 36)

What is equally significant, perhaps, is that although the French
element of *Appreciations* is noted by a number of reviews which
construct it as 'foreign' (whether approving or disapproving), its
address to the project of English literature is hardly recognised or
commented upon, except for comments on individual essays.
Only *Blackwood's* invokes Englishness outright. It would seem
that French literature as a literature had a higher profile at this
time than English which was only just emerging as a subject in
the older universities. In *Appreciations* (1889) French literature
serves to decentre the subject, and its reiterated presence
undermines the nationalist enterprise of English literature in
which Pater's book seems implicated; 'Style,' the title of the lead
essay, suppresses the name of Gustave Flaubert, in a manner
analogous to the displacement of William Morris by the title
'Aesthetic Poetry' later in the volume.

While the new titles signal the changed form and function of
recycled material, they also obscure controversial subjects. The
controversy surrounding the Morris essay pertains to the intertextuality of Pater's text, its hedonism rather than Morris's, on
the occasion of the initial appropriation of part of the 1868 review
as the 'Conclusion' to *The Renaissance* in 1873. Removed from the
second (1877) edition of that book, it was restored to the third
edition in 1888. A year later, a different fragment of the 1868
Morris text is introduced into *Appreciations*, and in a second act of
self-censorship it is withdrawn in the second edition of *Appreciations* in 1890. It is a testimony to the strength of the hegemonic,
that a mature writer such as Pater is sufficiently wary in 1890 of
charges in *The Spectator* which associate 'Aesthetic Poetry' with
degeneracy, 'rhapsodising' and 'affectation' (1889: 888) to with-
draw an essay from the public domain, material from the same
essay he removed twelve years earlier, as a younger and less
established author. But the controversy over Flaubert was
different from that concerning Morris: the former attached to
Pater's subject itself. From 1857 *Madame Bovary* attracted charges
of 'indecency', for which its author was tried in a French court,
and the general category of French realism which it heralded had,
by 1889, mutated into naturalism and the work of Zola, equally

problematic in Britain. A reference to the 'brutal frankness of Zolaesque truth' (Linton 1890: 11) in 'Candour in English Fiction' illustrates the perception of Zola's work by writers at the time. Inscribed in *Appreciations* are the destabilising notions of a modern international literature on the one hand, and French literary realism, on the other, with its attendant moral tolerance.

Both notions are part of other related debates in late Victorian Britain in which Pater and his fellows participated: the project of a Modern Languages degree at Oxford emerged simultaneously with the campaign for English, and the debate about moral purity was waged variously by W.T. Stead in the *Pall Mall Gazette*, George Moore in *Literature at Nurse*, and the circulating libraries of Mudie and W.H. Smith which refused to distribute books portraying aspects of sexuality or belief of which Average Opinion disapproved (Besant 1890: 8). That the campaigns for Modern Languages and moral purity palpably impinge on, even crowd, the subject of English may be read in the unease of *Appreciations*.

I want to go on now to some critical questions raised in *Appreciations* by its announced project of aesthetic criticism. They include the question of style and its relation to censorship; the attempt to establish the romantic tradition as the 'ground' of English literature; gender in literary discourse and culture; and the literary production of the aesthetic critic: the aesthetic book and its relation to the articles of which it is composed. Some of these 'questions' (of style, romanticism, gender, literature) are foregrounded in the text; in them contemporary culture may be seen to interrogate itself, but it should be noted that the culture in question is not static or unified, but various and differentiated over time: the questions in *Appreciations* are posed over the twenty odd years in which its writings were produced, as well as in the year 1889 in which it first appeared as a single text. Moreover some of these questions are those which preoccupy critical writing in our own time, gender, for example, and defining literature and defending criticism. Of the remaining questions, some are addressed far more indirectly in the text, such as the canon and university English, and the relation of the book to the periodical press. The identification of these questions as subjects derives from the position of this text, the one you are reading, in history. The historicity of the subject of this essay, aesthetics and *Appreciations*, is a complex matrix of time ranging from about 1790 to the present, and of readings from positions of positions:

Aestheticism on Romanticism, contemporary classicism, and itself; late twentieth-century cultural materialism on Aestheticism, late Victorian cultural production and gendered discourse. So the 'affray' of the title is constituted not only in the moment of production of *Appreciations* in 1889 but in the processes by which that text and this text produce meanings.

In a period such as the nineteenth century, when literature is linked publicly with responsibility for national morality and salvation, attempts to establish literary space outside of these constraints may come from a number of directions. Hardy and Moore ask, directly, for the link to be abandoned: concurring with the censors, they view the problem as one of subjectivity, and demand that censored issues – adultery, sexuality – be permitted to loom into view, irrespective of the effect on national morality. Pater takes a different tack, which addresses the problem obliquely, and avoids confrontation. Instead he, and others arguing from the aesthetic position, put forward formalist claims which minimise the question of subjectivity at which the censorship is directed. Proffering style as a subject is part of this strategy of resistance; it permits Pater, for example, in his essay on style to address the question of subjectivity only glancingly and tokenly, at the last moment possible. So style, whatever its positive values, is effectively a displacement of subjectivity in response to the demands on literature to articulate national and hegemonic morality. Pater's exclusion of the English novel in the essay (and in the book) also helps keep his critique implicit: the defence of imaginative prose in 'Style' does not emerge as a defence of the novel, but as an invitation to treat such prose – liberated from fact and the prosaic, and allied with the imagination – on an equal footing with imaginative poetry, which is not necessarily intrinsically distinct from prose or at the apex of cultural value.

The assault on extrinsic fact with which Pater supports this argument is part of a belief in the interiority of the experiential world which he articulated early in his work, in the 'Preface' to *Studies* when he appropriated Arnold's classical dictum by rewriting and transforming it to the romantic proposition, 'What is this song or picture to me?' In 'Style' the artistic quality of prose is made dependent on its 'imaginative sense of fact', truth lying with the former rather than the latter half of the phrase. Beauty is not qualitatively different from truth, but constitutes its extreme form, 'the finer accommodation of speech to that vision within' (1889a: 6). If much is made of 'truth' here (later in the essay it is rendered as 'vrai vérité' (1889a: 32), Pater makes it quite clear, through repetition, that 'truth' is subjective, relative and a function of language and readership. Where the relation between signifier and 'what it signifies' (1889a: 19) is discussed, the signified remains within the realm of ideas – 'the initiatory apprehension or view' (1889a: 19), in a mediated relation to the external world and in a transparent relation with *language*.

With an eye to the hegemonic constraints on fiction, 'Style' insists on the capaciousness of good literature, the 'eclectic' nature of the principle of 'vrai verité': 'how many kinds of style it covers, explains, justifies and at the same time safeguards! Scott's facility, Flaubert's deeply pondered evocation of "the phrase", are equally good art' (1889a: 32). This tolerance is evident too in the explanation of 'literary architecture', the image in 'Style' which most directly invokes the work of John Ruskin, one of those whose moral programme for art Pater is opposing. Like Ruskin, Pater welcomes variety in architectural design – 'an entire, perhaps very intricate, composition, which shall be austere, ornate, argumentative, fanciful' (1889a: 20). But instead of these diverse qualities attesting to formally anarchic and socially organic individualism, Pater with Flaubert requires 'a single, almost visual image, vigorously forming an entire, perhaps very intricate, composition' (1889a: 20). Here the substitution of the formal for the social/spiritual criterion for art is explicit.

Formalism after Marx, in a poststructuralist and postmodernist present, does not seem to have much to recommend it. But if the strategies of 'Style' are regarded as part of the discourse of resistance to the censorship of literature enforced by the institutions of the period, then the meaning of the advocacy of style may be enlarged to comprise not only formalist ends which establish the autonomy of art from culture. 'Style' may be viewed as an intervention in the literary politics of the day which allies itself with an alternative culture to the hegemonic culture – with realism and naturalism, with George Moore and Thomas Hardy, and with the liberation of what Hardy terms the 'monopolising' of 'literary space' (1889a: 17). 'Style' is part of a collective attempt in the late 1880s and early 1890s to topple certain cultural institutions and cultural values.

Nor does 'Style' limit itself to formalism. In the last paragraph of the essay, subjectivity appears in order to distinguish great art from good art. Formalist criteria pertain, in Pater's scheme, to good art, the great bulk of literature within print culture, which properly appears in the domain of circulating libraries and magazines. But in glancingly adumbrating criteria for the greatest art, Pater momentarily joins Hardy and Moore in a direct advocacy of an enhanced subjectivity, a 'greater dignity of its interests': 'It is on the quality of the matter it informs or controls, its compass, its variety, its alliance to great ends, or the depth of the note of revolt, or the largeness of hope in it, that the greatness of literary art depends' (1889a: 36). The only novel on Pater's list of the greatest literature is French, *Les Misérables*; overall, the list of four works – *The Divine Comedy*, *Paradise Lost*, the Hugo, and The English Bible – is catholic, European rather than English, and divided equally between poetry and prose. While it is not offered as exhaustive but exemplary, it is noteworthy that its historical range includes contemporary literature, and that the contemporary form is prose, and fiction. In its exclusion of classical Greek and Latin texts, it fulfils its function as the opening of a book on 'modern' and English literature, but in terms of the project of English, it is significant that it excludes Shakespeare and all drama; the absence of Shakespeare's work in the list contrasts with the attention to his work in the structure of *Appreciations* in which he is the sole author whose works are treated singly, and the only author accorded three essays, which appear at the core of the structure. One of many disjunctions in the volume, this double focus is the inscription of writing from divergent periods and discourses.

This last paragraph of 'Style,' which roots great art in cultures, histories and politics, has been regretted by formalists, but neglected by materialists. Rather than seeing it as an inexplicable *volte face* on Pater's part, or worse, a capitulation to the hegemonic, I want to suggest that the two positions in 'Style' – the formalism which makes up its bulk and the conclusion which enhances subjectivity – are both part of a strategy of resistance to the censorship of the novel in the period, a subject itself suppressed in *Appreciations*.

This question of the nature of the novel is part of a contemporary preoccupation with the nature of literature more generally. In Raymond Williams' discussion of the changing definition of 'literature' in *Keywords*, he notes the movement of the word away from an inclusive definition which takes in all print culture to one which locates literature in the more elitist domain of writing to distinguish it from journalism. A preoccupation with the definition of literature is unmistakeable in *Appreciations*, and on the whole Pater's conception is elitist not in terms of class *per se*, but in terms of education. It is elitist or, in another light specialised, self-consciously and contingently. That is, he claims no universal, essentialist character for literature ('Different classes of persons, at different times, make, of course, very various demands upon literature') (1889: 14), but adumbrates a particular class of readership, author and temperament for the definition he proffers. The author and reader are scholarly, attentive, susceptible and grave, the work possesses 'intellectual beauty' (1889a: 27), and is characterised by a dearth of ornament (*pace* Ruskin) which derives from a 'tact of omission' (1889: 15). The analogy is with 'fine art' (1889a: 27) free from 'vulgar decoration' (1889a: 15), and this structure of opposition between literary refinement and vulgarity is repeated in an image of opposition between 'a sort of cloistral refuge' afforded by literature from 'a certain vulgarity in the actual world' (1889a: 15).

All of this corroborates Williams' hypothesis of an attempt in this period to locate literature outside of the commercial sphere of journalism and publishing. But Pater's definition is tentative, consciously specialised, from an articulated position within higher education. Moreover, Pater notes the limitations of this perception of literature on two counts, both I think attaching to gender.

The first registration of the limits of the specialised kind of literature he advocates occurs early in 'Style' where he notes that the scholarly author or reader excludes most women 'under a system of education which still to so large an extent limits real scholarship to men' (1889a: 8). Debarred access to education, most women are debarred entry to Pater's categories of author or reader: 'In his self-criticism, he [the (male) author] supposes always that sort of reader who will go (full of eyes) warily, considerately, though without consideration for him, over the ground which the female conscience traverses so lightly, so amiably' (1889a: 8). This is the division of readership, between male and female, acknowledged by James, Hardy and Besant in the *New Review*. However, instead of resolving the problem by solutions which separate out 'realistic' fiction for male readers alone, Pater analyses it as one of culture rather than resorting to essentialism, or a unitary construction of woman. Pater's intervention is informed and topical; in the late 1880s the movement in

Oxford for higher education for women was engaged in managing its success, as the first Halls for women, Somerville and Lady Margaret Hall, had opened in 1879. Clara Pater, one of the two sisters with whom Pater shared a house, had a long association with the movement, and served as Resident Tutor at Somerville from 1881 to 1894. Her activities, and those of a number of his contemporary (male) Fellows, would have alerted Pater to the adverse position of women who sought higher education.

There is another gloss on gender in 'Style', which pertains to sexuality as an unacceptable subject of writing. Embedded in two other safe discourses in play, it is effectively obscured, except to those (largely male) readers alive to the codes of gendered discourse. Intertextuality is a key factor here, both in our reading and in the writing. Where 'Style' alludes to the self-censorship of writing in nineteenth-century Britain – which Walter Besant actually advocates in the *New Review* in his contribution to 'Candour in English Fiction' – it is in the discourses of theology and critical theory.

Blustering and bloody-minded, Besant simply demands self-censorship from British writers in his rousing concluding paragraph, and consigns sexuality in literature to the French language:

> The author, however, must recognise in his work the fact that such Love is outside the social pale and is destructive of the very basis of society. He *must*. This is not a law laid down by that great authority, Average Opinion, but by Art herself, who will not allow the creation of impossible figures moving in an unnatural atmosphere. Those writers who yearn to treat of the adulteress and the courtesan because they love to dwell on images of lust are best kept in check by existing discouragements. The modern Elephantis may continue to write in French.
>
> (1890: 9)

'Style' both defies this interdiction in its writing practice and addresses the issue of 'what can never be uttered' (1889a: 24) so circumspectly that self-censorship is articulated. In the text a theological mind-soul dichotomy is developed patiently, over a number of paragraphs (1889a: 22–4), with soul the presence of the '"the altar-fire"' (1889a: 23) in language. Beginning in theological discourse, the text moves explicitly to a discourse which is secular: 'But something of the same kind acts with similar power in certain writers of quite other than theological literature, on behalf of some wholly personal and peculiar sense of theirs' (1889a: 23). This secular discourse is apparently that of criticism, but it appropriates that of love, friendship, affinity – signalled by the substitution of the word 'perfume' for the word 'colour' (1889a: 23) – for a few explanatory culminating sentences which begin 'There are some to whom nothing has any real interest, or real meaning, except as operative in a given person'. Although 'soul' in writing is validated in this text through the laboured pursuit of the mind-soul opposition, the argument ends by positing the opacity and unutterability of soul due to the nature of language. Leading directly to that part of 'Style' in which Flaubert is introduced as 'the martyr of literary style' (1889a: 24), it ends in the contestation by Flaubert of the discourse of sexuality with that of literary criticism. So the text moves from the discourse of theology to that of literary criticism, and from an insistent introduction of the notion of 'soul' in literature to an allegation of its partial eclipse: 'it is still a characteristic of soul, in this sense of the word, that it does but suggest what can never be uttered, not as being different from, or more obscure than, what actually gets said, but as containing that plenary substance of which there is only one phase or facet in what is there expressed' (1889a: 24).

This gloss on 'soul' – 'what can never be uttered' – appears just before Flaubert and the text of his letters are introduced. That the discourse in which this gloss appears is gendered and sexual is clear not only from its position in the text and from the juxtaposition with Flaubert which follows, but also from another form of intertextuality, the provenance of the passage. The passage containing the parallel between the influence of art on the individual and that between living persons recalls 'Winckelmann' (and other early essays published eventually in *Studies* (1873), some versions of which appear in *Appreciations* such as 'Coleridge's Writings' and 'Poems by William Morris') in which the living-persons part of the equation is constructed as a passionate friendship between a male mentor and a younger male pupil or companion.

It seems clear that the definition of literature put forward in 'Style' is self-conscious, provisional and contingent on what are viewed as the conditions of nineteenth-century culture and language; while it is largely written by men for men, it can only 'suggest what can never be uttered' (1889a: 24). Pater's intervention in the censorship debate is written from a homosexual position which is never explicitly rendered visible in the argument. If the intervention of 'Style' in that debate is oblique compared with the visibility of those by George Moore, Besant, Hardy and Lynn Linton, the key lies in the relation of sexual politics, the discourse of gender and aesthetic questions, and in the construction of homosexuality and heterosexuality in the period.

The four essays on the modern poets, Wordsworth, Coleridge, William Morris and D.G. Rossetti, frame the collection after 'Style'. They comprise an historical critique of what is put forward as the English romantic tradition, with its first and second waves of Romanticism and Aestheticism. This construct engages with other contestants for dominance in the 'tradition' or discourse of English literature then being forged – notably, a 'salvationary' classical discourse authorised by the ancients as recommended by Matthew Arnold, and a 'moral' romantic discourse authorised by medieval Christianity advocated by John Ruskin. The 'grounding' of *Appreciations* in romanticism is reinforced by the concluding essay, 'Postscript.' Here opposition between 'classical' and 'romantic' is collapsed much in the way that difference between prose and poetry is tempered in 'Style': as the 'poetic' is brought into the remit of prose in 'Style', so the 'classical' is lodged on a continuum with the 'romantic' in 'Postscript.' Characteristically, Pater's tack is to avoid confrontation: to note difference, but to entertain its play, rather than deplore and eradicate it.

This crafty, cheeky, sleight of hand works by subversion and the undermining of rational argument rather than by the direct confrontations which can characterise Arnold's essays, strewn with surnames. The play of the text is one quality that distinguishes the discourses of *Appreciations* from those of Arnold and Ruskin.[3] Another can be identified in connection with the Rossetti essay. I have suggested that the discourse of gender is found throughout *Appreciations*, in 'Style', and in a particular and common form in the early essays included here. It takes yet another form in 'Rossetti' (1883), a later essay, and that is a defence of the 'fleshly'. Andrew Leng (1989) has recently suggested that the provenance of this piece, written when Rossetti's death permitted his inclusion in T.H. Ward's anthology *The English Poets*, is part of Pater's longstanding contestation of Ruskin's views; here Pater's strategy is construed as a claim of Rossetti for the Aesthetes just as Ruskin rejects him as a realist. What interests me here is the language of Pater's appropriation which introduces obliquely another, by now notorious, text into 'Rossetti', the pseudonymous piece by 'Thomas Maitland' (Robert Buchanan) in the *Contemporary Review* in 1871 called 'The Fleshly School of Poetry' of which Rossetti's work was the occasion and principal subject. While Buchanan's piece appeared over a decade before 'Rossetti' was written, it had been reinvoked in 1882 in obituaries of Rossetti. Pater also had particular reason to remember the article which virulently attacked the work of members of his circle – in particular the pictures and prose of Simeon Solomon, a close friend of Pater's in 1871, who was arrested in 1873 for homosexual offences, and subsequently ended his life as a vagrant, and destitute. Additionally it took as its subject of attack precisely the romantic discourse and tradition in English literature which *Appreciations* advocates:

> English society of one kind purchases the *Day's Doings*. English society of another kind goes into ecstasy over Mr Solomon's pictures – pretty pieces of morality such as 'Love dying by the breath of Lust'. There is not much to choose between the two objects of admiration, except that painters like Mr. Solomon lend actual genius to worthless subjects, and thereby produce veritable monsters – the lonely devils that danced round Saint Anthony. Mr. Rossetti owes his so-called success to the same causes . . . the man parades his private sensations before a coarse public . . . the fleshly feeling is everywhere.
>
> ([Buchanan] 1871: 338–9)

This part of the attack identifies Rossetti and Solomon as two of its objects, specifies a charge of sexual immorality, alleges it to be a ubiquitous cultural malaise, and valorizes Christian orthodoxy as the alternative position. If James Knowles's *Contemporary Review* in 1871 had a policy of open exploration of all aspects of a question, the cultural formation of the *Contemporary* is nevertheless within the religious press: the Christian orientation of the 'Fleshly School' is endorsed by the authority of the journal. Another discourse here is that of cultural, intellectual and economic elitism, whereby the work of Rossetti and Solomon is slurred by association with the coarse 'public' masses by way of the ubiquity of the malaise, the parallel with the *Day's Doings*, and the allegation of trivia or 'worthless subjects' (Buchanan 1871 : 339). It is this last phrase which suggests to me that Buchanan's text figures in the intertextuality of 'Style' as well as 'Rossetti'. Where 'Rossetti' addresses the charge of fleshliness (by embracing it), 'Style' turns the body-soul/expression-thought argument in Buchanan, exemplified here, on its head:

> The fleshliness of [Tennyson's] 'Vivien' may indeed be described as the distinct quality held in common by all members of the last sub-Tennysonian school, and it is a quality which becomes unwholesome when there is no moral or intellectual quality to temper and control it. Fully conscious of this themselves, the fleshly gentlemen have bound themselves to extol fleshliness as the distinct and supreme end of poetic and pictorial art; to aver that poetic expression is greater than poetic thought, and by inference that the body is greater than the soul and sound superior to sense; and that the poet, properly to develop his poetic faculty, must be an intellectual hermaphrodite, to whom the very facts of day and night are lost in a whirl of aesthetic terminology . . . *they* are creedless.
>
> (Buchanan 1871: 335)

Again, Christianity is valorized and abnormal sexuality alleged, but the body-mind, expression-thought dualities are additionally adduced, under the aegis of the 'aesthetic'. In 'Rossetti', in a passage which may be taken to invoke and reply to Buchanan without once naming him, the terms of the dualities are collapsed: a tradition is constructed on the authority of Dante whom Rossetti and Pater himself are then shown to follow:

> In our actual concrete experience, the two trains of phenomena which the words *matter* and *spirit* do but roughly distinguish, play inextricably into each other. Practically, the church of the Middle Age by its *aesthetic* worship, its sacramentalism, its real faith in the resurrection of the *flesh*, had set itself against that Manichean opposition of spirit and matter, and its results in men's way of taking life; and in this, Dante is the central representative of its spirit. To him, in the vehement and the impassioned heat of his conceptions, the material and the spiritual are fused and blent. . . . And here again, by force of instinct, Rossetti is one with him. His chosen type of beauty is one,
>
> > 'Whose speech Truth knows not from her *thought*,
> > Nor Love her *body* from her *soul*.'

Like Dante, he knows no region of spirit which shall not be
sensuous also, or material.

(Pater 1889a: 236)

All the terms of the Buchanan passage are here (in italic),
contested in the new text, apparently in connection with Rossetti's work. But that work, the subjectivity of 'Rossetti', is another,
second site of intertextuality: the essay may be seen to appropriate its apparent referent to its own textuality. The notion of
passionate friendship invoked in 'Style' and other essays in
Appreciations is attributed to Rossetti, as it is elsewhere to
Coleridge, Wordsworth and Morris:

> For Rossetti, then, the great affections of persons to each
> other, swayed and determined, in the case of his highly
> pictorial genius, mainly by that so-called material loveliness,
> formed the great undeniable reality in things, the solid
> resisting substance.

(1889a: 237)

Buchanan's charge against aesthetic poetry and painting –
'Fleshliness', the celebration of the body, the sensuous, the
material – is taken on board in 'Rossetti', and acknowledged as a
key characteristic of the aesthetic phase of the romantic tradition
constructed here. Inscribed in *Appreciations* is a materialist
discourse of gender in which corporeal sexuality – both homosexual and heterosexual – is a defended constituent.

Buchanan's disingenuous castigation of Solomon and Rossetti's 'private sensations' as 'worthless subjects' (1871: 339) is
another charge registered by *Appreciations*. It is addressed in
'Rossetti' where the poet's 'serious purpose' and 'serious beauty'
(1889a: 234) are likewise praised:

> Here was one , who had a matter to present to his readers, to
> himself at least in the first instance, so valuable, so real and
> definite, that his primary aim, as regards form or expression
> in his verse, would be but its exact equivalence to those data
> within.

(1889a: 229)

It is also addressed in 'Style' where its obverse, the worth of a
subject, is singled out as an important determining factor in
evaluating the greatness of literature. But the list of works
associated with this category, including as it does *Les Misérables*
and *Esmond*, clearly exemplifies a romantic tradition. In the

debate about the duality of mind and soul in art, 'Style' foregrounds the expression/soul side of the equation where Buchanan champions the 'moral or intellectual quality to temper and control it' (1871: 335), or mind.

If the profile of English literature in *Appreciations* gives generic pride of place to poetry through its four essays on Romantic and Aesthetic verse, and denies the English novel, it does include prose and drama. But these five essays at the core of the volume are notably lighter and shorter than the framing essays at its outer limits in which the weight and real engagements of *Appreciations* reside. A model for disengagement is offered in several of the core essays; it is 'the humourist', a word which figured prominently in the original title of 'Charles Lamb' when it appeared in the *Fortnightly* in 1878 as 'The Character of the Humourist: Charles Lamb'. It reappears in 'Sir Thomas Browne' (1889a: 131) where it is defined as one

> to whom all the world is but a spectacle in which nothing is really alien from himself, who has hardly a sense of the distinction between great and little among things that are at all, and whose half-pitying, half-amused sympathy is called out especially by the seemingly small interests and traits of character in the things or the people around him. Certainly, in an age stirred by great causes . . . that is not a type to which one would wish to reduce all men of letters. Still, in an age apt also to become severe, or even cruel . . . the character of the humourist may well find its proper influence, through that serene power, and the leisure it has for conceiving second thoughts, on the tendencies, conscious or unconscious, of the fierce wills around it.
>
> (Pater 1889a: 131–2)

It is clear that the three pieces on Shakespeare's plays largely take up this position of amused observation. Two – a *Love's Labour's Lost* and 'Shakespere's English Kings' – are characterized by a discourse in which beautiful (Richard II) or fashionable (Biron) males, whose links with homosexual culture are glancingly indicated, occupy centre stage. While exotic and morbid elements surface persistently in all of these compositions, they are inscribed in a disengaged, comedic discourse in which the aesthetic (in Lamb), the poetic (in Browne), the fashionable and the fop (in *Love's Labour's Lost*), poetic form (in *Measure for Measure* and 'Shakespere's English Kings'), and personal beauty (in 'Shakespere's English Kings') prevail. This discourse functions in a very similar manner to the way in which I suggested the emphasis on style functions in the context of late Victorian censorship, as an evasion of engagement with the question of the morality of the subject.

However, in *Measure for Measure*, the most serious essay of this core group and the earliest, the ethical and abstract question of the morality of art is raised materially, by means of intertextuality, through the morality play. To address the Victorian demand for morality in art in this oblique manner is a clever move. Rendered strange and crude, morality in art is viewed disadvantageously in relation to a distant historical period, and materially, through a literary form: 'The old "moralities" exemplified most often some rough and ready lesson' (1889a: 189); with the same sleight of hand, the claims of form over matter are positioned parenthetically rather than argued, and the ways in which morality is complicated by contingency are foregrounded. This 1874 essay is making a case entirely compatible with the position of 1889/9 in 'Style', though without participation in the larger, public censorship debate of the 1880s and 1890s which contributed to the ways in which this essay would be read in 1889 when it (re-)appeared in *Appreciations*. The link made here between style and the evasion of the demand for morality is very explicit:

> This ethical interest, though it can escape no attentive reader, yet, in accordance with that artistic law which demands the predominance of form everywhere over the mere matter or subject handled, is not to be wholly separated from the special circumstances, necessities, embarrassments, of these particular dramatic persons.
>
> (1889a: 188–9)

Morality is shown to be contingent, and the justice with which the play resolves this ethical element is termed 'poetic'; it is a function of soul rather than mind. Shakespeare too is corralled into the humourist category:

> the poetry of this play is full of the peculiarities of Shakespeare's poetry, so in its ethics it is an epitome of Shakespeare's moral judgments. They are the moral judgments of an observer, of one who sits as a spectator, and knows how the threads in the design before him hold together under the surface: they are the judgments of the humourist also, who

follows with a half-amused but always pitiful sympathy, the various ways of human disposition, and sees less distance than ordinary men between what are called respectively great and little things. It is not always that poetry can be the exponent of morality : but it is this aspect of morals which it represents most naturally.

(1889a: 190–1)

As discrete pieces of work, these core essays are shapely and engaging, but as parts of a cumulative outline of the canon or scope of an English literature they disappoint. *Appreciations* has none of the conviction or programme concerning English literature that is found in Hippolyte Taine's history for example, though it is *de facto* Pater's only collection of essays on English literature. We know from Pater's library borrowings that he knew of Taine's work from 1874 and, in 1886, three years before *Appreciations* appeared, Pater specifically addressed the question of English literature. At the height of the debate about the introduction of Modern Languages and English into degree status at Oxford, Pater like many of his peers published work on this question. In February he contributed an anonymous review of 'Four Books for Students of English Literature' to the *Guardian*, an Anglican weekly (17 February: 246–7); in November his statement on 'English at the Universities' in the *Pall Mall Gazette* (27 November: 1–2) showed him to be anxious to protect Classics; while cautiously welcoming the study of not only English but modern European literature, the basis of his approval is that literary (rather than philological) work in these modern literatures could aid students in their classical studies. It is at best a tepid endorsement, qualified by the complexity of the position from which it is written: Classical Fellow, reader and reviewer of modern European literature, and English author. I have already shown the ways in which French literature and fiction impinge on the Englishness of *Appreciations*, and I want also to suggest now that *Appreciations* represents a displacement of classical literature as well, a repression which is significantly more successful and ruthless.

After the painful aftermath of the publication of Pater's first book in 1873, traces of a number of projected books have survived. In late 1874 the *Academy* alerts readers to a series of essays on Shakespeare to follow *Measure for Measure*; from this, and from the preponderance of English literature in the books

Pater borrowed from libraries in the mid-1870s, Billie Inman argues that, initially, Pater's second book was to treat 'British authors, primarily Shakespeare' (Inman 1990: xxvi–vii); in 1878 plans for a collection successively titled *The School of Giorgione and Other Studies* and then *Dionysus and Other Studies* are put to Macmillan who produces proof, but the book is withdrawn before final printing.

How do the English, visual-art, and classical orientations of these successive projects relate to *Appreciations*, which could be said to represent the deferral of these aborted plans? The 1878 proposal does contain a number of the English essays of the 1889 volume: 'Wordsworth', the Lamb essay, and the two early Shakespeare pieces on *Love's Labour's Lost* and *Measure for Measure*; but it is far more eclectic than *Appreciations*, as it also has 'The School of Giorgione' (which looks back to the first book on Renaissance art) and four essays on Greek myths, two on Demeter and two on Dionysus. In addition it contains 'Romanticism', also in *Appreciations*, which is preponderantly about European literary culture.

What happens to these essays? The piece on Giorgione is viewed as a postscript to the visual arts work and added to the third edition of *The Renaissance* published in January 1888, almost two years before *Appreciations* appears in November 1889. The Shakespeare essays are built on, and 'Shakespere's English Kings' is written for *Appreciations* and published separately abroad, in *Scribner's* in April 1889, while *Appreciations* is in the press; the Wordsworth essay is utilised as the kernel of what becomes the English romanticism element of the volume, developed by the inclusion of the Coleridge, Morris and Rossetti essays; Lamb, the sole writer of English prose, is bastioned by the addition of 'Style' and 'Sir Thomas Browne'. Only the essays on Greek mythology are unaccommodated, and they remain unpublished in book form for the duration of their author's lifetime.

It is a significant suppression, one which attests to the power of the hegemonic between 1878 and 1894, the fear it endangered, and the self-censorship that resulted. While the fight for literary expression of heterosexual sexuality was publicly waged by the late 1880s in Britain, implicit expression of homosexual sexuality was still guarded, covert and fraught; explicit defence of homosexuality in public was illegal and impossible, even in 1895 by Wilde, who had conducted his life relatively flamboyantly. Greek culture in this period became a byword for homosexuality

(Tyrwhitt 1877) and Pater, much of whose work was manifestly sensuous, bold and risk-taking, would not leave himself open to such predictable censure. *Appreciations*, in fact, inscribes the position on English literature Pater takes in 1886: European literature is yapping at its heels, and insofar as English literature – denuded of fiction – is hegemonic and 'easy' (that is, less dangerous and more accessible) than classics (Pater 1886: 1), it does displace the classical in Pater's selection of work for *Appreciations*. Despite these measures, however, the *Blackwood's* reviewer of the volume is ominously percipient, identifying the classical and the French literatures behind the facade of the English volume: 'Greek as Mr. Pater is in soul, his models of style are all French' ([Oliphant] 1889: 144).

While the nature of this barbed remark inscribes the culture and politics of *Blackwood's Magazine*, that of a Tory periodical renowned for its fiction and which attracts in consequence a high percentage of female readers, it also offers a vantage point on *Appreciations*. Literature in English, the vernacular language, possessed gender and class qualities in the 1880s: among the literate, it was those deprived of access to higher, classical education, women and working men, who were among the most avid readers of English literature, and while the working men largely read science and social science, the women largely read fiction. By treating English literature, *Appreciations* itself moves into the sphere of female readership: for women in the 1880s probably constituted the majority of formal students of English literature (through Extension and other lectures), and also, through the circulating libraries, a significant portion of the general readership of fiction. By excluding English fiction from his book on English literature, Pater signals not only the censorship which results in the educated's apparent preference for French fiction and the low esteem of the English novel in comparison, but also the maleness of his book: its male vision of English literature accords with that of educated male readers who engage with the classical genres of English literature, poetry and non-fictional prose, which were viewed as more weighty than the novel. In its concentration on male perceptions of subjectivity, *Appreciations* resembles the contemporary periodical addressed to a male readership, the *Nineteenth Century*, which barred fiction and included just those subjects (religion and philosophy) excluded by *Cornhill* as unsuitable for a family readership. Margaret Oliphant, the anonymous *Blackwood's* reviewer, is registering the female territory that *Appreciations* appears to occupy in its map of English literature when she identifies its underlying French and classical elements as culpable.

I want to end with another reviewer's identification of disjunctions in *Appreciations*. William Sharp in the *Glasgow Herald* (28 November 1889) prominently poses the question whether *Appreciations* is a crude commercial venture 'composed simply of reprints' (1889: 9) or an aesthetic book possessing 'infinite charm . . . of an exquisitely refined style, of a thoroughly critical faculty, of an exceptionally acute and delicate insight' (1889: 9). As an anonymous reviewer writing a puff for his friend's book, Sharp is in no doubt that *Appreciations* belongs in the latter category. What is interesting is not his judgement but his view of literary production and the models which he juxtaposes – that of mass readership served by the 'mass of periodical literature' from which Pater's essays 'stood out in bold relief' (1889: 9) and the beautiful book for the delicate, refined, educated, rare sensibility. The review is at pains to distinguish Pater's book from its origins in the periodical press, and this is achieved by repeatedly noting the care, revisions and amplifications that the periodical texts have undergone before being consigned to the aesthetic book. The anxiety attaching to the danger posed by journalism to literature is manifest in the excessive claim that 'the book is as essentially one work as though the separate essays were but sectional parts for the reader's convenience: a unity of aim animates it throughout' (1889: 9). While acknowledging the expanse of years over which the essays were written, Sharp steadily attributes to the book the qualities of art and literature rather than those of journalism: unity, coherence, universality, refinement – not publishing to occasion, diversity, topicality and spontaneity. He also mistakenly identifies as 'new' the essay 'Aesthetic Poetry' and the 'Postscript' which older (or sharper) readers will recognise as reprints as well. What is of interest is that Pater's collection of critical essays on aesthetic questions is reviewed in the late 1880s in terms of material and cultural production, even if these dimensions are denied and categorically suppressed in favour of an oppositional high culture, art model.

I have read *Appreciations* as the cultural inscription of a highly specific period, the late 1880s and the early 1990s. Aesthetics may be seen to be a contingent order of knowledge, implicated here in the institutionalisation of knowledge, sexual politics and gendered discourse.

Notes

1. By my count Pater published 27 reviews out of 78 published items; of these, two treated English fiction and five French fiction. Including articles, imaginary portraits and reviews, Pater published far more on English literature – twenty-one items – than on French – eleven items; with eighteen publications on classical literature and art, including his only novel *Marius*, and with three unfinished essays on classical subjects at the Houghton library at Harvard, classics and English equally occupied his attention. But it also should be noted that seven or eight of the classics essays, those in *Plato and Platonism*, came out of his University work, and in his other work, as yet uncounted in this profile, a number of his fictional portraits treated classical revivals, mainly in Provencal France, and they combine the separate categories above.

2. *Esmond* figures in 'Style' as one of the examples of greater 'literary art' but does not quite make it into the list of 'great art' which includes *The Divine Comedy, Paradise Lost*, The English Bible and a French novel, *Les Misérables*.

3. Links between Pater's 'Wordsworth' (originally 1874) and Arnold's views on English Romanticism, and between Pater and Ruskin, have long since been claimed by scholars.

References

Besant, Walter. (1890). 'Candour in English Fiction', *New Review*, 2 (January), 7–21.

Bowker, R.R. (1888). 'London as a Literary Centre. Second Paper: The Novelists', *Harper's New Monthly Magazine*, 77 (June), 3–26.

[Buchanan, Robert W.] (1871). 'The Fleshly School of Poetry: Mr D.G. Rossetti', *Contemporary Review*, 18 (October), 334–50.

[Graves, C.L.] (1889). 'Mr Pater's Essays', *Spectator*, 63 (December), 887–8.

Hardy, Thomas. (1890). 'Candour in English Fiction'. *New Review*, 2 (January), 7–21.

Inman, Billie. (1990). *Pater and His Reading, 1874–1877*. New York and London, Garland.

James, Henry. (1891). 'The Science of Criticism'. *New Review*, 4 (May), 398–411.

Johnson, Lionel. (1890). 'A Note, upon certain Qualities in the Writings of Mr Pater; as Illustrated by His Recent Book'. *The Century Guild Hobby Horse*, 5 (January), 36–40.

Lang, Andrew. (1891). 'The Science of Criticism'. *New Review*, 4 (May), 398–411.

Leng, Andrew. (1989). 'Pater's Aesthetic Poet: The Appropriation of

Rossetti from Ruskin', *Journal of Pre-Raphaelite and Aesthetic Studies*, 2: 1 (Spring), 42–8.

Linton, E. Lynn. (1890). 'Candour in English Fiction', *New Review*, 2 (January), 7–21.

Moore, George. (1886). *Literature at Nurse*. London, Vizetelly & Co.

[Oliphant, Margaret]. (1890). 'The Old Saloon'. *Blackwood's Magazine*, 147 (January), 131–51.

Pater, Walter. (1891). 'A Novel by Mr. Oscar Wilde'. *Bookman*, 1 (November), 59–60.

—— (1889a). *Appreciations with an Essay on Style*. London, Macmillan.

—— (1889b). 'Shakespere's English Kings'. *Scribner's Magazine*, 5 (April), 506–12.

—— (1889c). 'The Bacchanals of Euripides'. *Macmillan's Magazine*, 60 (May), 63–72.

—— (1888a). 'Robert Elsmere'. *The Guardian*, 43 (28 March), 468–9.

—— (1888b). 'Style'. *Fortnightly Review*, 44 n.s. (December), 728–43.

—— (1886a). 'Four Books for Students of English Literature'. *Guardian*, 41 (17 February), 246–7.

—— (1886b). 'Sir Thomas Browne'. *Macmillan's Magazine*, 54 (May), 5–18.

—— (1886c). 'English at the Universities'. *Pall Mall Gazette*, 44 (27 November), 1–2.

[——] (1886d). 'Feuillet's 'La Morte'. *Macmillan's Magazine*, 14 (December), 97–105.

—— (1883). 'Dante Gabriel Rossetti', in *The English Poets: Selections*, T.H. Ward (ed.) 4 vols., 2nd edn. London, Macmillan, 633–41.

—— (1880). 'Samuel Taylor Coleridge', in *The English Poets: Selections*, T.H. Ward (ed.) 4 vols., London, Macmillan, 102–14.

—— (1878a). 'The Character of the Humourist: Charles Lamb'. *Fortnightly Review*, 24 n.s. (October), 466–74.

—— (1878b). 'On *Love's Labour's Lost*.' *Macmillan's* Magazine, 60 (December, 1885), 89–91.

—— (1877). 'The School of Giorgione', *Fortnightly Review*, 22 n.s. (October), 526–38.

—— (1876a) 'The Myth of Demeter and Persephone', *Fortnightly Review*, 25 (January and February), 82–95, 260–76.

—— (1876b). 'Romanticism', *Macmillan's Magazine*, 35 (November), 64–70.

—— (1876c). 'A Study of Dionysus. I. The Spiritual Form of Fire and Dew'. *Fortnightly Review*, 20 n.s. (December), 752–72.

—— (1874a). 'On Wordsworth'. *Fortnightly Review* 15 n.s. (April), 456–65.

—— (1874b). 'A Fragment on *Measure for Measure*'. *Fortnightly Review*. 16 n.s. (November), 652–58.

—— (1873). *Studies in the History of the Renaissance*. London.

[——] (1868). 'Poems by William Morris', *Westminster Review*, 34 n.s. (October), 300–12.

[Sharp, William] (1889). Review of *Appreciations*. *Glasgow Herald* (28 November), 9.

[Symons, Arthur] (1869). 'Literature', *Athenaeum*, 3242 (14 December), 813–4.

Tyrwhitt, R. St John (1877). 'The Greek Spirit in Modern Literature'. *Contemporary Review* 29 (March), 552–66.

5

'Inevitable relations': aesthetic revelations from Cézanne to Woolf

Rebecca Stott

> Let us hold painting by the hand a moment longer, for though they must part in the end, painting and writing have much to tell each other; they have much in common. The novelist after all wants to make us see.
>
> (Woolf 1966: 241–2)

John Berger in his essay 'The Moment of Cubism' talks of the early years of the twentieth century as one of those 'moments of convergence, when numerous developments enter a period of similar qualitative change, before diverging into a multiplicity of new terms' (1969: 6). This moment has been accounted for in a number of ways: there is an abundance of explanations of the character and causes of revolutions and transformations in the history of art. We have been offered philosophical, historical, economic and cultural explanations, yet the nature and causes of modernism remain nonetheless mysterious and elusive, characterized by an internationalism and an unusually close relationship between the arts, but particularly a coincidence between painting and literature. In this respect, the writings of Virginia Woolf have had a profound significance for those critics in search of a genetic type of experimental modernism. My aim is not to search for causes or influences, but to argue instead that to understand the full significance of the formal experimentation of Woolf's work one needs some grasp of the radical changes in the visual arts in the first decades of the century and some grasp too of the way in which they were understood and translated into

Mark Rigby

important systems of aesthetics by aestheticians and art critics such as Roger Fry and Clive Bell.

The formal experimentation of Virginia Woolf's work develops alongside the attempts of important art critics such as Roger Fry and Clive Bell to explain and interpret the radical art of the early Post-Impressionists which was arriving in England for the exhibitions organized by Fry himself. I will be arguing not only for the 'convergence' of the work of Fry, Bell and Woolf, but also that we must acknowledge that their attempts to develop a new system of aesthetics which would respond to the challenging new arts emerging from the Continent are themselves rooted in earlier nineteenth-century systems of aesthetics from Romanticism to Pater. Both Fry and Bell testify in their work to the inadequacy of language, to the problems of translating the visual radicalism of Cézanne and the Post-Impressionists into words. Both consider literature an imperfect, impure art form which is intellectual and rarely able to express 'pure inhuman emotion' (Bell 1914: 153), yet both these critics have given themselves the task of translating the visual into the written. Woolf was herself to attempt to translate with continuing frustration her moments of vision into words, into fiction rather than into aesthetic systems, as she recorded in her diary in 1928: 'what a little I can get down into my pen of what is so vivid to my eyes'.

The aesthetics of Bell and Fry

These two men, and those who worked with them, were not merely ivory-tower Bloomsbury aesthetes engaged in an obscure and elitist philosophical enterprise. Politically conservative and unarguably disdainful of aesthetic insensitivity, they nonetheless saw their work as part of an important re-education of the public eye. Fry's Omega Workshops must be seen as an attempt to 'develop a definitely English tradition' of the decorative arts which would train the public eye to appreciate the beauty of mass, colour and form.

Bell's *Art*, written in 1914, acknowedges his debt to continuing discussions with Fry whilst he also admits to differences of opinion between them. Less generous perhaps, Fry in his collection of essays, *Vision and Design* (collected in 1920), does not acknowledge Bell, although a reading of the two works indicates how closely their work is integrated and how much their differences are a stimulus to a formulation of relative positions. In the essentials of their creeds, however, their differences are less marked. These discussions were continued across the terrible years of the First World War and though Bell's system is formulated on the eve of this war and Fry's essays collected two years after its end, the chaos and death of the Great War are noticeably absent from their work. Yet the effects of the war are perhaps to be heard in their emphasis on emotional response, in their attempts to justify art ethically, in their solemnity, in Bell's arguments that periods of restlessness and turmoil are the moments of great art, and in his belief, too, in the stability and permanence of great art as a religion in itself able to redeem society.

Whilst Bell and Fry profoundly believed in the existence of a rare number of superfine aesthetic sensibilities, they also maintained that the eye and the emotions could be trained to see the 'Truth' of the new art forms. Fry wrote the introduction to the First Post-Impressionist Exhibition, which he had been courageous enough to establish in London. It is an introduction pervaded by the ecstasy of Fry's own revelation of Truth. After the furore caused by these works, Fry's subsequent work was to carry a bitterness, a Cassandra-like awareness of an inability to hear his prophecy of a new Truth, and a frustration with the medium in which he was forced to work: 'I tried in vain to explain what appeared to me so clear' (Fry 1920: 290). It is this bitterness that seems to fuel his rejection of socialism in 'Art and Socialism', and his belief that the people are bound to a hopeless conviction that 'the aim of painting is the descriptive imitation of natural forms' (Fry 1920: 239).

The shock of Cézanne

Bell and Fry's need for a revolutionary figure on which to build their systems of aesthetics was satisfied by the arrival of Paul Cézanne on the artistic stage of Europe. It was his work which shocked them both into recognition of the Truth of the new art forms which were replacing the scientific experimentation of Impressionism. Bell, always inclined more than Fry towards sentimentalism and a romantic mysticism, writes of Cézanne as a divine mystic, surprised by a revelation of Truth on the hillsides of Aix-en-Provence:

here came to him a revelation that has set a gulf between the nineteenth century and the twentieth: for, gazing at the

familiar landscape, Cézanne came to understand it, not as a
mode of light, nor yet as a player in the game of human life,
but as an end in itself and an object of intense emotion. . . .
From that time forward Cézanne set himself to create forms
that would express the emotion that he felt for what he had
learned to see. . . . Everything can be seen as pure form and
behind pure form lurks the mysterious significance that
thrills to ecstasy.

(Bell 1914: 209)

Roger Fry too in the retrospective essay which concludes *Vision
and Design* describes his search for the aesthetic absolutes of 'great
art'. This search had begun with the Impressionists, but here
something was missing: 'I came to feel more and more the
absence in their work of structural design' (1920: 287). This
absence took him to the visual arts of the Italian Renaissance 'in
the hope of discovering from them the secret of that architectonic
idea which I missed so badly in the work of my contemporaries'
(1920: 288). There was, he says, 'no modern art capable of
satisfying my predilections' because, he adds, 'none such was
known to me, but all the time there was one who had already
worked out the problem which seemed to me insoluble of how to
use the modern vision with the constructive design of the older
master' (1920: 291). This man was, of course, Cézanne, described
by Fry and Bell as a revolutionary and prophetic figure, the last
man on Fry's journey, the last piece in his jigsaw of aesthetic
theory.

In their subsequent search for the meaning of the new Truth
which these two men claim to have felt emotionally and
instinctively, they are both led back through the history of art,
finding the roots of Cézanne's Truth in the great art of earlier
ages: the Italian primitives, Blake, Negro Sculpture, ancient
American art and Mohammedan art. Their search is retrospective: having found Cézanne and having seen through his
eyes the vision revealed to him on the hillsides of Aix-en-
Provence, they believe that this new vision, once seen will be
seen again, but the eyes must be new. The search must not be for
verisimilitude, or imitative realism, or descriptive painting. None
of this is great art, it is only a 'pale reflex of actual appearance'
unable 'to arouse the conviction of a new and definite reality' (Fry
1920: 239) – the conviction, that is, of the Post-Impressionists.
'Like all sound revolutions, Post-Impressionism is a return to first

principles' writes Bell (1914: 44), and Fry later asserts: 'the modern movement was essentially a return to the ideas of formal design which had been almost lost sight of in the fervid pursuit of naturalistic representation' (Fry 1920: 290).

Form: a new and definite reality

In his search for the criteria of great art, Bell holds up what he calls Significant Form as the only common quality capable of arousing the aesthetic response which defines the art form as stable and unobscure. He rejects Beauty for there is a response to the beauty of natural forms (butterflies, flowers) which can be distinguished from the pure aesthetic response which Bell defines as arising from 'the depth's of man's spiritual nature' (Bell 1914: 76). Bell rejects all representational art, descriptive art and verisimilitude as lesser art, significant nonetheless, but once again unable to arouse the aesthetic emotion which is an ecstasy. Fry too argues that art touches our 'imaginative life', which he elsewhere refers to as the 'spiritual life':

> Art, then is, if I am right, the chief organ of the imaginative life; it is by art that it is stimulated and controlled within us, and, as we have seen, the imaginative life is distinguished by the greater clearness of its perception, and the greater purity and freedom of its emotion.
>
> (1920: 24)

Art goes beyond nature, he argues, in its order and variety, in its ability to elicit an appropriateness 'altogether beyond what Nature provides' (1920: 37). But, unlike Bell, Fry does not reject representation, although he questions verisimilitude, arguing that the Post-Impressionists 'do not seek to imitate form, but to create form; not to imitate life but to find an equivalent for life' (1920: 239). Fry calls the most significant criterion of great art 'architectonic form' or 'the scaffolding of the architectonic structure', a term which approximates to Bell's Significant Form: the expression 'by pictorial and plastic form' of 'certain spiritual experiences' of the artist (Fry 1920: 237). The aesthetic response to a work of art, he argues, is the pleasure we take in the recognition of order, 'the contemplation of the inevitable relations of all the parts in the whole' (1920: 81), and it is this contemplation which gives us the sense of harmony of the 'unity-emotion'. Architectonic form is what he had found lacking in the work of the

Impressionists: 'they, or some of them, reduced the artistic vision to a continuous patchwork or mosaic of coloured patches without architectural framework or structural coherence' (1920: 11). Impressionism, he argues, is still locked into accurate and 'scientific' representation, it is still of the surface. Unlike Bell, however, who calls Impressionism a 'blind alley', Fry can see how Impressionism 'paved the way' for Post-Impressionism.

Both critics argue that the new emphasis on the simplification and intensity of form (depth) rather than verisimilitude (the surface) was to liberate art from the shackles of materialism: 'Without [simplification] art cannot exist; for art is the creation of significant form, and simplification is the *liberating* of what is significant from what is not' (Bell 1914: 220, emphasis mine) and in the words of Fry: 'All art depends upon cutting off the practical responses to sensation of ordinary life, thereby *setting free* a pure and as it were *disembodied* functioning of the spirit' (Fry 1920: 242, emphasis mine). Release from the conventions of verisimilitude, likewise, is a liberation of the spirit, a movement from the particular to the universal, from the body to the soul.

The artistic vision

I have been emphasizing the 'mysticism' of these modernist aesthetics in an attempt to underline their roots in Romanticism, for both Bell and Fry premise their aesthetic theories on a shared conviction of the revelatory nature of the artistic vision. Both attempt (and neither achieve) an explanation of the process of artistic vision (Bell in 'The Metaphysical Hypothesis' and Fry in 'The Artist's Vision') which they see as a revelation of spiritual understanding experienced by the artist, realized in the art form and 'transmitted' through the art form to the viewer. It is a mystery beyond language, on the 'gulf' of mysticism, and it is at the point of discovering that he is on this 'gulf' in discussing aesthetic emotion that Fry's *Vision and Design* ends:

> One can only say that those who experience it feel it to have a peculiar quality of 'reality' which makes it a matter of infinite importance in their lives. Any attempt I might make to explain this would probably land me in the depths of mysticism. On the edge of that gulf I stop.
>
> (1920: 302)

Bell believes that art is not an expression of religious feeling but a religion in itself. He calls art and religion 'twin manifestations of the spirit; wrongly do we speak of art as a manifestation of religion' (1914: 2). Art and religion, he argues, 'belong to the same world'; the artist, like the mystic, understands that the physical world is a 'means to ecstasy' (1914: 81). Art as religion, he believes, has no priesthood and no dogmas, but, as a means to spiritual ecstasy, will redeem the world. Fry, never so categorical, nor so simplistic (these are the qualities that set him against what he implies is a sentimentality in Bell's thesis), nonetheless, like Bell, acknowledges the inadequacy of language and understanding to describe the mysteries of the artistic vision. It is transcendent, spiritual and transmitted only through the most 'refined aesthetic sensibility' (Fry 1920: 300).

Vision and design

The title of Fry's collection of essays affirms the two essential constituents of his system of aesthetics: the vision of the artist, a transcendent and mystical vision which is a revelation of inner form and spiritual truth, must be balanced by design, that 'inevitability of relations', that architectonic 'scaffolding'. It was to be in the design of a picture that the full force of the artist's vision communicated itself, a 'translation' of the revelation into the plastic and formal design which will enable the primary emotion (the artist's vision) to be 'transmitted' like an electric current through the art form to the viewer. Only the rarest of aesthetic sensibilities can receive the vision, can *see*. Reception of vision requires the most 'complete detachment from any of the meanings and implications of appearances' (Fry 1920: 51). The artist must apprehend passionately, in silence, detached from the ordinary phenomenal world. Yet whilst there is an anti-intellectualism in Fry's work, there is, too, an insistence that the emotionally comprehended vision must be combined with an intellectualism of design if there is to be a 'transmission' of the primary emotion, if there is to be great art. In the Italian Renaissance Fry finds an 'intellectual art', a curiosity about the phenomena of nature, perspective and anatomy, yet this passion for analysis can lead, he argues, to a conflict between the scientific spirit and art:

> . . . it is difficult to convince people that increased scientific investigation of phenomena, increased knowledge of how things present themselves to our sight, changes the mode

but does not necessarily increase the power, of pictorial expression.

(Fry 1920: 219)

Bell puts it in different terms when he rejects the scientific illusionism of some Renaissance painting. He argues that intellect had filled the void of emotion: 'By the end of the fifteenth century art is becoming a question of rules' not passion, and a true artist must 'apprehend form passionately' (Bell 1914: 150).

The artists whom Fry admires most are those who express emotion through inevitable relations, 'the general principles underlying all appearance' producing an art of intensity, simplicity and 'spiritual' expression. In Blake's work he finds the 'true power of symbolic expression' (1914: 219), his art 'more concentrated than most, gives us an experience which is removed more entirely from bodily and physiological accompaniments, and our experience has the purity, the intensity, and the abstraction of a dream' (1914: 220). Cézanne's great achievement, he believes, is his synthesis of the classical form of Poussin with the marked and expressive emotional states of El Greco. Only this rare synthesis of great passion and pure sight (vision) and the realization of inevitable relations in architectonic form (design) will excite the unity-emotion of great art. The mystical vision must be married to the architectural design. In Bell's words: 'The artist must know what he is about, and what he is about must be, if I am right, the translation into material form of something he has felt in a spasm of ecstasy' (Bell 1914: 233).

Continuities and discontinuities

I have mentioned earlier that the aesthetic systems of Fry and Bell, whilst responding to the entirely new aesthetic problems offered by Post-Impressionism, are nonetheless rooted in various nineteenth-century systems of aesthetics. They cross the gulf which they believe to have opened between the mimetic materialism of nineteenth-century art and the new Truth to Significant Form found in the experimentation of twentieth-century art. In their elevation of the artist into a prophetic seer endowed with a rare aesthetic and emotional vision, they echo the principles of Romanticism and the beliefs of Ruskin that the artist is an instrument of revelation. For Ruskin, the quality of seeing, the apprehension of essential form, are the qualities of the artist who is to reveal the essential truth of the phenomenal world. In their description of the course of Art as a stream which runs richly at times and thinly at others, they restate the principles of Arnold's description of culture in *Culture and Anarchy*, and in their emphasis on the emotional apprehension of Truth we hear Wordsworth's belief that 'the truth carried alive into the heart by passion' is radically different from one which is simply known.

Raymond Williams reminds us that the so-called 'new aesthetics' of Wilde and Pater (the 'new' doctrine of art for art's sake) are not so new but should be seen more accurately as a continuation from earlier traditions of aesthetics (Williams 1958: 169–75). Wilde's aesthetics, Williams argues, are rooted in Arnold's process of 'becoming', and Pater's work is little more than a restatement of an attitude which properly belongs to the Romantics, and the ideas of Wordsworth, Shelley and Arnold: the distinction between being and doing, the criticism of 'mere machinery' and the description of the true moral significance of art and poetry as culture, a 'summing-up of the long preceding tradition'.

But if Pater is saying no more than Mill said when he described poetry as 'a culture of the feelings', what more then is Fry stating when he defines art as 'the true organ of the imaginative [and emotional] life'? This preceding tradition which Williams describes as 'an emphasis of the function of certain kinds of thought and feeling in the whole life of man: a function properly described as moral' (Williams 1958: 171) is a tradition which Fry and Bell continue. Whistler, Williams argues, is distinct from Pater and Wilde in his rejection of the commonly-held assumption that life reflects art: '. . . Art feeds not upon nations, and peoples may be wiped off the face of the earth, but Art *is*' (quoted Williams 1958: 172), and it is Fry, not Bell, who aligns himself with this position – the self-containedness of art – whilst Bell argues, like Wilde, that the artist 'is not an isolated fact, but a resultant of a certain milieu and a certain entourage'. If we accept Williams' summary of the three principles of the 'new aesthetics' of Wilde – first, 'that "art never expresses anything but itself"; second, that "all bad art comes from returning to Life and Nature, and elevating them into ideals"; third, that "Life imitates Art far more than Art imitates Life"' (Williams 1958: 173) – then we can see the continuity of the aesthetics of Fry and Bell with the preceding tradition more clearly.

Yet, if not discontinuities exactly, there are changes of emphasis in these aesthetic systems of the early twentieth century.

There is a stress on the simple line and abstract simplification, a rejection of the chaotic Untruth of realism and verisimilitude in favour of a realization of the 'essential thing' – the Truth of Significant Form hidden from the eye beneath the surface confusion of the object. There is a new movement, too, from the physical to the spiritual, from the body to the soul (the 'disembodiment' that Fry talks of in his description of the aesthetic emotion), from the ornate 'Catholicism' of 'nineties aestheticism to a new, more austere 'Puritanism' of form, from surface to depth, from noise to silence. Quentin Bell has argued for the 'Catholicity' of Fry's tastes (the emphasis on the 'instinctive', mystical response to art) and argued, too, that there is a conflict in Fry's work between catholicity and formalism (see McLaurin 1978: 19). Other critics have seen only Fry's 'native puritanism' (see McLaurin 1973: 20–1), but this puritanism is not to be found in a rigid dogmatism but in the native austerity of Fry's temperament, a puritanism he shared with Ruskin and a temperament which gave him more pleasure (in terms of Truth) in contemplating the plastic form of the Post-Impressionists than the 'marvellous texture of Impressionist painting'. It is this conflict which we hear in the title of his collection: *Vision and Design*. It is a conflict, too, which, I will argue, is one of the driving creative energies of Woolf's *To the Lighthouse* seen in the opposition between the marvellous surface texture of the butterfly's wing and the formal austerity of the cathedral.

Woolf's 1910

In May 1924 Virginia Woolf delivered a paper on modern fiction to the Heretics at Cambridge entitled 'Mr Bennett and Mrs Brown'. It was, as Quentin Bell states, 'as near as she came to an aesthetic manifesto' (1972: 104). It has the confidence and the declamatory tone of a manifesto: 'I will hazard a second assertion . . . to the effect that in or about December 1910 human nature changed'. In this lecture she does not explain the significance of the date, but it will have been obvious to all present: December 1910 was the date of the notorious First Post-Impressionist Exhibition organized by Roger Fry in London. In the following spring she had travelled with a party of friends including Fry to Constantinople, the home of Byzantine art, where she was to spend a great deal of time with Fry during the illness of her sister, Vanessa.

In this lecture Woolf attempts to draw a distinction between the writing of those she calls the Edwardians and the Georgians, or to use a different terminology, the writing of the late Victorian realists and the experiments of those we would call the early 'modernists'. Her point concerns the fictional revelation of character. The Edwardians – Wells, Galsworthy, Bennett – faced with the task of recreating a character perhaps met with on a train – a Mrs Brown – would tell us about her family, her house, her rent and what her mother died of, but not the real Mrs Brown. Yet these tools, she argues, are no longer adequate:

> I knew that if I began describing the cancer and the calico, my Mrs Brown, that vision that I clung to though I knew no way of imparting it to you, would have been dulled and tarnished and vanished for ever. That is what I mean by saying that the Edwardian tools are the wrong ones for us to use. They have laid an enormous stress on the fabric of things.
>
> (Woolf 1924: 106).

Whilst new tools are being found she asks her audience to

> tolerate the spasmodic, the obscure, the fragmentary, the failure. Your help is invoked in a good cause. For I will make one final and surprisingly rash prediction – we are trembling on the verge of one of the great ages of English literature. But it can only be reached if we are determined never, never, to desert Mrs Brown.
>
> (111)

Delivered in 1924, it was a surprisingly late statement about modern aesthetics, but nonetheless it takes its place in a series of aesthetic formulations from Bell's *Art* (1914) to Fry's *Vision and Design* (1920). I would argue that the novel, *To the Lighthouse*, published three years later in 1927, also belongs to that series. However, Woolf's tendency to use painterly analogies to describe her struggle with literary form increases throughout her diaries: they begin in 1915 and continue until her death in 1941. She refers to the drafts of her books as 'canvases' and refers, too, to the final re-typing of a novel like *Mrs Dalloway* as a good method 'as thus one works with a wet brush over the whole, and joins parts separately composed and gone dry' (Saturday, December 13 1924). But there is more than the borrowing of a technical metaphor, for her problem is so often one in which the aesthetics of the visual arts provide her with a language which literary aesthetics cannot:

> The look of things has a great power over me. Even now, I have to watch the rooks beating up against the wind, which is high, and still I say to myself instinctively 'What's the phrase for that?' and try to make more and more vivid the roughness of the air current and the tremor of the rook's wing slicing as if the air were full of ridges and ripples and roughness. They rise and sink, up and down, as if the exercise rubbed and braced them like swimmers in rough water. But what a little I can get down into my pen of what is so vivid to my eyes, and not only to my eyes; also to some nervous fibre, or fanlike membrane in my species.
>
> (Saturday, August 12 1928)

Is this not recognizably, too, the fine emotional quiver which Fry describes as that rare aesthetic response? It is a response which she finds in the 'epiphanies' of Joyce as described in her essay 'Modern Fiction': a movement away from the 'materialism' of the Edwardians to the new 'spiritualism' of the Georgians:

> In contrast with those whom we have called materialists, Mr Joyce is spiritual; he is concerned at all costs to reveal the flickerings of that innermost flame which flashes its messages through the brain, and in order to preserve it he disregards with complete courage whatever seems to him adventitious, whether it be probability, or coherence, or any other of those signposts which for generations have served to support the imagination of a reader when called upon to imagine what he can neither touch nor see.
>
> (Woolf 1957: 190–1)

In 'A Sketch of the Past' Woolf allies herself with Fry's aesthetics, describing the artistic vision – her own – as a spiritual ecstasy beyond words, a 'shock' and a 'moment of being':

> I always feel instantly that [these moments] are particularly valuable. And so I go on to suppose that the shock-receiving capacity is what makes me a writer . . . it is . . . a revelation of some order; it is a token of some real thing behind appearances; and I make it real by putting it into

words. It is only by putting it into words that I make it whole.

(Woolf 1985: 81)

The shock-receiving capacity of these moments can be related to what Fry and Bell refer to as the transmission of a vision through the art work to the viewer. It comes as no surprise that Woolf wrote this description of these 'moments of being' as late as 1939, as a distraction from the frustrations of writing her biography of Roger Fry. The words are his, the vision and recognition of rare sensibility are hers.

From Manet to Cézanne

Woolf's aesthetic search seems to take her on a journey, like Fry's, from the scientific illusionism of the Impressionists to the plastic form and design of Cézanne. (The significance of the work of the Post-Impressionists comes to her late, for at the time of the first Post-Impressionist exhibition she had little time, Quentin Bell tells us, for the new art.) The early novels, much discussed by Clive Bell in correspondence with Woolf, show her searching for 'atmosphere' which Bell refers to in a letter about an early draft of *The Voyage Out*: 'We have often talked about the atmosphere that you want to give; that atmosphere can only be insinuated, it cannot be set down in so many words' (quoted in Quentin Bell 1972: 211). But her doubts about this early writing show a concern about how Impressionistic it is. As she says to Bell: 'I want to bring out a stir of live men & women, against a background. I think I am quite right to attempt it, but it is immensely difficult to do . . . but you have no notion of how *pale* and *transparent* it reads to me sometimes' (quoted in Quentin Bell 1972: 211–2, emphasis mine). Reading back over the novel some years later, she adds: 'such a harlequinade it is – such an assortment of patches', which is precisely Fry's rejection of Impressionism: 'they have reduced the artistic vision to a continuous patchwork or mosaic of coloured patches without architectural framework or structural coherence' (Fry 1920: 11). Woolf is searching at this time for an open, loose form as indicated in early notes for *Night and Day*: 'all crepuscular, but the heart, the passion, humour, everything as bright as fire in the mist' (McLaurin 1973: 33). McLaurin argues that whilst these early novels show Woolf using an impressionistic technique comparable to that of Joseph Conrad, by *Night and*

Day (1919) she is already moving towards a more solid geometri-
cal structure as she begins to search for a grid or net on which her
impressions can fall.

To the Lighthouse

This novel, written only two years after Woolf's delivery of 'Mr
Bennett and Mrs Brown', dramatizes many of the aesthetic
problems which she had discussed in that lecture and with which
she was struggling in her diaries. The confrontation of Lily
Briscoe (abstract painter) and Mr Bankes (who favours sentimental representational art) is central to this novel, and restates
the arguments of Woolf's lecture (a dramatization of an imaginary conversation between a Georgian and an Edwardian). Lily
Briscoe, painting her canvas outside, suffers the curious attention
of Mr Bankes, who asks her to justify her abstract art:

> What did she wish to indicate by the triangular purple shape,
> 'just there?' he asked.
> It was Mrs Ramsay reading to James, she said. She knew
> his objection – that no one could tell it for a human shape. But
> she had made no attempt at likeness, she said. For what
> reason had she introduced them then? he asked. Why
> indeed? – except that if there, in that corner, it was bright,
> here, in this, she felt the need of darkness. Simple, obvious,
> commonplace, as it was, Mr Bankes was interested. Mother
> and child then – objects of universal veneration, and in this
> case the mother was famous for her beauty – might be
> reduced, he pondered, to a purple shadow without irrever-
> ence.
> But the picture was not of them, she said. Or, not in his
> sense. There were other senses, too, in which one might
> reverence them. By a shadow here and a light there, for
> instance. Her picture took that form, if as she vaguely
> supposed, a picture must be a tribute. A mother and child
> might be reduced to a shadow without irreverence. A light
> here required a shadow there. He considered. He was
> interested. He took it scientifically in complete good faith.
> The truth was all his prejudices were on the other side, he
> explained. The largest picture in his drawing-room, which
> painters had praised, and valued at a higher price than he
> had given for it, was of the cherry trees in blossom on the
> banks of the Kennet. He had spent his honeymoon on the

banks of the Kennet, he said. . . . The question being one of the relations of masses, of lights and shadows, which, to be honest, he had never considered before, he would like to have it explained. . . .

(Woolf 1927: 52)

As fiction it is a much more subtle (and amusing) confrontation than that outlined by Woolf in her lecture. Woolf shows an uncertain modern painter trying to explain (as Fry was doing) her anti-representational aesthetics: 'if as she vaguely supposed, a picture must be a tribute'. Lily's experimentation is still beyond words for her ('she could not show him what she wished to make of it'), although Bankes, with a tradition of representational aesthetics and 'value' behind him, is more articulate, falling easily into terms such as reverence and irreverence, which Lily finds difficult to resist. Hers is no confident aesthetic manifesto but an intuitive sense of the Truth and power of her vision as she tunnels her way into her picture, largely in silence, watching Mrs Ramsay, fellow artist, merge 'unrelated passions' so that 'in the midst of chaos there was shape'.

The essential thing

Lily is searching, like Woolf, for the new tools which will convey a new and more definite reality. Like Fry she rejects the verisimilitude of the Paunceforte school ('pale', 'transparent') in favour of an abstraction which will capture not only the surface but the 'essential' depths of a Mrs Brown. Here is Mrs Ramsay based on Woolf's memories of her mother:

But why different and how different? she asked herself, scraping her palette of all those mounds of blue and green which seemed to her like clods with no life in them now, yet she vowed, she would inspire them, force them to move, flow, do her bidding to-morrow. How did she differ? What was the spirit in her, the essential thing, by which, had you found a glove in the corner of a sofa, you would have known it, from its twisted finger, hers indisputably?

(1927: 49)

Georges Braque writing in 1910 also refused to paint what he called the 'factitious woman'. His search was for the beauty of volume, of line, mass, what he called the Absolute:

I couldn't portray a woman in all her natural loveliness . . . I haven't the skill. No one has. I must, therefore, create a new sort of beauty, the beauty that appears to me in terms of volume, of line, of mass, of weight, and through that beauty interpret my subjective impression. Nature is a mere pretext for a decorative composition, plus sentiment. It suggests emotion, and I translate that emotion into art. I want to expose the Absolute, and not merely the factitious woman

(Braque 1910: 47).

Lily's vision at the end of the novel confirms her realization of the need to balance the massy dualities of her composition. The line that she places at the centre of her canvas achieves the synthesis for which she has been searching. It is an instantaneous vision, it comes to her through the passionate apprehension of the form of her subject, the essential thing beneath all the surface detail. She is described, too, as a diver in this last section, quivering on the edge of a board above the 'waters of annihilation', searching for 'some common feeling which held the whole together' (177). Yet 'for whatever reason she could not achieve that razor edge of balance between two opposite forces' (178) until,

With a sudden intensity, as if she saw it clear for a second, she drew a line there, in the centre. It was done, it was finished. Yes, she thought, laying down her brush in extreme fatigue, I have had my vision.

(192)

The aesthetic search of the novel is not only thematic but formal, for the very problems which confront Lily are those with which Woolf herself is struggling as she writes this novel. In her diary she describes the formal problems of the ending: 'the problem is how to bring Lily and Mr Ramsay together and make a combination of interests at the end' (September 1926).

The novel shows a new awareness of formal and architectural design more complex perhaps than the brilliant merging oppositions of *Mrs Dalloway*, in which the figures of Septimus Smith and Clarissa Dalloway are carefully counterpointed and finally joined at Clarissa's party (parties, like Mrs Dalloway's dinner party, are so often the canvases for structural union in Woolf's work). It has a tripartite form with two longer sections shaped around the impressionistic and diachronic 'Time Passes' which McLaurin describes as a parenthetical framing device (McLaurin 1973: 199).

The important use of multiviewpoints is one which Lily comes to understand: 'One wanted fifty pairs of eyes to see with, she reflected. Fifty pairs of eyes are not enough to get round that one woman with, she thought' (182), a device used by Cubist painters to realize the object's multifacetedness and to achieve unity in time and space. The novel itself is multiviewpointed: we inhabit the consciousness – the 'eyes' – of numerous primary and secondary characters. The novel has, too, the 'broken frame' characteristic of Post-Impressionist art: the opening sentence of *To the Lighthouse* takes us into a conversation already long begun.

The fundamental search of both the novel's author and her counterpart, the fictional artist Lily Briscoe, is for a balance of design, a balance of masses, a balance of light and dark, a balance of the tripartite form, a balance of the massy figures of Mr Ramsay and Mrs Ramsay and above all a balance between surface and depth, vision and design. As Lily herself notes as she stands before her painting, 'one must hold the scene – so – in a vice, and let nothing come in and spoil it' (186).

Yet Woolf has not abandoned her search for atmosphere and fluidity. It is the great achievement of 'Time Passes': the 'crepuscular' mistiness or wateriness of this section, an openness of form, a beauty of surface texture. But there is also an attempt to combine surface beauty with the architectonic sense that Fry recognized in the great art of all ages, that 'scaffolding' of design. This union is to be found most powerfully expressed in the recurring image of girder and fabric, cathedral and butterfly's wing, surface and depth, which becomes part of Lily's under-standing of art as well as part of the artistic integrity of the novel:

> She could have done it differently of course; the colour could have been thinned and faded; the shapes etherealized; that was how Paunceforte would have seen it. But then she did not see it like that. She saw the colour burning on a framework of steel; the light of a butterfly's wing lying upon the arches of a cathedral.
>
> (48)

Woolf had remembered her early novel, *The Voyage Out*, with dissatisfaction, recalling how 'pale and transparent' it seemed to her in retrospect. But the shape and form she is searching for here

are those of Lily Briscoe whose colours burn on a framework of
steel, though the surface itself must not be lost to the scaffolding:

> Beautiful and bright it must be on the surface, feathery and
> evanescent, one colour melting into another like the colours
> on a butterfly's wing; but beneath the fabric must be clamped
> together with bolts of iron.

(159)

However, there is another element of this central opposition
(framework and fabric) which indicates that there are other
syntheses of dualities going on in the novel. During the dinner-
party scene Mrs Ramsay listens to the intellectual reasoning of
the men around her table and remarks to herself:

> she [Mrs Ramsay] let it uphold her and sustain her, this
> admirable fabric of the masculine intelligence, which ran up
> and down, crossed this way and that, like iron girders
> spanning the swaying fabric, upholding the world, so that
> she could trust herself to it utterly.

(98)

During the sentence Mrs Ramsay becomes the 'swaying fabric'
upheld by the girders: 'she could trust herself to it utterly'. In a
sense Mrs Ramsay does represent the 'fabric' of the novel, she is
so often exemplified for Lily by the shawl which loosens and falls
in 'Time Passes', carrying for us the full significance of her death,
whilst Mr Ramsay's intelligence and intellectualism is associated
with things hard and straight, such as tables, iron posts marking
spots in the sea and the girders of masculine intelligence. We
leave Mrs Ramsay's shawl wound around the pig's skull at the
end of the first section of the novel. Mrs Ramsay had wound her
fabric around that symbol of 'death', spinning it around the
skeleton, 'fabricating' simultaneously for her children a visionary
world of fairies, mountains and castles, which acts as a correlative
to her ability to bring things together, to merge and make
coherent disparate needs: James wants the skull, Cam does not.
For 'the whole of the effort of merging and flowing and creating
rested on her', the cohering centre of the novel. Yet in the middle
section of the novel (in which we hear the destruction of the war),
the shawl falls, the marvellous texture of Mrs Ramsay's imagination falls from the pig's head, leaving only the emptiness at the
centre of the novel.

Woolf's novel comes as the last in a series of aesthetic

statements, another attempt to translate the visual truth into words. After the direct and startling visual 'Truth' of Post-Impressionist painting, that primitivism which Bell and Fry so admired, how could they consider any art form which used the medium of words to be anything other than inadequate to their needs? Woolf was never to agree with Fry on the subject of the inferiority of literature as an art form, believing as she did that 'painting and writing have much to tell each other: they have much in common'. Yet if Woolf's chosen tools for her task are linguistic they are nonetheless, like all tools, sometimes defective, imperfect communicators of the artistic vision: 'The urgency of the moment always missed its mark. Words fluttered sideways and struck the object inches too low. . . . For how could one express in words the emotions of the body? express that emptiness there?' (Woolf 1927: 165). Fry's inability to account for the artist's vision in anything but the language of mysticism and the abrupt ending to his *Vision and Design* testify to a frustration with language which Woolf was to try to overcome in her formal experimentation with fiction: 'a revelation of some order . . . a token of some real thing behind appearances; and I make it real by putting it into words. It is only by putting it into words that I make it whole' (Woolf 1985: 81).

The synthesis of Impressionism and Post-Impressionism in this novel, expressed through the careful repetition of the iron girders/butterfly wing opposition, suggests, too, that this is a pivotal novel in which Woolf moves from the surface texture and 'atmosphere' of Impressionism to embrace an art which bears the visionary design of the iron girders and architectonic 'scaffolding' of Post-Impressionism. But neither replaces the other in her work, for like Fry she realizes not that surface realism and beauty is 'bad' art, but that the beauty of the surface texture must be 'clamped together on a framework of steel'. These are the inevitable relations, the Significant Form of modernist aesthetics – not 'factitious' realism but Absolute Beauty seen in terms of mass, weight, line and volume. In her autobiographical 'A Sketch of the Past' Woolf weaves present time with anecdotes from her past. Written during 1939 whilst she was also engaged in the gruelling task of writing Roger Fry's biography, she recalls a dinner party with the artist, Mark Gertler, the night before, during which he had talked of the inadequacy of literature to describe her 'Mrs Brown' in contrast to the 'integrity of painting'. Woolf adds, 'Yet if one could give a sense of my mother's personality one would have to be an artist. It would be as difficult to do that, as it should be done, as to paint a Cézanne' (Woolf 1985: 95).

References

Bell, Clive. (1914). *Art*. London, Chatto and Windus. (1930)

Bell, Quentin. (1972). *Virginia Woolf: A Biography*. London, Hogarth Press. (1982)

Berger, John. (1969). 'The Moment of Cubism' in *The Moment of Cubism and Other Essays*. London, Weidenfeld and Nicolson.

Braque, Georges. (1910). 'Personal Statement', *The Architectural Record*, New York, May 1910.

Fry, Roger. (1920). *Vision and Design*. London, Chatto and Windus. (1925)

McLaurin, Allan. (1973). *Virginia Woolf: The Echoes Enslaved*. Cambridge, Cambridge University Press.

Williams, Raymond. (1958). *Culture and Society: 1780–1950*. Harmondsworth, Pelican Books in association with Chatto and Windus. (1977)

Woolf, Virginia. (1924). 'Mr Bennett and Mrs Brown' in *The Captain's Death Bed and Other Essays*. London, Hogarth Press. (1950)

—— (1925). 'Modern Fiction' in *The Common Reader: First Series*. London, Hogarth Press. (1957)

—— (1927). *To the Lighthouse*. London, Hogarth Press. (1984)

—— (1966). *Collected Essays*. Vol. I, London, Hogarth Press.

—— (1985). 'A Sketch of the Past' in *Moments of Being*. Ed. and with an introduction by Jeanne Schulkind. London, Hogarth Press.

Nicola Bettison

6

Marxism and modernist aesthetics: reading Kafka and Beckett

Geoff Wade

Although the rudimentary techniques and motifs of modernism can be detected earlier than the 1850s (in, say, Sterne's *Tristram Shandy*; in Swift's writings; in the later Quartets and the Symphonies – notably the 3rd and 9th – of Beethoven), that decade, to all intents and purposes, announces the birth of modernism in Europe. In Paris, initially, it represented a challenge to Enlightenment Reason, organized religion, Louis Napoleon, and the laborious selectivity and categorization of anything and everything that could be listed on an inventory or positioned on a graph. Later, some aspects of modernism came to be associated with a fractured consciousness emanating from the debacle of the collapse of an older Europe into the blood and mire of the Somme and Ypres – and the battlefields of East Prussia and Asia Minor – with their millions of dead and dismembered humans. It was related, also, to the inspiration of the revolutionary proletariat, and the fear of revolution, the demise of a culture, as T.S. Eliot lugubriously records in *The Waste Land*. For Eliot and his peers, all that remained was a world to be scorned or feared; a world held together by electric machines, 'whiggery' and parochial philistinism.

From the outset, then, modernism had an international flavour, yet in many quarters a reactionary one. Terry Eagleton asserts that modernism 'cuts indifferently across cities, societies, art-forms, languages, national traditions. . . . It belonged in this way to the new, rootless semiotic networks of monopoly-capitalist Europe, floating in and out of Berlin, Paris, Zurich,

Vienna, as easily as the pound' (Eagleton 1989: 23). In Western Europe modernism shifted increasingly to the Right; and with notable exceptions, such as Pablo Picasso and Bertolt Brecht (and those close to them), there dwindled, to almost nothing, any objective socialist content. There was, though, a drive against the expanding technology of the age (aspects of which will later be celebrated by postmodernism); consequently, modernism found itself taking refuge in mythology: the *Rite of Spring*, the 'Fisher King', 'Daedalus', *The Celtic Twilight* and 'Cuchulain'. As Eagleton notes, modernism swept parochial experience up, not into a progressive movement, but into 'great global mythological cycles'. As a result modernism effectively 'cut itself off from what was still potentially alive and politically subversive'. But not all factions, 'isms' and 'schools' have been reactionary. There were elements within German Expressionism which were radically left wing; and for a time, before its drift into the polarities of fascism and anarchism, Brecht was one of those elements. Not all modernists were attempting to re-establish myth in the age of capitalist technocracy: to the East was the progressive arm of Futurism (as opposed to Italian Futurism) with Mayakovsky in its ranks; a movement not interested in Teutonic gods and long-dead Irish kings, or their Slav and Tartar counterparts. Its advocates perceived themselves as an intrinsically active current within the Russian Revolution; and a number of (mainly French) Surrealists had concomitant sympathies and aspirations. Eventually, at the behest of Stalin, modernism in the Soviet Union was suppressed, and a new cultural regime was enforced by his cultural thug, Zhdanov. It is worth bearing in mind the total conditions prevailing in the USSR, rather than judging this suppression in the context of a modern 'democracy' which in its turn has its own – albeit respectably subtle – ways of marginalizing and suppressing that which it fears and/or derides.

In the Soviet Union the crushing of modernism, as an impure 'bourgeois affectation', was accompanied by the promotion of 'socialist realism', offering us (in its worst forms) inventories of footwear and combine-harvester production, and stories of the boy-meets-tractor variety, but also, it must be said, giving the world the brilliant, committed and lucid novels of Mikhail Sholokhov, with their vivid depiction of Soviet life, related from a critical but avowedly Marxist-Leninist position. However, it remains a sad irony that the first consolidated socialist state based on the proletariat should be responsible for the demise of modernist art forms that stood in opposition to Salvador Dali and Ezra Pound. What did issue, though, from all of this is a vast and profound debate on modernism within Marxist thought. This debate – or series of debates – has centred on works, particularly the writings of Franz Kafka and Samuel Beckett, which are ideologically ambiguous in ways that (for example) *Middlemarch* and *Oliver Twist* are not. It may seem grotesque to many Western Europeans that such politically charged discussions of art should be elevated to such prominence and entered into with such fervent complexity, especially in places where banishment, ostracism and even imprisonment could be the wages of literary production and literary criticism. But in post-1917 Eastern Europe and in the Soviet Union, art has been a tremendously public affair, inextricably bound up with the dynamics of civic, industrial and political life, not something tucked away in libraries, galleries and museums, to be peered at periodically by a populist agglomeration of intellectuals, shop-keepers on holiday, and people waiting for the pub to open. Mayakovsky recited his verse in the factory yard; his poems appeared frequently in newspapers; Brecht's plays are distinctly 'agitprop'. It is characteristic of this debate, however, that Georg Lukács (like Brecht, a Marxist-Leninist) for years regarded Brecht as 'degenerate', while Theodor Adorno scoffed at his drama. Adorno and Lukács adopt, indeed, very different stances: where the latter reveres socialist realism, the former strongly asserts the social importance of modernism. It is on the positions of these two theorists that I shall now concentrate.

The public importance of art is thematically emphasized throughout *The Meaning of Contemporary Realism*, where Lukács maintains, for example, that characters such as Flaubert's Frederic Moreau or Sophocles's Philoctetes exhibit a certain loneliness, but here this is merely a 'phase' applicable to a given set of circumstances, whereas with modernists, such loneliness is presented as a 'central fact of human existence' (Lukács 1979: 20–1). He asseverates: '[This] ontological view of leading modernist writers is [that 'man' is] solitary, a-social, unable to enter into relationships with other human beings'. Modernism in this sense is private in itself, and it portrays an equally private existence. For Adorno, on the other hand, characterization in modernism is far more realistic than in classical realism; a stress on isolation has a ring of 'authenticity' about it: 'Beckett's works . . . enjoy what is today the only form of respectable fame . . . a highly concrete reality: the abdication of the human subject. Beckett's *Ecce Homo* ['behold the man'] is what human beings have become' (Adorno 1977: 190). But Lukács protests at a lack of what he terms 'concrete potentiality', this being sacrificed to 'negative potentiality' which 'belongs to the realm of subjectivity', unlike the former which is 'concerned with the dialectic between the individual's subjectivity and objective reality' (1979: 23–4). Modernism also, in Lukács's opinion, is seen to promote the nature of humans as unchanging and unchangeable; a world depicted in which there is no way out of the conditions from which modernism sprouts in the first place. If individuals do escape, it is by retreating into their own subjectivity. But Adorno insists that

> Kafka's prose and Beckett's plays, or the truly monstrous novel *The Unnamable*, have an effect, by comparison with which, officially committed works look like pantomimes. Kafka and Beckett arouse the fear that existentialism merely talks about. . . . The inescapability of their work compels the change in attitude which committed works merely demand.
> (Adorno 1977: 191)

One of the things Adorno seems to be arguing here is that situations are created – things are said – which provoke their opposites; for instance isolated and helpless figures impel an urge for collective action. The reader – in Brechtian fashion – is 'estranged' from what is happening, is forced away from emotional attachment, and searches for alternatives. The texts make Lukács angry; that is the point: they are intended to make us angry (they are intended to amuse us too at times, but Adorno and Lukács are not renowned for their sense of humour). Without doubt, in Kafka's novels *The Trial* and *The Castle*, and in many of the short stories, this compulsion to change the world is thrust upon the reader:

> Kafka . . . uses formal devices in his text[s], disruptions of conventional narrative time, for instance, which show that this alienated reality has weak points and cracks in it. By both reproducing and exposing the way reality is, Kafka's books work to give a negative knowledge of it.
> (Forgacs 1983: 158–9)

But for Lukács there needs to be a clear socialist drive; without it, he insists, one is left with no more than gratuitous gestures (though we might ask where the socialist drive is in Thomas Mann, whom Lukács reveres). Lukács also advocates works that force a 'critical detachment' on the part of the reader. My argument, following Adorno, is that many modernist works do in fact force a critical detachment.

Now these contentions are as much about 'form' as they are about 'content'; and Adorno avers that 'form' can be as revoutionary as 'content' in its social significance. He asserts that Kafka uses 'formal structures', but importantly, it is the way in which he does this that is so effective. Adorno refers here to Kafka's employment of 'naturalist' modes which he utilizes in uniquely modernist ways: Kafka, 'by zeroing in on the dregs of the administered world . . . laid bare the inhumanity of a repressive social totality. . . . That form is the key to understanding social content, can be shown concretely in Kafka's language' (Adorno 1984: 327). There exists in Kafka a contrast, Adorno goes on to say, 'between stylistic sobriety and highly imaginary happenings. This contrast . . . brings what seems distant and impossible into menacingly close range' (327). This may be accurate as far as it applies to Franz Kafka (and some of his peers and contemporaries), but it is not valid, I would argue, as a generalized description of modernist art. As Brecht has remarked, writers can liberate themselves 'from grammar' without 'freeing themselves from capitalism'; and as Linda Hutcheon comments, 'art can just as easily confirm as trouble received codes, no matter how radical its surface transgressions. Texts could conceivably work to dismantle meaning in the name of right-wing irrationalism, as easily as left-wing defamiliarization critique' (Hutcheon 1988: 183). This is undoubtedly true of T.S. Eliot and Ezra Pound, Céline and Salvador Dali. Numerous modernists envisaged freedom from capitalism only in terms of regressing historically into some pre-capitalist 'organic' age; others (Conrad for instance) were content to make faces at imperialism. Of course Lukács is clearly aware that Kafka uses devices borrowed from Realism and Naturalism in the ways described by Adorno:

> We have only to think of Kafka, where the most improbable, fantastic statements appear real through force of descriptive detail. Without this realism in detail, Kafka's evocation of the spectral nature of human existence would be no more than a sermon, not the inexorable nightmare it

is. Realistic detail is a precondition for the communication of a sense of absurdity.

(1984: 48)

But Lukács does not share Adorno's enthusiasm, and he goes on to say: 'Good realistic detail often in itself implies a judgement on . . . conflicts. The question of what we mean by the *norm* and by *distortion* is also involved'. He continues:

These categories – norm and distortion – can be used to determine an individual's relation to society; but they can only do this if the literary technique allows of equal treatment being given to both aspects of human nature. A realistic work of art, however rich in descriptive detail, is always opposed to naturalism. But an artistic method which reproduces the dialectical – social-and-individual – totality of human existence, must relapse . . . into naturalistic arbitrariness. It will then be incapable of seeing distortion as distortion.

(1979: 75)

This brings us to the contingent epistemological problems of perception and intelligibility. Adorno pursues his refutation of the authenticity of realist perception in the following way:

Kafka's works seem to violate the reader's sensibilities . . . yet it is this violation that renders them easily accessible to all. The view trumpeted by Stalinists and Westerners alike, that modern art is unintelligible, is empirically correct. But it treats reception as though it were a constant, and overlooks the impact that unintelligible works can have on the consciousness. In the administered world the only way to appreciate art-works is one where the incommunicable is communicated, and where the hold of reified consciousness is thus broken.

(1984: 280)

For Adorno, 'The greatness of works of art lies solely in their power to let those things be heard which ideology conceals' (1984: 155). But this autonomous function which Adorno ascribes to certain artefacts comes dangerously close to being a new 'form of "reification", thus reproducing what it resists' (Eagleton 1990: 351); for, 'The transcendence of the artefact lies in its power to dislocate things from their empirical context and reconfigurate them in the image of freedom; but this also means that art works "kill what they objectify, tearing it away from its context of immediacy and real life"'. However, 'even in the most sublimated work of art there is a hidden "it should be otherwise", . . . as eminently constructed . . . works of art . . . point to a practice from which they abstain: the creation of a just life' (Adorno 1977: 194). In modern life, according to Adorno, we are enveloped in a 'petrified and alienated reality'; it is 'in its mimetic relation' to this that art can claim its 'modernity' (1977: 31). This is what he terms a 'negative sense of reality' (28). The relationship, then, between the authentic artefact and the 'administered world' is (albeit in a somewhat Hegelian manner) dialectical, and any reification of such artefacts renders itself transparent through its transitory nature. We can, if we wish, mentally 'dismantle' the artefact and 'see through' it. Georg Lukács, need it be said, is having none of this; he is adamant that such forms of art – and such critical explanations of them – refuse to separate the 'pathological', i.e. that which is 'distortion', from a 'concept of the normal', i.e. that which must pertain if we are to 'measure one type of distortion against another'; failing to do this is to 'arrive necessarily at universal distortion' (1979: 33). What troubles Lukács here is (*inter alia*) the lack of a shared cognition of normalcy which needs to be hitched to a realizable political goal. In his estimation we need alternatives to 'chaos', 'absurdity' and 'alienation'. Lukács claims that in Kafka's works the emotion of 'fear', which was 'originally a subjective experience, becomes an objective entity'. He goes on to assert that although 'Kafka's artistic method differs from that of other modernist writers, the principle of presentation is the same: the world as an allegory of transcendent Nothingness. With Kafka's followers the differences grow smaller or disappear altogether'; he suggests that 'With Beckett . . . a full stylized nihilistic modernism is the end product'. Again, Lukács fails to perceive just what is at work here. In opposition it might be argued that there are several levels of complexity in Kafka's writing. First, he uses flat, pedestrian language; he also presents the most absurd situations in this matter-of-fact way. But he does so with fine detail, neurotically, monotonously and self-consciously, so that the text advertizes its production *as a text*. We are made aware of the process of writing, thus we become critically detached. Second, as this essay will go on to show, there are innumerable situations in Kafka that suggest alternatives to life as it is. Third, the frustrating helplessness of the solitary, estranged individual, antagonizes the reader into a recognition of the need for collective action.

We now have a fairly substantial sketch of the debate between Adorno and Lukács. The former's remark that modernism 'compels the change in attitude which committed works merely demand' and the latter's yearning for alternatives to 'chaos' will bear heavily on what follows. But before moving on to the literary monuments of Beckett and Kafka themselves, it would be interesting and helpful, I think, to quote briefly from other critics of Kafka, some of whom attended the 1963 conference on Kafka in Czechoslovakia. Many of these standpoints are reflective of the conflicting views of Lukács and Adorno; others are severer; still others, mediatory. Kozak, abrasively – and with die-hard Marxist-Leninist rhetoric – declares that 'Kafka-ism is a contagious disease that infects the blood of socialist countries. It is a knife that severs the progressive arteries of tradition between socialist avant-gardism and revolutionary ideas' (Järe 1972/3: 60). On a more conciliatory note, Dimitriy [sic] Zatonsky believes that 'Joyce, Proust and Kafka had certainly "meant well", but [that] their books are "useless in the fight"'. However, Zatonsky also mentions that Kafka sided with the workers, criticized capitalist exploitation, and took an interest in socialist ideas' (57). Again there is an attempt by Zatonsky to 'accommodate' Kafka:

> Kafka was 'not a deliberate reactionary'; he rejected and dissociated himself from surrounding reality, 'but could not understand the meaning and logic of social progress'. His imitators describe the world in a state of absurd chaos; he is exploited by those who try to degrade men to the level of a helpless victim of irrational forces.
>
> (Järe quoting and paraphrasing Zatonsky, 1972/3: 57)

Kafka's writings had been banned under most Eastern European socialist administrations, and Ernst Fischer makes what is no less than an appeal for full rehabilitation: 'we do need Kafka. We need him not only because he is a great writer, and because the socialist world should not ignore any writer of his stature, but also because he stimulates us to passionate thinking about the problems of modern reality' (Flores 1977: 53). Now Brecht cautions that 'literary works cannot be taken over like factories; literary forms of expression cannot be taken over like patents' (1977: 81), but like some of his fellow-travellers, he maintains that although Kafka had important things to say on the subject of alienation, 'he never found a solution, and never woke from his nightmare' (1977: 88; and in Benjamin 1988: 108). Whilst some of these views are accepted in their particular context by this essay, others will be interrogated and challenged. What seems to be an embarrassment for many Marxist-Leninists is that alienation, which socialism was to obliterate, often merely changed shape under much socialist administration. Forms of alienation persisted, partly because a formal change in the economic power base cannot emancipate social consciousness overnight and partly because of the incredible bureaucracies that socialism inflicted on itself.

It now remains to examine the works of Kafka and Beckett with particular reference to *The Trial* and *Metamorphosis* (Kafka) and *Murphy* and *Waiting for Godot* (Beckett). In *The Trial* we as readers can readily perceive Joseph K.'s working life, along with his social and domestic life, as shallow and quotidian. For Joseph, however, they are security and satisfaction; at least, that is, prior to the infringement of his privacy by the Court's arresting officers, at which point his regulated serenity is destabilized. His position at the bank now seems to be in jeopardy, because of his tarnished reputation. His petit-bourgeois (but bachelor) domesticity is disrupted; items of clothing are purloined, as is his breakfast; and he refuses to eat food obtainable at the nearby grubby night-cafe as a possible substitute, thus asserting his middle-class pride and respectability. From this juncture, Joseph suffers *angst* and alienation, both at work and in a wider social and juridical sense. If Marxist theory is correct, then as far as the first of these is concerned Joseph had been under the sway of 'false-consciousness'; true, he is a senior bank employee, not a machine operator or a bus conductor, but Kafka was as aware as Marx was of a cunning dialectic wriggling away here: we do not have to be machine operators to be alienated within the capitalist mode of production and exchange. Joseph is sandwiched between the proletarian and the capitalist, and therefore caught up in a capitalist system which is a 'system of dependencies, which go from the inside out, and from the outside in, from above to below. All is dependent, all stands in chains . . . Capitalism is a condition both of the world and of the soul' (Flores 1977: 157). But until we 'enter' the novel, as it were, Joseph 'is oblivious to the alienating character of his work', as Goldstein notes (Flores 1977: 165). To explain this properly, and to explain its importance in relation to what follows here, we need to glance at *Metamorphosis*.

Alienation is exhibited in *Metamorphosis*, but with the dialogue and action taking place in the diminutive world of the home. In Gregor's case, even though capitalism only once intrudes directly into the home (in the shape of the company agent), it continues to insinuate itself with devastating cunningness. Goldstein comments brilliantly:

> Here the external world exerts power, not only because of the exigencies of living, but because it is experienced as something rigid, objective and permanent, rather than as something which has been created by humans, and therefore is subject to change and alteration. In the face of the apparent impregnability of their environment, people do not recognize . . . the subjectivity and creative energies responsible for their modes of existence.
>
> (Flores 1977: 165)

The Samsa family undergo two principal metamorphoses: the first after Gregor has ceased to be provider, and the second when Gregor ceases to live. The pervasiveness of capitalism ensures that all are, in one way or another, alienated. After Gregor is forced to discontinue his employment, parasites and host change places (his family lived from his labour). His new situation is substantially an exaggerated repetition of the previously obtaining situation: he is shut away from his family, only now the economic dependence has become inverted. Now we encounter Gregor starkly as estranged labour; he is aware of his alienation, but has neither the energy nor the inclination to alter things. It is only when crippled and dying that he becomes wholly conscious of the full implications of his material footing and psychological state – the debilitating outcome of a brutal competitiveness forced upon human relationships. He maintained his preoccupation with finance, time-schedules and work-loads, almost to the harrowing end. On approaching death itself, Gregor tries to reach his family to counsel them; he is too late, and we see them, as it would seem, fertile, energetic and confident to assume the world, ready to enter the economic milieu that has mutilated their son and brother. These signs of optimism and fecundation, as the sorry tale draws to a close, are resoundingly false and ironic: they are entering a world in which they credulously presuppose happiness and security will be available for themselves, when in fact the pathetic cycle is about to be resumed. Now Lukács *et al.* would seize on this as deterministic pessimism, and they may have a point; but they would miss the irony. The end is a tongue-in-cheek comment on the family's 'one-dimensional' view of life, the 'eternal' bourgeois view.

In *The Trial*, by way of contrast, we accompany Joseph, who has suddenly been ousted from his middle-class conventionality and smugness, into a new realization of the teeming capitalist city with its slums (wherein the Court is situated) and its sordid financial relationships. The city's sinister institutional corridors appear as a reified monster; Joseph's own place of work is abruptly transformed in his mind into an organization thriving on greed, hypocrisy and maniacal competitiveness. We are not, however, merely presented (as Lukács would have it) with a horror that is unchangeable. Alternatives (usually noted by critics only as 'existential decisions') are foregrounded; additionally, potential alternatives are implied *by their opposites*. Bearing in mind that Joseph now has consciousness of his alienation – though still somewhat confused as to its source(s) – he does have certain choices; it is only part of the story that he does not 'dare disturb the universe', and as a consequence is killed. At times Joseph refuses to act when the reader may think he should act, and acts when he should refuse to act. Nonetheless, he is made sharply aware of his potential several times; for instance if he refuses to recognize the Court, then it is reduced to so much ideological rubble. The spell of reification is blasted: 'it is only a trial if I recognize it as such' (49). And Joseph aggressively informs the Court that he will not attend a further hearing; this must register with the Bench, for when he does return the court-room is empty. Also Joseph had made a positive assertion prior to attending the first hearing, when he boldy declined an offer from his superior at the bank to spend a week-end with him (thus, at a stroke, resisting vaulting ambition and deference). But Joseph's main failings are grounded in the fact that he has an incomplete grasp of the true nature of his alienated state; from this short-coming arises the inconsistency of his resolutions. But what the text does not seek is that Joseph should revendicate his bourgeois pseudo-superiority and values, which served in part to tighten the grip of alienation in the first place. Indeed, as Walter H. Sokel shrewdly observes, 'Joseph is continually punished for his snobbish-bourgeois contempt' and 'his general arrogance, in both thought and behaviour' (Sokel [ed. Kuna] 1976: 8). Further, 'By summoning him to the slums, the Court shows [Joseph] K. a . . . setting which had been unknown to his bourgeois . . .

existence' (9). The 'warders' were whipped in Joseph's presence (as Sokel apprehends these harrowing/comic scenes) because he had insisted on his 'property rights'. Joseph is thus shamed. The importance of this is not whether Joseph does or does not become some kind of born-again proletarian hero over whom the Soviet Minister of Culture and Georg Lukács may go into rhapsodies, but that we as readers see through the reified processes of life and become aware of the alternatives.

Similar motifs and themes are at work in *The Castle*. As Christian Gooden argues, the Castle is itself much more delicately placed than it appears at a surface reading: 'It is arguable . . . that if K. . . . were to act according to his critical consciousness, the Castle would come crashing down, K. achieve his goal, and the relationship between Castle and village, official and subject, be altered or reversed' (Flores 1977: 102). In the first few pages of *The Castle* K. wastes much time on futile efforts to solicit some recognition from the Castle. Eventually, with some resolution, he grabs the telephone receiver and engages in a positive dialogue. 'Ironically, and not without humour', Gooden notes, 'success comes when he apparently contradicts the Castle'. Gooden continues:

> Later in the novel K. achieves another success. Without having done any land-surveying he receives an unsolicited letter from [Herr] Klamm congratulating him on the good work. Generally speaking . . . it seems to be an ironic truth [that in] Kafka's works . . . the following ploys are most effective: not bothering, contradiction . . . non-recognition, non-compliance . . . seizing the reins. . . . To interpret this, it seems that an alternative, successful mode lies in the rejection or reversal of the submissive . . . quest mode, such as is pursued by the K.s.
>
> (Flores 1977: 104)

But the imagery is essentially dark. *The Castle* is much possessed by death; there is a perpetual sense of foreboding; and many of the characters are figurations dominated by images of gloom and dying (about half the action takes place at night). 'Schwarzer' is not only German for 'black', it denotes in Austria the Devil; 'Klamm', with a small 'k', has connotations of 'Abyss'; and etymologically the messianic Hebraic connotations of K. as 'Land-surveyor' – at least in New Testament terms – are associated with sacrificial death. Also, 'Jeremiah' (most of the time) gives the impression that he is already 'in a state of decomposition, a corpse escaped from the grave'; and we cannot miss the Charon-like appearance of Gerstäcker. At the close of the novel, it is difficult to make a diremption of the optimistic and the pessimistic, as the narrative descends into a Heideggerian mini-Apocalypse: '[K.'s] head-on clash with the authorities resolves itself by his hard-won acceptance of the primary condition of human existence: its inevitable end in death' (Flores 1977: 136). But we are cautioned early in the novel to be prepared for irony and ambivalence, that everything may not be as it first appears. Amusingly, yet with obviously intended sinister over-tones, there is a 'Gothic' dimension to the Castle, which like another famous castle does have a 'Count' of sorts, when the pedant admonishes K. for speaking of the Castle in front of 'innocent children'.

It should be clear so far that while this essay accepts a certain abiding gloom in Kafka – even at times a hint of inevitability – it is not accepting his writings in themselves as a form of resigned pessimism; quite the reverse in fact. I mentioned earlier the importance of the ways in which the reader reacts to the K.s' predicaments, and also the importance of things being provoked by their opposites, plus the speculation on reverse courses of action. What Adorno argues (see above) is crucial in the context of commitment, recognition and resolution: there is almost continu-ously a 'double reality' facing us in Kafka's works. In this, there is the utilization of a related but rather different manner of alienation from the socio-economic alienation already discussed, one with a markedly Brechtian flavour, and it concerns the way in which we as readers perceive potential courses of action. Kafka's employment of fine (neurotic?) detail to express the absurd estranges us from the protagonist: we are eavesdropping on what is both real life and not real life. The text advertizes its own creative impulses and techniques, its own self-conscious method of production ('naturalism' here is a parody of 'form'); we are jolted out of an emotional attachment (or out of one attachment into another). The reader must evaluate and re-evaluate all that is happening: (a) to perceive the nervousness behind the fine detail, as it painstakingly tries to seal off all loop-holes through which the protagonist may escape from attack or deception, or by which he may fully understand what is besetting him; (b) to find alternative directions for the protagonist; and (c) when the reader is informed categorically that such-and-such *is*, to detach critically from the words on the page and to become aware that the *opposite* is (or could be) the case. When Joseph converses with the 'Commercial Traveller', for instance, there are several pages of tightly-knit discourse, but the Traveller (who never travels anywhere, but spends all his time in the Advocate's dwelling) then remarks in a pedestrian manner: 'Occasionally a group [of defendents] believes it has found a common interest, but it soon finds out its mistake. Combined action against the Court is impossible . . . common action is out of the question.'

The effect can be explosive: this homily may serve to confuse Joseph further, but we can be antagonized into repudiating the Traveller's tale. Joseph dismisses the Advocate from his service, and collective action from his mind, and he lurches perplexed toward death; but we know – and we have seen the hold of reification broken previously – that he need not have done so.

A couple of decades hence, the existential philosopher Jean-Paul Sartre will work a theoretical transformation whereby the solitary moral 'agent' becomes a revolutionary, a member of a social class – and reading Kafka's letters one can be convinced that some idea of community was important to Kafka. It may be that he had some reservations about the projected outcome of working-class revolutionary action, but that something of the sort was on his mind, despite his interest in existentialism, is evidenced by the texts. The 'man from the country' who cannot, or will not, go through the door (there are lots of doors in Kafka, both inviting and prohibitive) to the Law, is emblematic of the existential dilemma that can be translated into a collective dilemma; one that requires a collective solution. The structure of the parable in *The Trial* would only change numerically. But in any case, as Roger Garaudy comments, even if Kafka 'could not "draw revolutionary conclusions from his knowledge of alienation", the effect of his writing can be revolutionary' (Flores 1977: 53).

Before moving to the writings of Samuel Beckett, I would like to stress two further significant aspects of Kafka's work. First, the psychological, frequently oedipal, themes and motifs that run through Kafka's texts are crucial to a substantial understanding of his novels (and letters). For Marxists, psychological states or 'complexes' are culturally and historically determined, rather than innate. One would have thought, then, that Marxist critics, generally, might have payed some close attention to them in Kafka, rather than ignoring them, or rejecting them as nugatory fragments of bourgeois ideology. I mention this because Gregor Samsa, K. and Joseph K. embody psychological states and psychotic inclinations which are contrapuntally, dialectically and ineluctably caught up in the processes of alienation and re-ification dicussed above. In *The Trial* the psychoanalytical sym-bolism – the 'Fatherly' Court, the Advocate as 'analyst', the 'phallic' knife (at the close of the novel) which Joseph still dare not grasp as it passes tantalizingly back and forth over him – are inseparable from his estranged 'being', a condition wrought from reified capitalist institutions, and thus ultimately linked to economic friction and power. In *Metamorphosis* the spiritual condition of the whole family is grounded in sundry economic 'metamorphoses'. The repossession of the phallus by the father (his restored mastery and virility) and the sexual metamorphosis of Gregor's sister (with thinly veiled suggestions of an erstwhile incestuous liaison between herself and Gregor) become promi-nent at times of economic change. Changes take place in the home, but are dialectically and paradigmatically connected to economic exigencies and tensions of a broader kind; indeed the wider implications are devastating, if we transpose what hap-pens in the Samsa household to modern human societies as a whole. And here, too, in the Samsa abode, the human 'condition' is not unchanging and unchangeable. But important phenomena are often not considered by those discussing the inevitability of human 'nature': under certain conditions people will react in very similar ways, as they are moulded by those conditions as much as they react *to* them. Also, as humans have very few instincts, compared with other animals, they tend to guard themselves in certain ways which become so ingrained as to take on 'second nature', usually banding together for the purpose, and so giving the impression of a universal 'condition'.

The second point is really to stress once more – but now in a lighter-hearted manner – the irony (and self-irony?) in Kafka. Christian Gooden draws our attention to this succinct passage (the 'Little Fable') which seems to summarize in one fell swoop the whole of Kafka's *oeuvre*:

'Alas' said the mouse, 'the world gets smaller every day. At first it was so large that I was afraid [*hatte angst*], I ran on and was glad when I finally saw walls to the right and left in the distance, but these walls are closing in so quickly that I am already in the last room, and there in the corner is the trap into which I run'. 'You only have to alter your direction' said the cat, and ate the mouse.

(Flores 1977: 101)

In Kafka's writings, irony, self-irony, 'authorial intention' and so on, are important; but as we have seen, a lot more is 'happening' in the texts and this unfortunately passes unnoticed by the majority of critics; the writings have a powerful 'unconscious' engendered by their socio-economic conditions of production. When we turn to Beckett we are again confronted with irony and multiplicity of meaning, with lubricous signification. As with Kafka, a critical distance is hollowed out between reader and text, but there is a stronger use of parody.

Let us examine, as a start, some different approaches or 'readings' – in a fairly straightforward way – of Beckett's *Murphy*. On one level the novel can be understood as a serious study of a man estranged from and disillusioned with his society; a world that has failed both him and itself. It is replete with the 'burnt-out ends' of broken promises; it is the narrative of a man thrown back on superstition and idealist philosophy for comfort, that is, on horoscopes and the diremption, à la Descartes, of 'mind and body'; and the existentialism of Martin Heidegger (though admittedly this latter is hardly a 'comfort'), who views life as a brief moment of consciousness experienced between Nothing and Nothing. What is implicit throughout *Murphy* is explicit in *Waiting for Godot*: 'They give birth astride the grave, light gleams an instant, then it is night'; and the obstetrician and the 'gravedigger' melt into each other. Heidegger also sees everyday conversation ('prattle') and entertainment as diversions from the appalling awareness of the inevitability of Death. What is an extended and oblique metaphor in *Murphy* is again expressed explicitly in *Waiting for Godot*: 'Let us not waste time in idle discourse'. Such a reading would be essentially one of existential gloom.

But *Murphy* can also be read as a humorous novel (something that would not necessarily occur to Lukács and Adorno). A gradual awareness of the 'intellectual' nature of the puns, quips and parodies may undercut this, just as conversely the comedy in the first reading would intervene, undermining the seriousness. There is in fact a parodic tragi-comic parallel between Descartes's life-experience and philosophy, and Murphy's own: Descartes, in his *Meditations*, early assures himself against madness; but then, in 'Meditation III', he proceeds to indulge in lunacy by imagining himself first as devoid of hands and feet, then the limbs to which they seem ordinarily attached. Descartes was kept in later years as a pet philosopher by Queen Christina of Sweden, and when not engrossed in philosophical disputation with her, resided in a cubby-hole warmed inadequately by a stove; in the Winter of 1649/50 he died of pneumonia. Murphy, after his solipsistic gesturing (chapters one and six and *passim*) – sometimes indulged in from a rocking-chair into which he tied himself – takes a job as an auxiliary in a psychiatric hospital: the Magdeline Mental Mercyseat (MMM). Here he lives in a chilly garret whose only source of heating is a highly unreliable make-shift gas heater, which one day malfunctions and kills him. Like Descartes, 'Murphy felt himself split in two, a body and a mind'. The tone and idiosyncratic narrative of chapter six displace any cosmic relevance, as does the biographical parody. Yet we cannot escape the fact that here is a man striving to depart from a totally unacceptable world. There is an implicit rejection of the optimism of Enlightenment Reason in the mimicry and parody, but there is no *expressed* optimistic alternative. I shall come back to this.

Still another reading of *Murphy* may convey impressively the employment of the techniques of the modernist novel, although as in Kafka these techniques are dependent upon 'naturalism' and realism. There is the creation of a certain suspense, and unlike Kafka and many other modernists, Beckett pulls together the various elements into a fairly conventional dénouement (Kafka's characters often burst into the text, only to disappear from it). All this, I suggest, is a parody of the 'novel' form. As Adorno remarks, Beckett only referred to his prose stories as 'novels' sardonically. What is unmistakably modernist is that *Murphy* is held together primarily by stylistic paradoxes, through which the characters lurch from crisis to crisis. And here we are in the realm of the Absurd, which is anathema to Lukács. For Murphy, life is a sort of purgatory lodged between the polarities of birth and death. He tries to make his mind into a purifying refuge from his pursuers and from life in general. Ultimately failing, he meets death head-on. The novelistic ironies seem geared to this *raison d'être*. And as already noted, Murphy – in true Heideggerian style – neither indulges in nor will countenance 'small talk'. Celia's nagging of him to find work comes under this heading, but also he is insensate to her admonishments because they refer to the essentially physical, and physicality is of no consequence to Murphy, for whom the body is merely a surface inscription; it is something to be the target of derisive laughter, as with Rosie Dew's thighs and posterior, and the garrulous inventions of Miss Carridge, to say nothing of her malodorous flesh. This absurdity, however, has profound implications: try as he may, whatever Murphy contemplates in life, it is 'In vain'. There is only the 'freedom of indifference, the indifference of freedom . . . a murk of irritation from which no spark could be excogitated'. And if his mind is divorced most of the time from his more corporeal self, the other bits are divorced from the rest of society. Even in the MMM, where sympathy and empathy with the inmates is reciprocal, he remains only 'a speck in Mr Endon's unseen'. The seeming utter meaninglessness of human existence is accentuated when Murphy's remains (his 'ashes') are scattered on a bar-room floor, to be trodden first into the spit and sawdust, then swept ignominiously away. With Adorno we can perceive the realism of *Murphy* as depicting the ways in which modern life has perverted the human subject. But as I have (I hope) shown, there are many ways of 'reading' the novel. It defies any linear interpretation; no sooner do we think we have a secure interrogative toe-hold than it crumbles away. And emphatically, Murphy and his pursuers (parodying the Quest for the Holy Grail?) are only a part of the overall tapestry. We may laugh with Murphy, sympathize with him or scorn (like Lukács) the stylistic despair. On the other hand we may concede the portrayal of what is the sad fate of millions of people. We can, too, be antagonized by Murphy's incorrigible inertia and pessimism; and we can note with satisfaction Marx's Eleventh Thesis on Feuerbach, as Cartesian epistemology and Heideggerian Nothingness are displayed as irrelevant in the face of the pressing need to change life as it is. Crucially, through Celia's ability to cope with and expedite the substance of her decisions, we are made aware that some necessary accommodations can be made with life, and some radical alterations brought about. It would not be implausible, I think, to assert that Celia is perhaps the most developed of Beckett's female characters, and perhaps of all his characters.

If in *Murphy* we puzzle over the inertia and despair – and laugh, but uneasily – the impressions of *Waiting for Godot* arise from a still darker world; the enigmatic smile is transformed into a horrid cackle. This is a world being re-erected in the nightmare shadows of Belsen and the Warsaw Ghetto; a world twitching in the shadow of Hiroshima, and the atomic 'mushroom' clouds issuing from Pacific islands ('pacific' seeming like a helpless protest in such a context). It is also a world that has been familiarized with the crimes and philistinism of Stalin and his minders, distortions that many perceive as the Soviet Union failing itself and them, despite the heroism of the Sieges, the battles for Kursk and Berlin, and other undeniable and more structural achievements of Soviet socialism. For the fainter-hearted still, socialism as a concept – as a feasible and optimistic possibility – and an answer to the violent psychosis of crisis-ridden capitalism and imperialism is now shamefully redundant and obsolete.

Appropriately, then, in *Waiting for Godot* language and action fail to agree; time has become at once irrelevant and frustratingly ambiguous; nothing and nobody can be relied upon; violence and peace, night and day, veracity and mendacity are dissolved as meaningful categories. They are not simply labile, but wisps of absurd murmuring. Often the impression is that past, present and future, subject and object – nothingness and materiality – are actually all in collision. On discovering that some leaves have mysteriously appeared on the single tree, Estragon and Vladimir engage in the following 'conversation':

> *Estragon*: Leaves?
> *Vladimir*: In a single night.
> *Estragon*: It must be the Spring.
> *Vladimir*: But in a single night!
> *Estragon*: I tell you we weren't here yesterday. Another of your nightmares.
> *Vladimir*: And where were we yesterday evening according to you?
> *Estragon*: How do I know? In another compartment. There's no lack of void.

As with Kafka, there obtains a frantic paranoia:

> *Pozzo*: Who is Godot?
> *Estragon*: Godot?
> *Pozzo*: You took me for Godot?
> *Estragon*: Oh no sir, not for an instant sir.
> *Pozzo*: Who is he?
> *Vladimir*: Oh, he's a . . . he's a kind of acquaintance.
> *Estragon*: Nothing of the kind, we hardly know him.

Now apropos Kafka's Joseph K. we can say with Goldstein that

> K.'s sense of his own self as a function of a financial
> institution, and his identification with the man [from the
> country] as victim of an intractable antagonist prevent him
> from understanding the parable. And because K. is at home
> in a reified world, there can be no dialectical relationship
> between his empirical and his ontological experience of
> human existence. . . .
>
> (Flores 1977: 168)

But in *Waiting for Godot* there is not even this locatedness; only, it
seems, isolated souls lost in a vast desolation, where an immense
terror of 'them' – 'Don't leave me, they'll kill me' – far exceeds the
K.s' psychic isolation and frustration. The K.s are surrounded by
possibilities, chances of a grip on their environment; in *Waiting for
Godot* there is only someone who may come with 'reinforce-
ments', but doesn't. And with Kafka there is progression of some
kind; in *Waiting for Godot* (and *Watt* and *The Unnamable*) everything manages to be both open-ended and terminal; both
symmetrical and crazily cyclical.

To leave the theatre, or put down a copy of the text, resignedly
agreeing that this is what the world has become – even to say,
with Adorno, that there can be no lyric poetry that is not obscene
after Auschwitz, is to be compliant with capitalism and imperialism. As Sarah trenchantly declares in *I'm Talking About Jerusalem*
(Wesker 1984: 214): 'A Rasputin comes, you oppose him . . . a
Hitler comes, you oppose him! They won't stop coming, and you
don't stop opposing'. Otherwise, the 'garden'll get covered with
weeds', i.e. the legacy will be the spiritual and temporal
wilderness inhabited by Estragon and Vladimir and others.
'Redemption' *is* held out in many modernist writings and other
art forms, but to ensure the ultimate coming to pass of that
redemption we must ceaselessly spell out just what we are being
redeemed from (or averting, as the case may be). Stalingrad,
Belsen, the London Blitz, Vietnam, Pinochet's Chile, apartheid,
etc., etc., *ad nauseam*, must not be allowed to shrink from the
public mind; we must visit and revisit, mentally, the sites of
alienation and waste, aporia, torture and death; 'if the advertizing slogans for Pepsi-Cola sound out above the collapse of
continents', then emphasis on horror must never be relaxed
(Adorno and Horkheimer 1989: 221). Naturally the art-work –

realist or modernist – can never become a totality of representation because its function is referential, though it can be a
component in a greater struggle against exploitation and war.
Unfortunately there is ever the threat (all too often actualized) of
incorporation, 'canonization', and frequently, marginalization.
Nevertheless, as Terry Eagleton notes: 'artefacts for Adorno are
ridden with inconsistencies, pitched battles between sense and
spirit, astir with fragments which stubbornly resist incorporation. Their materials will put up a fight against the dominative
rationality which rips them from their contexts' (1990: 353). Both
realism and modernism spring from the Enlightenment 'Project',
which ended, as far as Adorno is concerned, in the death-camps;
but Adorno is not relinquishing the aspirations inherent in that
huge historical expedition. Rather, there must be a fresh and
urgent re-examination: 'The task to be accomplished is not the
conservation of the past, but the redemption of the hopes of the
past' (1989: xv). Lukács would not disagree with these sentiments; but if the texts of Kafka and Beckett disturb him, then that
is what they are intended to do. The problem is that he misses the
point of the urge for redemption that has been thrust at him.

   Finally, I would like to try clear up what I think are often
serious misreadings of Adorno, and misunderstandings of the
nature of his integrity as a Marxist socialist. Because of his stress
on the crucial function of art, and certain forms of art at that, it is
all too frequently assumed that he is promoting culture in a
neo-Arnoldian sense; and theorists such as Linda Hutcheon
denounce Adorno for an 'aristocratic viewpoint' (1988: 26),
basing their criticism on Adorno's aversion to 'pop' music,
electronic sound reproductions and texts which are readily
accessible; in other words he is dismissed as 'elitist'. True,
Adorno could at times veer towards an elitist stance – and at other
times (especially when pontificating on jazz or ridiculing Brecht's
incorporation of 'tin-pan alley' and 'pop' music for progressive
ends) he could be aesthetically blind and naive – but primarily his
theories of aesthetic value are sharply and politically Marxist.
Adorno does not always discriminate on grounds of quality, in
the usual sense of value. What concerns Adorno, as should be
clear from the foregoing, is what art and entertainment do to
people, and what they can deprive them of. 'Culture', for
Adorno, can be oppressively totalitarian, with many aspects of
modernism itself (in Stravinsky for instance) being saturated with
fascist impulses. In 'classical' music (and he glorified Beethoven)

Adorno suspects a 'sinister link between the flamboyant, domi-
nating conductors and the *Führerprinzip* of fascism'; 'the true
"musical subject" is . . . "not individual", but collective' (Jay
1985: 138–9). As Jay also stresses, 'The Marxist in Adorno . . .
deeply distrusted any concept of culture that forgot its tainted
origins in social inequality' (113). Mills and Boon romances and
Wagner alike are parts of a monolithic 'Culture Industry' which
'cheats' us, undermining our capacity for critical and political
thinking about art, entertainment and social existence. The
Culture Industry cannot recognise the horror and suffering
which the works of Beckett and Kafka, Schoenberg and (the later)
Beethoven reveal as the truth of modern humanity. Where for
example *Jane Eyre*, Count Basie or selected items from grand
opera as sung by Pavarotti can be incorporated into the Culture
Industry, Schoenberg and Beckett defy any such incorporation.
The bulk of what constitutes the Culture Industry simply imitates
imitation, until

> this imitation finally becomes absolute. Having ceased to be
> anything but style, it reveals the . . . secret: obedience to the
> social hierarchy. Today, aesthetic barbarity completes what
> has threatened the creations of the spirit since they were
> gathered together as culture and neutralized. To speak of
> culture is always contrary to culture. . . .
>   (Adorno and Horkheimer 1989: 131)

Popular culture for Adorno is nothing more or less than something cynically imposed from above by commercial and oligarchi-
cal hoodlums; consequently, it comes as no surprise when we
observe that 'In the most influential . . . magazines . . . a quick
glance can now scarcely distinguish advertizing material from
editorial picture and text' (1989: 163). And there is an incessant
'plugging of names' and a 'group ego' which inevitably leads to
the 'reawakened irrationality' of 'fascism' (Adorno [ed. Roazen]
1985: 89); for, 'the objective aims of fascism are irrational in so far
as they contradict the material interests of . . . those whom they
try to embrace' (99). Fascism, Adorno goes on to argue, only has
to seize on ready-made material: 'the children of today's standardized mass culture'.

Theodor Adorno in many respects can be pessimistic, for
ultimately art cannot save us from our festering socio-historical
wounds. Within the capitalist system, art – to survive the rigours
of the market place – must be pre-planned in such a way as to

destroy the primary function of art; that is to say, human beings are transformed into stereotypes. And Adorno has no programme to overthrow capitalism (indeed he has grave doubts about the possibility of such a feat). As for the proletariat, he asserts that they have no consciousness of their class position, much less the ability to be revolutionary; so what remains is such art as can at best give us an imprint of Truth. But as Terry Eagleton comments generously: Adorno still 'join[s] the ranks of Mikhail Bakhtin and Walter Benjamin as one of the three most creative, original cultural theorists Marxism has yet produced' (1989: 363–4).

References

Adorno, T.W. (1984). *Aesthetic Theory*. Boston, USA and London, Routledge and Kegan Paul.

—— (1977). 'Reconciliation Under Duress' and 'Commitment', in *Aesthetics and Politics*, London, New Left Books.

—— (1985). 'Freudian Theory and Fascist Propaganda', in *Sigmund Freud* (ed. P. Roazen), New York, De Capo Inc.

—— and M. Horkheimer (1989). *Dialectic of Enlightenment*. London, Verso.

Beckett, Samuel (1988). *Waiting for Godot*. London, Faber and Faber.

—— (1973). *Murphy*. London, Picador.

Benjamin, Walter (1988). *Understanding Brecht*. London, Verso.

Brecht. B. (1977). 'On the Formalistic Character of the Theory of Realism' and 'Popularity and Realism', in *Aesthetics and Politics*. London, New Left Books.

Craig, D. (ed.) (1975). *Marxists on Literature*. Harmondsworth, Penguin.

Descartes. R. (1972). *Philosophical Writings* (ed. Anscombe and Geach). London, Nelson.

Eagleton, Terry (1990). *The Ideology of The Aesthetic*. Oxford, Blackwell.

—— (1989). 'Modernism, Myth and Monopoly Capitalism', in *News from Nowhere* 7.

Flores, A. (1977). *The Kafka Debate*. New York, Gordian Press.

Forgacs, D.(1983). 'Marxist Literary Theories', in *Modern Literary Theory* (ed. Jefferson and Robey). London, Batsford.

Gooden, Christian (1977). 'The Prospect of a Positive Existential Alternative' (in Flores).

Hutcheon, L. (1988). *A Poetics of Postmodernism*. New York and London, Routledge.

Järe, Harry (1972/3). 'Kafka in Eastern Europe', in *The Wiener Library Bulletin* XXVI, 3/4.

Jay, Martin (1985). *Adorno*. London, Fontana.

Kafka, F. (1926). *The Castle*. Harmondsworth, Penguin. (1976)

—— (1916) *Metamorphosis and Other Stories*. Harmondsworth, Penguin. (1975)

—— (1925): *The Trial*. Harmondsworth, Penguin. (1953)

Lukács, G. (1971). *History and Class Consciousness*. London, Merlin.

—— (1979). *The Meaning of Contemporary Realism*. London, Merlin.

Marx, Karl and Friedrich Engels (1985). *The German Ideology*. London, Lawrence and Wishart.

McLellan, David (1978). *The Thought of Karl Marx*. London, Macmillan.

Sokel, W.H. (1976). 'Oedipal and Existential Meanings in *The Trial*', in *On Kafka* (ed. Kuna). London, Elek Books.

Warnock, Mary (1988). *Existentialism*. London and New York, Oxford University Press.

Wesker, Arnold (1984). *The Wesker Trilogy*. Harmondsworth, Penguin.

7

Lost correspondence: aesthetics, ideology and Paul de Man

Robin Jarvis

'Seeing a distant segment of one's past resurrected gives one a slightly uncanny feeling of repetition', wrote Paul de Man in 1983 (the year in which he died), in the foreword to the revised edition of *Blindness and Insight*. Repetition does not, of course, exclude difference, but the sense here is that de Man perceives the outlines of an uncanny correspondence between his current preoccupations as a critic and theorist and what he acknowledges may well be regarded as 'earlier and unresolved obsessions' (1983: xii). If the concept of the uncanny implies at the very least a tremor of unpleasure, one can only guess at what his feelings would have been had he lived to witness the public resurrection of a much more distant segment of his past: to witness, that is, the discovery and re-republication of his wartime journalism. One is only too graphically aware, however, of the intense alarm and unpleasure experienced as a result of these revelations by the literary-critical profession, and more specifically by the interpretive community associated with de Man's theoretical project. In a vivid collective instance of what Freud termed *Nachträglichkeit* – the traumatic reinterpretation of the past in the light of fresh experience or knowledge –, this community has had as a matter of urgency to re-appraise the over-familiar critical legacy of thirty years' academic work, thus to explore and redefine the nature of the correspondence between the young and the mature Paul de Man.

That de Man himself emphatically resisted, in the uniquely compelling logic of his theoretical writings, any future

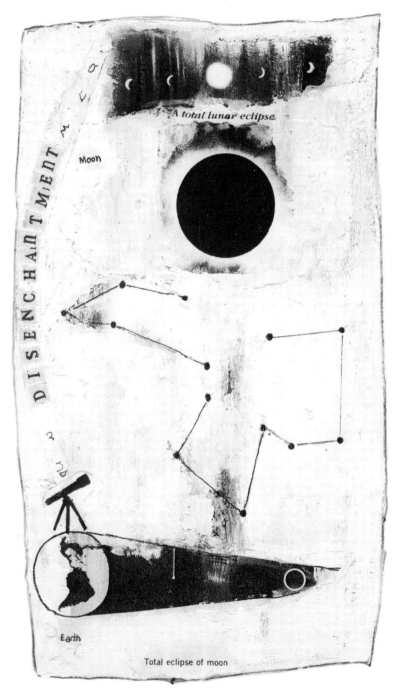

A total lunar eclipse.

Moon

DISENCHANTMENT

Earth

Total eclipse of moon

Anna Gay

elaboration of such correspondences, can now offer little comfort to anyone; still less has it offered de Man himself any posthumous reprieve from the aggressive dismantling of his reputation. It is true that de Man, as Christopher Norris points out in his impressively acute and judicious study of the man, habitually decries any tendency to read his work in a biographically developmental way; but it is equally true, as Norris also asserts, that there is no longer the possibility of acceding to such a demand: even if we do not see de Man's entire post-war production as 'a species of cryptic autobiography, a confessional record that merely masquerades as textual exegesis, philosophy of language, or *Ideologiekritik*', it is inescapable that his early experience had left so deep an impression that 'one cannot simply separate . . . the "man who suffers" from "the mind that creates"' (Norris 1988: 192). Nothing is more representative of the 'de Man affair' than the fresh, merciless ironies found to nestle previously unobserved in a statement like the following from one of the most celebrated of critical ironists:

> [The] apparent coherence *within* each essay is not matched by a corresponding coherence *between* them. Laid out diachronically in a roughly chronological sequence, they do not evolve in a manner that easily allows for dialectical progression or, ultimately, for historical totalization. Rather, it seems that they always start again from scratch and that their conclusions fail to add up to anything. If some secret principle of summation is at work here, I do not feel qualified to articulate it . . .
>
> (1984: viii)

The more conspicuous irony here was always that whereby the most remorseless of deconstructionists, whose commitment to 'dialectical progression' and 'historical totalization' might be assumed to be less than wholehearted, wryly apologizes for the very discontinuity and indetermination in the *sequence* of his writings which, individually, they proclaim as the irresistible insight of any responsible rhetorical criticism. The deeper and more sinister irony, now apparent, undoes this show of regret and exposes it as the disingenuous subterfuge of a man who had every reason to welcome the fragmentation of history, or the disengagement of the past from the present. In his analysis of the structure of irony in 'The Rhetoric of Temporality', de Man posited ironic discontinuity as the master-trope of undeluded temporal consciousness – experience, that is, seen as divided between 'a past that is pure mystification and a future that remains harassed forever by a relapse within the inauthentic' (1983: 222). This grim temporal predicament contains the promise of 'self-destruction and self-invention' (1983: 220), but only in the shape of a 'relapse' into inauthenticity, because the desired fullness of being is not compatible with one's finite situation: desire re-engenders itself as the ever-inadequate present is negated through further acts of ironic distantiation. De Man would seem to have rigorously eschewed such relapses: otherwise, who would not prefer such inauthenticity to the alternative of an organic temporality in which one's present self is genetically related to a past self one shrinks from resurrecting? But even if de Man forgoes the false gratifications of a mystified self-development, it is arguable that the model of history as rupture and discontinuity, or, in individual terms, the exposure to time as a series of moments which 'always start again from scratch' and invariably 'fail to add up to anything', have more perverse comfort to offer him than the ideal of organic coherence and progression that is ostensibly relinquished only in the interests of existential authenticity or philosophical rigour.

In this essay I propose to examine some correspondences now discernible between the writings of a former arts correspondent of a Belgian newspaper and various of the academic essays of the professional critic Paul de Man. These correspondences in turn entail reflection on the correspondence or non-correspondence of aesthetics and ideology, a potentially troubling interpenetration of discourses which de Man arguably failed to perceive as such in his wartime writings, but which was to become one of the keynotes of his mature work. It suits my own interests and competence to focus on de Man's direct engagement with literary texts, from which I believe we can unravel the important threads in his treatment of aesthetics just as well as from his more 'philosophical' essays, and I shall consider in particular his enduring fascination with two poets, Wordsworth and Baudelaire, against whose privileged texts the decisive movements in his thought are calibrated.

It is unlikely that I am presuming too great a familiarity with the de Man affair, which reached the proportions of a public scandal in America and continues to provide fuel for the most prestigious critical journals. Nevertheless, a few expository notes may be in order.[1] It is now well known that de Man, who came from a well-off middle-class Flemish family and had his education at the Free University of Brussels interrupted by the invasion of Belgium in May 1940, obtained a job writing a column for the largest circulation French language daily paper in Belgium, *Le Soir*, which was published under German censorship and edited from the time of the occupation by a member of the ultra-right Rexist party, Raymond de Becker. The 170 articles de Man wrote for *Le Soir*, together with ten articles in a Flemish newspaper, *Het Vlaamsche Land*, and less important writings in three other journals, came to light only in 1987 and have now been made available in largely unedited form (de Man 1988). De Man left his job towards the end of 1942 in somewhat obscure circumstances (by his own very dubious account, when 'nazi thought-control did no longer allow freedom of statement' [Hamacher *et al.* 1988: 476]), and worked for a book publisher and distributor till the end of the war. In 1948 he moved to America and began what was effectively a kind of second life, predicated on the suppression of his wartime activities: ten years of part-time work, including teaching, ended in de Man becoming a tenured professor at Cornell University, from where he moved to Zurich, to Johns Hopkins, and finally to Yale, where he was in post when he died of cancer in 1983. There was an eleven-year silence between de Man's journalistic forays in the war and his first publications as a professional literary critic.

Those journalistic pieces have now received minute and exhaustive analysis. I do not propose here to rehearse the ritual condemnation of the most obnoxious and objectionable elements of that output: outrage at the most notorious of the articles, 'Les Juifs dans la littérature actuelle'(de Man 1988: 45), in which de Man apparently lends support to the planned forcible deportation of Jews to Madagascar, can scarcely be overdone, but has been amply expressed. The most unsparingly juridical analysis of the wartime writings that I have read is by John Brenkman, and the majority of his deposition, leading to the chilling conclusion that de Man 'responded, consistently and actively, to an entire range of ideological imperatives associated with European fascism and political imperatives specifically directed by the Third Reich' (1988: 34), I find persuasive. For my own part, I shall merely highlight certain aspects of the journalism which are germane to my own argument concerning de Man's early investment in aesthetic values and resources: for I take a central paradox of these essays to be that of a repeated insistence on the autonomy of literature, the separation of the aesthetic from the ethical and political realms, that nevertheless goes hand in hand with a blindly aestheticized political creed.

On the autonomy of literature, de Man's column of 2 December 1941 ('Sur les possibilités de la critique') is representative, albeit in a subdued form. Here he sets out to define the responsibilities of the literary critic by first stressing the need to free oneself of all preconceptions, especially 'extraliterary' ones. He wishes, it seems, to demarcate aesthetics from epistemology and ethics just as severely as Kant:

> La littérature est un domaine indépendant qui a une vie, des lois, des obligations qui n'appartient qu'a lui et qui ne dépendent en aucune manière des contingences philosophiques ou éthiques qui se meuvent à ses côtés. Le moins qu'on puisse dire est que les valeurs artistiques qui régissent le monde des lettres ne se confondent pas avec celles du Vrai et du Bien . . .
>
> (1988: 168)

However, as de Man goes on to assert a requirement constantly to adapt one's methodology to changing aesthetic norms, which he says in passing renders one's theoretical superstructure of greater interest than the literary judgements themselves, the autonomy of literature begins to blur before the ever-widening historical perspectives which the critic is asked to contemplate. It is, in fact, no less than the evolving history of Mind that is accessible in literature, the close analysis of which becomes of secondary importance to the totalizing aspirations of *Zeitgeist* theory: 'Ce qu'il importe avant tout, c'est de rechercher dans la tendance d'une oeuvre ou d'un écrivain le côté par lequel il s'intègre aux tendances de son ere et l'apport que sa production apporte aux développements ultérieurs' (1988: 169). To attempt anything less than this, de Man adds, would be to produce work that was futile and fragmentary – an uncanny prediction of his lament forty years later, in the preface to *The Rhetoric of Romanticism*, for the 'fragmentary aspect of the whole' and the 'failure to make the individual readings coalesce' (1984: viii) that result from his renunciation of the task of defining Romanticism historically.

The tendency evident in this essay to look for some overarching grand narrative to which individual works of literature can be sub-plotted, to see the spiritual life of nations, or of humanity generally, as an organically developing whole, is the same tendency that leads elsewhere in the wartime writings to crudely stereotypical characterizations of French and German literature, and a persistent denigration of the former's shrivelled rationality in favour of the latter's metaphysical depths. As Jeffrey Mehlman has stated, there is 'an odd sense in which the more insistent target of de Man's collaborationist articles is not at all the Jews, but the French' (1988: 327). On 26 May 1942, for example, reviewing a translation of Goethe's *Elective Affinities*, de Man praises Goethe's union of French and German qualities within a single novel, but its formal 'vertus "françaises"' are clearly subordinated to the symbolic resonances and higher ethical imperatives which link it to the 'génie germanique'. With an impatient backward allusion to French classicism, de Man writes:

> un certain nombre de passages suggèrent qu'il se trouvent quelque chose *au delà* de l'explication psychologique et que tout ne se clarifie pas par la simple raison. Au dessus du conflit des caractères plane une puissance surnaturelle, échappant à toute analyse, et conférant aux actions humaines un éclat céleste. . . . Il flotte, dans ce roman d'apparence si raisonnable et si cérébrale, un subtil parfum de rêve. Alors qu'une oeuvre française paraît toujours aboutir à une limite, atteindre un stade où tout a été dit et compris, il demeure ici une échappée sur des profondeurs insondables, un sentiment métaphysique de l'infini, propre à la pensée allemande.
>
> (1988: 238–39)

Although de Man's comments here refer specifically to *Elective Affinities*, he makes it clear that he is adducing the characteristics of a privileged national mentality. Goethe is praised as one of the elect in whom from time to time the diverse national riches of western culture are concentrated and unified; but it seems plain that 'le génie universel' only makes its appearance by virtue of 'le génie germanique' incorporating and sublimating the lesser and more terrestrial French virtues. Such sentiments may appear no more than romantic hyperbole when considered abstractedly as a piece of literary criticism, but they appear far from innocuous when one takes into account the circumstances of their publication (a large-circulation national newspaper financed and censored by the propaganda department of the German military administration) and the political realities of the world into which they were launched (among other things, increasing discontent among some collaborationist parties at the ideologically-driven policy of annexation being vigorously pursued by the Nazi occupation authorities). The manifest preference accorded to German culture within de Man's enveloping aesthetics of nationhood has clear political import; the appeal beyond reason to some higher and more mysterious level of being and significance is congruent with fascist reliance on collective passion and mystified ritual; and one would not need to look far for a contemporary equivalent of the great, semi-mythologized individual who embodies in himself the destiny of the West and becomes the 'génie universel'.

The collaborationist position implicit here – which I concede is considerably more complex, even double-edged, in the ensemble of de Man's wartime journalism, as Jacques Derrida (Derrida 1988) and others have tried to argue – is less mistakable in some of the transparently political pieces, as in the review of Jacques Chardonne's *Voir la Figure* (28 October 1941), a book which envisaged a hegemonic Germany at the centre of a unified Europe: de Man can only share Chardonne's relief at the prospect of displacing the effete structures of bourgeois individualism, which left everyone to make their own salvation, and suggests that 'Ce n'est pas une des moindres innovations des régimes totalitaires que d'avoir substitué à cette imprécise anarchie un cadre d'obligations et de devoirs définis auxquels chacun doit adapter ses talents' (1988: 159). However, it is worth looking at how these views are carried through into the seemingly blander 'literary' pieces, not so much to determine the extent to which politics was capable of co-opting aesthetics, but to reinforce the contrary point that the politics de Man espoused at this time took its own origins precisely in a potent aesthetic ideology – an ideology in which national identity, or reciprocally the identity of the nation, is construed as an essential outgrowth of a people's unique, organic language and culture, within which the false antinomies of self and other, individual and collective, part and whole, are effortlessly transcended. In the manner of the subjective universal postulated in Kant's third *Critique*, in the aestheticized State everyone is truly themselves , but at the same time is entirely at one with everyone else. Furthermore, in the nation conceived as an art-object, people's lives are infused with a transcendental meaning and purpose in a fashion reminiscent of the Coleridgean symbol, with its 'translucence of the Eternal through and in the Temporal'. If literature enjoys an autonomy within de Man's cultural theory, therefore, this is not because literature will tolerate no intrusions from history into its rarefied domain, but because, within the borders of a national tradition, literature and history are perfectly consanguineous – and if they are not, they should be.

To underline this point, and to answer the question it raises as to what happens when the autonomy of a nation and culture are threatened from without, let us turn to an essay which directly addresses 'Le Problème Française' (28 April 1942). Here de Man argues that France has for some time been treading water economically, politically and spiritually to its own detriment. Its backwardness in industrial organization is matched by an arrogant, narrow-minded nationalism in politics that is completely opposed to what de Man calls the 'new European idea', according to which distinct national virtues must be 'adapted' to those of neighbouring countries. A lot hinges, of course, on the exact basis on which the trans-national European super-state presumably ensuing from the desired 'unification of occidental culture' would be constituted. De Man's opinions on this matter are signalled unmistakably when he turns to consider the intellectual or spiritual aspects of the French Problem, whereupon his writing assumes an almost rhapsodic quality:

> les forces qui semblent avoir pris la conduite de l'histoire ne sont guère conformes à l'âme specifique de la France. Il suffit, pour s'en rendre compte, d'examiner l'opposition . . . entre une certaine forme de la raison française, qui cherche partout à fixer des limites et à établir des mesures, et ce sens de la grandeur et de l'infini qui parait bien caractériser les tendances de l'heure. Nous entrons dans une ère mystique, dans une période de foi et de croyance, avec tout ce que cela suppose de souffrance, d'exaltation et d'ivresse.
>
> (1988: 227)

De Man is at some pains to assert that the French tradition of secular rationality, together with its formal correlates in art and literature, should not be destroyed or pensioned off completely, however anachronistic or maladjusted it seems to him to be. But it is clear that his sympathies are heavily with the counter-forces comprising 'les tendances de l'heure' or 'l'orientation générale', and that this counterculture, with its sublime reaching beyond the historically contingent and its reliance on impassioned belief, belongs unequivocally to the Germans even though they are not mentioned by name. It therefore seems that it is the business of a distinctive national culture, when faced with the manifest superiority of an adjacent culture, to allow itself to be incorporated by some dialectical process into a greater whole, its function being thereby reduced to one of maintaining the 'equilibrium' of that whole, and its destiny being enveloped within that of the parent-culture. Two days after the installation of a new Vichy government, and the day after censorship was imposed by the Germans for the first time on occupied France, to accuse France of parochialism (*esprit de clocher*) and urge it to open its borders (metaphorically) and be more receptive to foreign influences can hardly be an innocent or casual intervention. What we see here is the way an aesthetics of harmony, reciprocity and complementarity becomes the perfect ideological vehicle for a counsel of non-resistance towards, and collaboration with, the occupying forces. The goals of literature and politics converge precisely in an aesthetic ideology in which the essentialization of any structure, having suppressed its internal differences, leaves it ill-equipped to counter the imperial tendencies of some larger whole, whose respect for its autonomy and individuality may be less real than apparent. It is a fascism of the text, that is, that promises French literature (or Belgian literature, or Flemish literature) its autonomous survival within some larger European cultural bloc which intends rather to annex and assimilate it to its own nature, and the relation of such textual politics to more material manifestations of fascism need not be insisted upon; but once one has taken the step of thinking in terms of organic culture and authentic national destiny one is well on the way to admitting such an outcome, since one will always be vulnerable to the attraction of some more powerful foundational and validatory myth.

In looking for the correspondence between de Man's early life and suppressed wartime writings and the mature critical productions for which he is best known, there are certain ways of being wise after the event which I wish to avoid. One is illustrated by the flip sophistication with which Shoshana Felman, having eulogized de Man in a *Festschrift* published shortly after his death 'for having taught us, even through the process of your loss of life, how life can triumph' (Felman 1985: 9), will later find his entire post-war destiny cunningly and unflatteringly prefigured in his translation, towards the end of the war, of Melville's *Moby Dick*.[2] But in another sense, de Man has forced us to be wise after the event, and such wisdom is necessary to the re-estimation of whatever value his work should still hold for us. Christopher Norris's consideration of de Man's analysis, in 'Wordsworth and Hölderlin', of Wordsworth's 'recoil from the claims of political action' in Book VI of *The Prelude* – which entails the discovery 'that our actions can never know their ends, that consciousness is always "in arrears *vis-à-vis* the actual act", and that therefore reflection must inevitably lead to a mood of political quietism' (Norris 1988: 6, 9) – is exemplary of the kind of fruitful re-envisioning which a reading of de Man's mature work against what is now known of his early life can bring about.[3]

Norris suggests that de Man's radical scepticism about the efficacy of revolution in this early essay is prefigurative of the entire project of his later work, which developed, had we but realized it, as 'an agonized reflection on his wartime experience', and which 'can best be read as a protracted attempt to make amends (albeit indirectly) in the form of an ideological auto-critique' (1988: 190). This auto-critique had as its implicit target the insidious aestheticizing of politics and nationhood which, as we have seen, seduced de Man in its manifestation in National Socialism in the 1940s; but it usually takes the rigorously impersonal form of a deconstruction of mystified conceptions of language and art: by exposing, for instance, at a certain remove, the internal stresses of the organicist myths and metaphors that underlie such phenomena as cultural nationalism, he undertakes a ritual self-cleansing from the kinds of totalitarian thinking that had entrapped him as a youth.

In order to demonstrate the workings of this auto-critique, I intend to spend a little time exploring de Man's peculiar fascination with a particular poem of Wordsworth's, and to force certain correspondences between this poetic obsession and the argument of an important fugitive essay recently translated for the first time. The poem in question is the piece describing the Boy of Winander, often known simply by its opening words ('There was a Boy'), first published separately in the 1800 edition of *Lyrical Ballads* and later incorporated into Book V of *The Prelude*:

There was a Boy, ye knew him well, ye Cliffs
And Islands of Winander! many a time

At evening, when the stars had just begun
To move along the edges of the hills,
Rising or setting, would he stand alone
Beneath the trees, or by the glimmering Lake,
And there, with fingers interwoven, both hands
Press'd closely, palm to palm, and to his mouth
Uplifted, he, as through an instrument,
Blew mimic hootings to the silent owls
That they might answer him. – And they would shout
Across the watry Vale, and shout again,
Responsive to his call, with quivering peals,
And long halloos, and screams, and echoes loud
Redoubled and redoubled; concourse wild
Of mirth and jocund din! And when it chanced
That pauses of deep silence mock'd his skill,
Then sometimes, in that silence, while he hung
Listening, a deep shock of mild surprize
Has carried far into his heart the voice
Of mountain torrents; or the visible scene
Would enter unawares into his mind
With all its solemn imagery, its rocks,
Its woods, and that uncertain Heaven, receiv'd
Into the bosom of the steady Lake.

This Boy was taken from his Mates, and died
In childhood, ere he was full ten years old.
– Fair are the woods, and beauteous is the spot,
The Vale where he was born; the Churchyard hangs
Upon a Slope above the Village School,
And there, along that bank, when I have pass'd
At evening, I believe that oftentimes
A full half-hour together I have stood
Mute – looking at the Grave in which he lies.
                (Wordsworth 1970: 77–78; *The Prelude*, V, 389–422)

De Man is preoccupied with this passage in some of his earliest
significant essays from the 1960s, and he is still returning to it in a
very late essay such as 'Phenomenology and Materiality in Kant'
(first published in 1984). By the time of the latter, 'There was a
Boy' has become a paradigmatic instance of the disabuse of
aesthetic ideology, even 'the undoing of the aesthetic as a valid
category' (de Man 1990: 107). The 'blank' which introduces the
second part of the poem, in which the boy's death is recorded, is

taken to disarticulate the happy continuity of nature, mind and language which the boy had seemed to enjoy spontaneously, and which the first part of the poem had promised to recapture on the level of art. In 'Wordsworth and Hölderlin', however, de Man offers a closer reading of the poem that shows us the phenomeno-logical antecedents of this late anti-aesthetic stance. He points firstly to the seemingly perfect analogical correspondence be-tween nature and the boy's consciousness in the description of the exchange and intermixture of sound and echo in the first fifteen lines – promising that faultless mutual adaptation of the mind of man and the natural world which Wordsworth postu-lated in the Preface to *Lyrical Ballads*, and celebrated in such poems as the well-known 'Prospectus' to *The Excursion*. How-ever, as the poem continues, de Man argues, the impression of delightful reciprocity gives way before the suspenseful silence in which the boy 'hung / Listening' (the word 'hang' being cited by Wordsworth elsewhere as exemplary of the imagination and its partial liberation of language from thraldom to the senses), and a feeling of anxiety before the prospect of an *'uncertain* Heaven' (only partially recuperated by the depth and stability of the 'steady Lake'). For de Man, this anxiety is explained, in an act of necessarily deferred reflection, by the second section of the poem describing the premature death of the boy and the place of his burial:

> The boy's surprise at standing perplexed before the sudden silence of nature was an anticipatory announcement of his death, a movement of his consciousness passing beyond the deceptive constancy of a world of correspondences into a world in which our mind knows itself to be in an endlessly precarious state of suspension: above an earth, the stability of which it cannot participate in, and beneath a heaven that has rejected it.
>
> (1984: 53–4)

All hinges, therefore, on the admission of mortality and muta-bility by consciousness, by which means, and via a disturbing loss of 'correspondence' between inner and outer, an 'uncertain' future takes the place of an 'inauthentic past'.

In a related, and partially overlapping, essay from 1967, which was only published posthumously, de Man expands on the nature of the transition which the boy undergoes, glossing the above comments on earth and heaven more adequately: it is as if, he says, 'we were left "hanging" from the sky instead of standing on the ground'; the 'fundamental spatial perspective is reversed; instead of being centered on the earth, we are suddenly related to a sky that has its own movements, alien to those of earth and its creatures' (de Man 1987: 7). The spatial heaven of the first five lines has, in fact, become a temporal heaven inscribed with the foreknowledge of death. In this essay de Man discusses at greater length the steadying effect achieved by the lake image at the end of the first section, associating it with the meditative half-hour in the churchyard described in the second: noting that the first version of 'There was a Boy' was written entirely in the first person, de Man concludes that the poem 'is the autobiography of someone who no longer lives written by someone who is speaking, in a sense, from beyond the grave' (1987: 9). What Wordsworth is doing, through this depersonalization and tortuous temporal structuring, is anticipating a future from which he can reflect serenely and dispassionately on his own death. This death, or return to the warmth and solidity of earth, is conceived very much as repose, and is furthermore a transcendence of the perpetual self-division of a time-bound consciousness – just as origin and end are fused in the textual coupling of village school and churchyard. In some interesting annotations made to this essay in 1971 or 1972, after his so-called 'rhetorical turn', de Man emphasizes that whatever reassurance the poem has to offer emanates from the figural rather than cognitive resources of language: namely, a metaphorical substitution of persons and a metaleptic reversal of past and present which together create the illusion that one can anticipate what is strictly unimaginable. It is precisely this confusion of linguistic and natural reality which de Man, in his later work, defines as the hallmark of ideology, but what we see in 'There was a Boy', if we follow de Man's reading, is a potent instance of specifically *aesthetic* ideology (seen in this essay as more deluded than it was in 'Wordsworth and Hölderlin') in which the contingencies of historical being are reckoned to be overcome through the august mediation of certain privileged tropes.

In the severely ascetic mode of his later, deconstructionist essays, as represented by 'Phenomenality and Materiality in Kant', de Man seems to regard the transition between the two sections of 'There was a Boy' as marking one of those points where 'language frees itself of its constraints and discovers within itself a power no longer dependent on the restrictions of cognition' (1990a: 96). This need not be the power of tropes, which can themselves be thought of as pseudo-cognitive, but may be the power of performativity. Wordsworth's poem moves from the depiction of an intoxicating world of correspondences, to the intuition of an alien nature bleached of any determined human significance, to a proleptic representation of the self reflecting tranquilly on its own death. This passage is similar to the modulation from 'shocked surprise' to 'tranquil admiration' which de Man traces in Kant's analytic of the sublime, in which the imagination curtails its revelling in the might of natural forces in order to facilitate reflection on the power of a mind whose transcendental longings are incapable of bedding down in a world of appearances: the imagination 'achieves the highest degree of freedom by freely sacrificing its natural freedom to the higher freedom of reason' (1990a: 103). However, just as Kant's argument, for all its ostensible analytical rigour, may be shown to be governed chiefly by 'the laws of figural language' (1990a: 105), so, in 'There was a Boy', is Wordsworth's contemplative poise and superiority undermined by the rhetorical sleight-of-hand which demonstrably produces it. In Kant's *Critique* aesthetics has the responsibility of articulating the realms of pure reason and sensuous intuition, but here, as in Wordsworth, the articulation is threatened by the presence of 'linguistic structures that are not within the author's control' (1990: 105): language, that is, stands in the way of that perfect adaptation of an unknowable world to one's cognitive faculties, which was the cornerstone of Kant's transcendental psychology.

To conclude this section on de Man's fascination with 'There was a Boy', which helps to open up multiple correspondences between his preoccupations as a literary theorist and those of his lost wartime correspondence, I want to turn to an essay which makes no reference to the poem at all: 'The Temptation of Permanence', first published in 1955 but translated into English for the first time in 1983. This essay begins with a rebuttal of the view of de Man's new home, America, as a valueless technological desert: for him, the brutal incursions of technology are as yet engulfed by the vast lands and 'immense skies' of America, which provide a more authentic dwelling-place for existential man, driven away from the 'false serenity' of the mythologized organic communities of his ancestors into the strife of his interior life:

Man in the center of space, man whom nothing protects from the sky and the earth is no doubt closer to the essential than the European, who searches for a shelter among beautiful houses polished by history and among fields marked by ancestral labor. For he is in the midst of his own struggle: the elaboration of his history with this physical entity that is given to him and that, with Heidegger, one could name the Earth.

(de Man 1989: 31)

The earth here equates with an 'opaque' material world resistant to human aspirations, while the sky connotes the liberty and transcendence which the fatigued spirit, always susceptible to 'seeking refuge in the earth', nonetheless desires and seeks. Such refuge, de Man adds, though it is a sign of weakness, may perversely take the shape of a 'promise' or 'alleviation', and constitutes the 'temptation of permanence' announced in the title of the essay. De Man's argument, which is prosecuted in connection with certain novels of André Malraux, is that this temptation, the temptation of becoming one with the earth, partakes of death in a more urgent sense than does the alternative of a conscious embrace of historical process, which can also appear as deathly in its discontinuity and groundlessness. The opposition is therefore one between *becoming* and *being*: de Man argues that Malraux reductively construes historical conscious-ness as the passive acceptance of one's mortal destiny, with the consequence that artistic creation is conceived, in a betrayal of its quintessential freedom, on the model of slow organic growth and the teleology of natural form. In such a capitulation to the temptation of permanence, we lose 'the precarious situation of being *on* the earth to become creatures *of* the earth', and achieve an art which amounts only to 'a sediment without life'.

The crucial mistake of such a manoeuvre, according to de Man, is to biologize the life of the mind and refuse to think negation positively, and it is at this point that a rare political optimism seeps into his writing:

While the moment of discontinuity is certainly that of a death, it is nevertheless also that of a renewal, difficult and uncertain, but possible. . . . Far from being antihistorical, the poetical act (in the general sense that includes all the arts) is the quintessential historical act: that through which we become conscious of the divided character of our being, and consequently, of the necessity of fulfilling it, of ac-complishing it in time, instead of undergoing it in eternity.

(de Man 1989: 32–3)

Poetry, therefore, far from offering the refuge of organic form, the reassuring curves of the well-wrought urn, should instead co-ordinate with historical deed in rejecting passive fate, and, in acknowledging the impossibility of complete fulfilment, gesture towards a better future that can come into being only through struggle in the present. As opposed to the fatigue which finds its political correlate in a 'nationalistic conservatism', to 'conserve being in its truth is to conserve the incessant struggle that constitutes it, and it is consequently to think in a necessarily insurrectionary mode' (1989: 33). De Man ascribes such a conservatism to modern America, which he rather sardonically describes as 'the Western country that has the least to conserve'. However, we are now in a position to observe a chiastic relationship between de Man's political and cultural philosophy in this 1950s essay and that of his wartime journalism in *Le Soir*. Whereas in 'The Temptation of Permanence' authenticity is identified with an insurrectionary freedom, and opposes itself politically to 'nationalistic conservatism' and philosophically to the fatal sarcophagal attractions of organic form, in the wartime journalism the revolutionary forces of the time, aligned with German hegemony and military expansionism, are synonymous with a fervent cultural nationalism and are grounded philosophically in organicist concepts of national/racial identity and historical destiny. This is a reminder that the organicist myths and metaphors one assimilates to Romantic ideology need not present themselves as a passive refuge from the active stress of historical being, but can themselves ground a programme of radical intervention in the historical process. One can *act in the name of* such beliefs, even if one's actions disguise their own volitionality as predestination and even if the effects of those actions are those of a radical discontinuity quite foreign to conventional notions of organic form.

If 'The Temptation of Permanence', with its grim characterisation of 'the great fatigue of the century' in which 'history has . . . become painful', invites comparison with de Man's collaborationist writings in *Le Soir*, it also provides a fascinating sidelight on his lasting obsession with Wordsworth's 'There was a Boy'. For what is the Winander Boy, enthused by his initial success at fashioning an inarticulate language proximate to nature's, then jolted out of this illusory world of correspondences by nature's resistance to his appeals into a premonition of death as he confronts the 'uncertain Heaven' above him – what is he but a version of de Man's existentialist subject, caught 'in the center of space', disdaining the earth but incapable of attaining the sky to which he aspires, and locked therefore into a perpetual struggle to keep faith in the life of the mind and in the possibility of historical renewal? And would not de Man therefore see the second section of the poem, to borrow the tone and terminology of 'The Temptation of Permanence', as a capitulation, a rhetorical contrivance through which the depleted spirit of the speaker vicariously seeks a repose not available in life? Wordsworth, one can imagine de Man arguing, succumbs to the temptation of permanence precisely in the transition from the first to the second part of the poem: for it is clear that the narrator/spectator ruefully contemplates the permanence of the boy at rest within his grave – a boy who has accepted the promise of a 'refuge in the earth' – from the unstable position of historical *becoming*. Far from constituting nostalgia for lost youth, the poem breathes a nostalgia for the inorganic calm of death, or perhaps for that amalgamated state of peaceful natural endurance which Wordsworth ascribed indifferently to rocks and stones and trees. The imaginative trick by which the speaker pays his respects to his deceased alter-ego may appear redolent of creative freedom, but in fact amounts to little more than 'a sediment without life'. That de Man, resettled under 'the immense skies of America' but carrying the painful memory of his past errors and compromises, should prefer the prospectivism of a discontinuous history to a morbid acquiescence in destiny, or to the chthonic fantasies of an imagination recoiling from the full burden of temporal, historical consciousness, should cause no surprise. Having once made camp (to borrow Christopher Norris's phrase) on 'the dangerous ground of "blood and soil"' (Norris 1988: 159), the earth now holds little temptation for him.

I would like to look more briefly at de Man's treatment of another poem which seems to have held a peculiar fascination for him: Baudelaire's much-anthologized sonnet, 'Correspondances'. De Man is aware of this poem in his wartime writings, where he seems to succumb fully to its seductive symbolism, but in his mature work it comes to serve as a concise exemplification of the disjunction of truth and trope, epistemology and aesthetics. Here is the full text of the sonnet:

La Nature est un temple où de vivants piliers
Laissent parfois sortir de confuses paroles;
L'homme y passe à travers des forêts de symboles
Qui l'observent avec des regards familiers.

Comme de longs échos qui de loin se confondent
Dans une ténébreuse et profonde unité,
Vaste comme la nuit et comme la clarté,
Les parfums, les couleurs et les sons se répondent.

Il est de parfums frais comme des chairs d'enfants,
Doux comme les hautbois, verts comme les prairies,
– Et d'autres, corrompus, riches et triomphants,

Ayant l'expansion des choses infinies,
Comme l'ambre, le musc, le benjoin et l'encens,
Qui chantent les transports de l'esprit et des sens.

(Baudelaire 1986: 61)

In one of his contributions (6–7 July 1942) to the Flemish-language newspaper, *Het Vlaamsche Land*, on 'Contemporary Trends in French Poetry', de Man names Baudelaire as the first to break with the rationalist traditions of French literature: he is said to eschew logical connections of spirit and feeling and to discover 'a deeper, instinctive, irrational correspondence between the things of the earth'. The sonnet 'Correspondances', he adds, 'is a magnificent poetic representation of the mysterious alliance of nature with man's inner essence and experience' and signals poetry's entrance into 'the dark domain of the unconscious and the inexplicable' (de Man 1988: 317).

Nothing could be further from the interpretation of the same sonnet offered in one of de Man's last essays, 'Anthropomorphism and Trope in the Lyric' (in which, referring dismissively to those who put to the poem the 'casually historical' question, 'When can modern French lyric poetry . . . be said to begin?', he introduces the ghost of his wartime self). Here, the notion of an alliance of nature with man's inner essence is taken to be one of the recurrent delusions of canonical readings of the poem, which have anthropomorphically misread its central metaphor of forest as temple, linking nature with art, as the expression of some sort of intimate communion of man with the natural world, rather like, but in a more esoteric way, the Winander Boy's improvised dialogue with the owls. De Man begins this essay, in fact, by calling into question the status of anthropomorphism, which he considers to be misleadingly bracketed with metaphor and metonymy in Nietzsche's famous definition of truth as a mobile army of tropes. A trope such as metaphor, according to de Man, is a form of proposition, and to call truth a collection of tropes is to construe it as 'the possibility of definition by means of infinitely varied sets of propositions'; somewhat disingenuously, therefore, he concludes that 'there is nothing inherently disruptive in the assertion that truth is a trope' (de Man 1984: 241). Anthropomorphism, on the other hand, in taking one entity for another, implies 'an identification on the level of substance' and is tantamount to the ascription of a proper name. It makes a more overweening truth-claim than metaphor: starting out as a trope, it hubristically calls a halt to the endless substitutability of metaphor and enthrones itself as unquestionable essence. As such it coheres with the ideological: in a somewhat bizarre formulation, de Man states that 'tropes are the producers of ideologies that are no longer true' (1984: 242).

Approaching Baudelaire's sonnet itself, de Man carries through this precept that metaphorical substitutions cannot be *substantiated* as anthropomorphisms, and that language remains an estranging medium that will not broker the redomestication of the spirit within nature, or its accession to a higher order of truth. In a surgical and deliberately counterintuitive analysis, he remorselessly points up the ambiguities and antinomies that stand in the way of a transcendental reading, forbidding any lazy conflation of sensory (aesthetic) pleasures with rational conviction. He begins by overturning the assumption that there is indeed an anthropomorphizing of a sylvan nature in train in the opening four lines: highlighting the prominence of terms connected with language in lines 1–8, he suggests that 'vivants piliers' may be in simple apposition to 'l'homme' two lines later, and that the 'forêts de symboles' may designate not natural trees in some mysterious converse with man, but instead 'the verbal, rhetorical dimension within which we dwell and which we therefore meet as passively as we meet the glance of the other in the street' (1984: 246). The 'temple' would therefore not connote a sacramental view of the natural world but a 'verbal building' in which are performed the ritual death and rebirth of meaning. 'Passer à travers' in line 3, correspondingly, would denote mere errancy rather than the positive crossing of a threshold favoured by a transcendental reading.

I can, of course, only provide a sketch of de Man's extended analysis, which incorporates Baudelaire's 'complementary' poem, 'Obsession' (which is said to recuperate the indeterminacies of the earlier poem in naturalistic and psychological terms). Its main thrust is to query the strategy whereby the chain of analogical, often synaesthetic tropes which constitutes the poem is taken to sublimate at a higher level of supersensory significance, this transcendence being announced in the first quatrain and ratified at the end by the 'transports de l'esprit' which correspond to the infinite expansion of certain perfumes. What impedes this movement towards a mystical oneness of thought and perception is, as always with de Man, the material resistance posed by language itself as an impersonal system of arbitrary signs, of grammatical and rhetorical structures and patterns. This comes across most fully in his tenacious discussion of the word on which the poem's many similitudes hinge: 'comme'. In particular, de Man alleges a consequential double syntax affecting the final 'comme' in the poem: if, he says, 'comme' relates to 'l'expansion des choses infinies', then it marks a comparative simile like the rest, and 'links the finite senses to an experience of infinity'; if, on the other hand, it relates to 'parfums', then it does no more than introduce a series of *examples*, and an arbitrarily truncated one to boot. Therefore,

> Instead of analogy, we have enumeration, and an enumeration which never moves beyond the confines of a set of particulars: 'forêt' synthesizes but does not enumerate a set of trees, but 'ambre', 'musc', 'benjoin', and 'encens', whatever differences or gradations one wishes to establish between them, are refrained by 'comme' ever to lead beyond themselves; the enumeration could be continued at will without ceasing to be a repetition, without ceasing to be an obsession rather than a metamorphosis, let alone a rebirth.
>
> (de Man 1984: 250)

De Man may appear to some to be overplaying the different effects of these two readings, but one can see how the underscoring of this kind of enumeration, or repetitive metonymy, re-enacts his familiar subversion of the transcendental privileges thought by Hegelian and Coleridgean aestheticists to inhere in metaphor and symbol. The banalization of meaning which results from such a brusque dispersal of potential totality is then capped by the rereading of 'transports' in line 14 not as ecstasies but as the literal spatial displacements of transportation: instead of the poem placing us on an escalator to some ineffable realm of peace and stasis, that is, it would condemn us to an endless, shuttling series of changes and connections in the Metroland of language. The correspondence of de Man's analysis of 'Correspondances' to his recurrent engagement with Wordsworth's 'There was a Boy' should be clear: in both cases he is concerned, whether explicitly or not, to expose what he terms in 'Anthropomorphism and Trope' the 'aesthetic ideologization of linguistic structures'. However, the differences between a late essay such as the one I have just examined, and de Man's writings of the 50s and 60s, should also be apparent: the positive implications of his earlier critique of Wordsworth's surrender to the temptation of permanence, or the glimpsed possibility of renewal in the discontinuities of history in the essay of that name, here give way to a much bleaker, purgatorial refusal of any prospect of redeeming the paralysing unintelligibility of the world – or rather the radical non-correspondence of phenomenal cognition with forms of intellection – which the enmortgagement of consciousness to language imposes. The 'reconciliation of knowledge with phenomenal, aesthetic experience' (1984: 258) is now a 'phantasm' pure and simple. To historicize is to do no more than fallaciously metaphorize figural patterns: the latter would seem, paradoxically, to be the only literal truth one can hang on to, and to be all that de Man has in mind when he speaks of 'the materiality of actual history' (1984: 262). At the furthest possible remove from our contemporary upsurge of interest in the public, performative, end-oriented aspect of rhetoric, de Man can authenticate as 'language power', and define as 'historical', only the 'blind violence' (1984: 262) with which we are driven, with no epistemological certainty, from one trope or text or interpretation to another.

So, the network of correspondences and revisionary links between various of de Man's writings from the 1940s to 1980s that I have traced should have made the broad trajectory of his aesthetic thought reasonably clear. It is a trajectory that begins in the politicized aesthetics and aestheticized politics of his wartime journalism, with its culpable and disreputable alignment with the organic myths of language, culture and nationhood propagated by the Nazis; and ends, as we have seen, with a severely sceptical refusal to anthropomorphize the sign, to breathe life into the

dead letters of language. The nature and extent of the renunciation involved in this trajectory should thus also be apparent. For
it is arguable that in a guilt-driven effort to rid his thought of any
trace of the aesthetic ideology which had captivated him as a
young man, de Man both engaged an unbalanced and political
disempowering view of ideology and assumed an unnecessarily
hostile stance towards aesthetics. The latter point has been put
well by Terry Eagleton in his recent study of *The Ideology of the
Aesthetic*, both briefly in specific reference to de Man and at large
in the argument of the book as a whole: for him, the positive
components of de Man's critique of ideological thought are
bought at the 'enormous cost' of suppressing 'the potentially
positive dimensions of the aesthetic' – 'the whole prospect of a
creative development of the sensuous, creaturely aspects of
human existence, by pleasure, Nature and self-delighting
powers, all of which now figure as aesthetic seductions to be
manfully resisted' (Eagleton 1990: 10).

As for ideology, de Man's mature concept of it as the 'confusion
of linguistic with natural reality, of reference with phenom-
enalism', is often cited from his justly celebrated late essay, 'The
Resistance to Theory' (1982: 11). A related and equally interesting
definition can be found in a posthumously-published review-
article on Roland Barthes dating from 1972. Here he begins by
positing the 'gratuity, the lack of semantic responsibility' of
fictional signs, which, being more persuasive than facts and
accountable only to themselves, are 'the defenseless prey of any
interest that wishes to make use of them'; furthermore,

> When they are . . . being enlisted in the service of collective
> patterns of interest – including interests of the 'highest'
> moral or metaphysical order – fictions become ideologies.
> One can see that any ideology would always have a vested
> interest in theories of language advocating the natural
> correspondence between sign and meaning, since they
> depend on the illusion of this correspondence for their
> effectiveness. . . .
>
> (1990b: 183)

However, despite the vaguely approving reference here to
'interests of the "highest" moral or metaphysical order', the
undeniable trend in de Man's work of the 1970s and 80s is
towards a paranoiacally indiscriminate suspicion of *all* collective
patterns of interest, and this seriously handicaps the progress

made in that work towards positive political utility. Again, Terry Eagleton points the finger in accusing much poststructuralist theory of slackly entertaining 'a vision of the hegemonic ideologies of the West as centrally reliant upon apodictic truth, totalized system, transcendental signification, metaphysical groundedness, the naturalization of historical contingency and a teleological dynamic' (1990: 379), thus obscuring the vital distinction between liberal capitalist and fascist societies – a charge, indeed, which he has levelled before specifically (and rather more unsympathetically) at Paul de Man in *The Function of Criticism* (1984: 100–2).

The conclusion to draw from this would seem to be that one should be continually wary of *particular* aestheticizations of ethics and of politics, but that to renounce all such potential alliances of ends and means would be to relinquish a valuable resource. As the evidence mounts that poststructuralism is finally despairing of its own scepticism, it may be that this is one of the enduring lessons of de Man's life-work, with all its freshly disinterred correspondences and deferred significances. The fact that this construction of a *felix culpa* from his now tarnished career may be out of sympathy with the rough justice now being administered by large sections of the academic community should not, I think, be allowed to inhibit its aim.

Notes

1. Much fuller biographical and historical contextualization (inevitably slanted in one way or another) can be found in many of the essays collected in Hamacher *et al.* 1988, especially Ortwin de Graef's 'Aspects of the Context of Paul de Man's Earliest Publications' (96–126), Werner Hamacher's 'Journals, Politics' (438–467), and Thomas Keenan's collection of 'Documents: Public Criticisms' (468–77). The volume also has a useful Chronology linking de Man's early life to European events in the period 1919–1949. Lindsay Waters's introduction to his edition of de Man's uncollected essays and reviews (de Man 1989) is also worth mentioning.
2. Like Ahab, the argument goes, de Man is to make a radical break with the past, leaving his wife and children behind in embarking on his new life; like Ishmael, the narrator, who goes to sea as a substitute for committing suicide, he does so as a way of annihilating his former self; but like Ishmael too, who begins his conclusion by quoting from Job, 'And I only am escaped to tell thee', he survives to bear witness to the impossibility of such escape. See Felman 1989.
3. Among other examples one might mention, Morrison (1990) offers a

measured and eloquent case for finding more threatening continuities between the wartime journalism and de Man's mature work than either Norris or I find compelling.

References

Baudelaire, Charles. (1986). *The Complete Verse*. Ed. and trans. Francis Scarfe. London, Anvil Press.

Brenkman, John. (1988). 'Fascist Commitments', in Hamacher et al., pp. 21–35.

De Man, Paul. (1982). 'The Resistance to Theory', *Yale French Studies*, 62, 3–20.

——. (1983). *Blindness and Insight: Essays in the Rhetoric of Contemporary Criticism*. 2nd ed. London, Methuen.

——. (1984). *The Rhetoric of Romanticism*. New York, Columbia University Press.

——. (1987). 'Time and History in Wordsworth', *Diacritics*, 17, 4–17.

——. (1988). *Wartime Journalism, 1939–1943*. Ed. Werner Hamacher et al. Lincoln and London, University of Nebraska Press.

——. (1989). *Critical Writings, 1953–1978*. Ed. Lindsay Waters. Minneapolis, University of Minnesota Press.

——. (1990a). 'Phenomenality and Materiality in Kant'. In Hugh J. Silverman and Gary E. Aylesworth (eds), *The Textual Sublime: Deconstruction and its Differences*. Albany, NY, State University of New York Press, pp. 87–108.

——. (1990b). 'Roland Barthes and the Limits of Structuralism', *Yale French Studies*, 77, 177–90.

Derrida, Jacques. (1988). 'Like the Sound of the Sea Deep within a Shell: Paul de Man's War', *Critical Inquiry*, 14, 590–652.

Eagleton, Terry. (1985). *The Function of Criticism: From 'The Spectator' to Post-Structuralism*. London, Verso.

——. (1990). *The Ideology of the Aesthetic*. Oxford, Basil Blackwell.

Felman, Shoshana. (1985). Tribute in *Yale French Studies*, 69 ('The Lesson of Paul de Man'), 8–9.

——. (1989). 'Paul de Man's Silence', *Critical Inquiry*, 15, 704–44.

Hamacher, Werner, *et al.* (1988). *Responses: On Paul de Man's Wartime Journalism*. Lincoln and London, University of Nebraska Press.

Mehlman, Jeffrey. (1988). 'Perspectives: On De Man and *Le Soir*', in Hamacher *et al.*, pp. 324–33.

Morrison, Paul. (1990). 'Paul de Man: Resistance and Collaboration', *Representations*, 32, 50–74.

Norris, Christopher. (1988). *Paul de Man: Deconstruction and the Critique of Aesthetic Ideology*. New York and London, Routledge.

Wordsworth, William. (1970). *The Prelude* (1805). Ed. E. de Selincourt, corrected Stephen Gill. London, Oxford University Press.

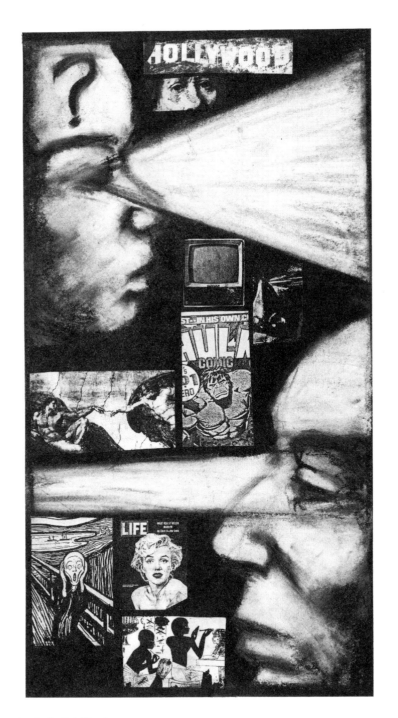

Justin Ruffel-Ward

8

Aesthetics and English Studies

Adrian Page

In the course of writing about literary criticism, T.S. Eliot shows a curious respect for aesthetics: the 'critic who remains worth reading', he tells us, has asked both 'what is poetry?' and 'Is this a good poem?' (1933: 16). Furthermore, these questions 'imply each other': the most worthwhile critics have pondered the nature of literary art as well as evaluated particular examples. This respect for the consideration of aesthetic issues is curious because Eliot also remarks that criticism never arrives at an adequate definition of poetry, and even if it did, he says, 'I do not know what use such a definition would be'. The definition of literary art has often seemed to critics to be superfluous to any genuine critical activity in much the same way that a definition of time would be irrelevant to a person's punctuality. Nonetheless, there seems to be a connection between the value of criticism and its implicit aesthetic theory.

Eliot is apparently arguing that aesthetics has no immediate effect on issues of practical criticism: the critic must decide anew in each case whether particular criteria apply. In this sense aesthetics can be of no direct help in criticism. On the other hand, aesthetics may provide a set of criteria which helps to ensure consistency in evaluation and to focus the sense of value which a critic is attempting to refine. The example of ethics may help to illustrate the paradoxical situation which Eliot describes, where the value of criticism is dependent on an intellectual issue logically divorced from it. The definition of 'good' will not automatically produce a set of principles of good behaviour. On the other hand, any moral code will presuppose some notion of what 'good' means for mankind. In translating a notion of good into practical principles, a methodology such as Utilitarianism has to be employed. In this sense it could be argued that any morally righteous person has a concept of good, but the real business of morality is to apply that sense.

It is also possible to develop a literary methodology without ever articulating its aesthetic presuppositions. The problem is that whereas a mistake in the concept of 'good' can be shown to invalidate a moral argument drawn from it, a mistaken aesthetic theory may have little impact on the worthiness of criticism in English Studies. It seems generally true that if a theory in science can be shown to be inconsistent, then no valid conclusions can be drawn from it. In literary criticism, however, a muddled aesthetic theory may nonetheless lead to illuminating critical observations. The concerted attack on Leavis and his views on literary criticism have not noticeably diminished his stature as a major critic. For many practitioners of English Studies, literary criticism was an entirely 'natural' activity which implied no conscious theorizing at all. William Golding suggests that 'writing, when you get down to it, like running, like eating, like pursuit, is a simple, direct thing, uncomplicated, natural, like the act of being, a wholeness which is in itself a defier of analysis' (1982: 200). Even such a negative statement, however, is susceptible to some kind of analysis. The theory that art is unanalysable leads to the conclusion that critical writing is in the nature of 'further descriptions' in Wittgenstein's words. All we can do is continue to lavish descriptive language on the matter in defence of our opinion. In this sense the concept of what literary art is will have an impact on literary evaluation.

It is still difficult to resist the feeling that, as de Man once remarked, literary matters are 'relatively autonomous', in that they can be settled without reference to a grand theory. In particular, it is arguable that the reason why critics who disagree about the nature of the work of art can nonetheless discuss the same novel or poem coherently is that the true focus of English Studies is not the work of art but some other item such as the text.

Ian Small and Josephine Guy have recently suggested a reason for the apparent 'failure' of literary theory to clarify the discipline of English Studies and proposed criteria by which the nature of the discipline could be made more rigorous (1990: 3). The fundamental reason for the lack of progress in this matter is the failure of the major proponents of literary theory to define the 'object of study' with which English Studies can be said to concern itself. Without such a preliminary theoretical step, they argue, the discipline of English can never advance, since without an object of study, the methods employed, like their object, will expand infinitely to encompass everything. Small and Guy argue that the examples of the theory in other disciplines show that the definition of an agreed goal enables the competing theories to contest specific issues and also clarifies the relative success of theories in achieving their ultimate aims. Literary theory, according to Small and Guy, has conspicuously failed to demonstrate how to differentiate between good and bad theories. Its lamentable failure is shown in the fact that divergent theories of the same text are entertained by its practitioners. Theorizing about literature has become ideological warfare.

The example of linguistics illustrates the kind of theory which Small and Guy would like to bring to bear on literature. Linguists agree on the 'object' of their studies, whatever theoretical perspective they adopt. Language may be vast, but its prior existence can be safely assumed in any theoretical enquiry. Furthermore, whether linguists espoused the cognitive approach of Chomsky, the structural approach of Bloomfield or the sociolinguistic theory of Halliday, they were generally agreed on their objective: to explain the human capacity to generate infinite examples of grammatical sentences. In this field of enquiry the definition of the concept of language, however, was not as important as the agreement on a shared goal, a criterion by which success in linguistics could be measured. The advance in linguistics which has left Halliday more fashionable than Chomsky and Bloomfield, testifies to this. The agreement that language was a common object of study solves very little. It is possible for each theorist to define language differently and still adopt the same criteria for a successful theory.

Small and Guy begin to recognize this point when they write that 'Even if we failed to find a closed set of features which would define the "literary", we need not assume that literature does not exist. Literature may be defined in terms of its functions' (1990: 195). The classic question of aesthetics, however, is whether 'the beautiful' could be defined in terms of the properties of beautiful objects or the properties which an observer assumed or believed them to have. In literary terms, this raises the question of whether we can circumscribe the works to be called 'literature' by identifying certain qualities which such works all possess, or whether we can only describe the kind of relationship which must exist between a reader and the text. Small and Guy first appeal for a closed definition of the object of literary study which would restrict the items which could conceivably be called 'literature', and then concede that such a definition may not be either possible or necessary. If the function of objects, defined their literary status, then we could not define the objects, only what they did.

The aesthetic theory that Terry Eagleton adopts in *Literary Theory* (1983) is known as the 'aesthetic attitude' (Stolnitz 1960). Rather than defining literature in advance, which would beg many questions of value, Eagleton chooses to find the essence of the literary in the relationship which exists between reader and text. It is the way that the text is regarded that makes it literature. This shifts the burden of explanation to ask instead for a definition of the appropriate mental state which invests potential texts with literary qualities, but it does not avoid the issue of the 'object of study'. Rather than failing to address certain matters in aesthetics, Eagleton is, in fact, simply proposing another traditional answer: 'Anything can be literature' (Eagleton 1983: 10). In a similar vein, aestheticians have argued that, in principle, anything can be beautiful.

Although the problems associated with the theory of the aesthetic attitude are also considerable, it does show that the concept of the object of study is sufficiently nebulous to warrant relatively little attention. The *objects* of various theories of language may be said to be much wider than language itself, for example. With Chomsky it could be said to be the functioning of the mind itself; for Halliday it might be said to be the field of communicative social practices. In the literary sphere, differing theories might propose various 'objects' which are much greater in scope than the literature which refers to them. For feminists the object of literary studies might be the social construction of women; for linguistic critics it might be the nature of language itself, and Eagleton has recently claimed that the object of literary theory is history (Eagleton 1990a). Agreement on the object of study which yields access to these much greater goals is not agreement on a definition of literature. Small and Guy maintain that the development of theory in the natural sciences is linear in that there is a succession of theories, as each is replaced by a stronger alternative which refutes its predecessors. They cite no less an authority than Karl Popper to uphold this view of science.

Popper, however, distinguishes between 'a preconceived

selective point of view', such as the interests of the working class or women, and theories. In Popper's opinion, such restricted approaches constitute examples of 'historical interpretation' rather than full-scale theories of history itself. 'Historicism mistakes these interpretations for theories' (Popper 1957: 151). Different literary theories may draw on aesthetic ideas to defend their approach, but they are not always theories of *literature*, rather they constitute an attempt to demonstrate their own interests at work in literature. The linguistic critic and the Marxist may have entirely different objects in mind when they write about literature; hence they cannot contradict or refute each other. Todorov also rejects the notion that science offers an example of absolute agreement on objects of study:

> The literati are inclined to admit, with equal willingness, an analysis of literature based on linguistics, then another based on psychoanalysis, then a third, based on sociology, then a fourth based on the history of ideas. . . . The unity of all these procedures is constituted, we are told, by their unique object: literature. But such an assertion is contrary to the elementary principles of scientific research. The unity of science is not constituted by the uniqueness of its object: there is not a 'science of bodies' to a 'chemical analysis,' a 'physical analysis,' and a 'geometrical analysis.' It is hardly necessary to repeat that method creates the object. . . .
>
> (Todorov 1981: 8)

The object of a particular literary approach does not precede it, in other words, but is composed by it. The scientific analogy which Todorov employs shows that the same item can be several different objects in this sense for a number of scientific disciplines. Similarly, the same piece of literature can serve to illustrate radically different points of view.

If, however, we accept that literary theories can or in fact must bypass each other and do not even contest the same territory, then it seems that theory is open to the charge that it simply allows ideological bickering and fails to address the substantial questions about the nature of literature. Small and Guy maintain that major aesthetic questions, such as the object of study, should be settled independently of ideological controversies. Others would insist that aesthetics is itself imbued with ideology and cannot be purely neutral; hence to attempt to resolve aesthetic questions is only to re-open the ideological debates.

The controversy in aesthetics over the nature of the work of art can throw some light on this difficulty. Rather than presuming that all works of art have something in common, it has also been proposed that there is a 'family resemblance' between them (Mandelbaum 1965). The term is borrowed from the philosopher Wittgenstein, who uses it to show that games, for example, may have nothing in common except a striking resemblance to each other. If this is the case, then there can be no rules of games in general. Each practice is unique and demands a unique form of compliance with its peculiar rules.

If each literary theory similarly constructs its own objects, then it may also simultaneously construct its own methodology for the correct application of its principles. Aesthetics may have no general conclusions about the nature of all works of art which directly assist in this process. By analogy, science may have no general theory of stones which informs the methodology of the different scientists, such as geologists, physicists and chemists who study stones from their particular perspectives. Patrick Parrinder seems to overlook any such distinction when, in *The Failure of Theory* (1987), he uses the example of Poe's essay 'The Philosophy of Composition' to illustrate the fundamental rationalist fallacy of literary theorists. Parrinder takes exception to the theorists' attempt to divest literature of its mystery by fully accounting for it: 'theory, as a systematic explanation of phenomena, tends to reduce its objects – whether literary works or the cosmos itself – to the subordinate status of phenomena to be explained' (1987: 14). This is only true if each literary theory sets out, as Terry Eagleton did in his early Marxist days, to 'explain' the literary work (Eagleton 1976). The recognition that theories do not attempt to offer exhaustive readings allows them to admit of other plentiful possibilities beyond their own scope. Parrinder assumes here that the 'object' of every theory is the entire work.

Literary theory, where it can be distinguished from literary *theories*, is not, given the preceding argument, a general account of literature itself. Although individual theories of sectional interests may not be refutable by reference to other interest groups, there is a question of methodology which can be used to differentiate between good and bad applications of interested positions such as feminism or Marxism. Small and Guy make a plea for a variety of literary theory which will advance pedagogical concerns in English Studies, and we surely have to concede that recent theory has compelled us to re-think the issue of methodology. When T.S. Eliot declared that 'There is no method but to be very intelligent' (1933: 89), with reference to literary criticism, he was voicing the *reductio ad absurdum* of the idealist position whereby literature is the immediate expression of an individual mind. Since there is no means other than intuition to discover the intangible relationship between words on a page and a (possibly deceased) writer's mind on this account, there can indeed be no systematic principles by which to proceed.

Catherine Belsey begins her controversial work *Critical Practice* (1980) with a refutation of the principles on which this opinion of Eliot's and other theories or anti-theories are based. The expression theory of art, as it is known to aesthetics, was recognized as an absurdity as long ago as the eighteenth century, and possibly far earlier. The discrediting of this particular position does not constitute an attack against aesthetics on ideological grounds, but an aesthetic criticism of what was the thinly-disguised ideological position known as liberal humanism. Where there is no possible methodology to implement the approach, the theory must fail. The example of liberal humanism shows how aesthetics can be harnessed to refute a position which is primarily ideological: it is not a case of aesthetic theories being undermined by ideology, but of ideology being undermined by aesthetics. Liberal humanism is not a 'preconceived selective point of view', as Popper conceives of such, but a comprehensive theory of humanity, which is open to Popper's objection that it therefore cannot discriminate amongst the infinite strands of literary history to find a coherent viewpoint.

Literary theories are more properly, then, accounts of the ways that the interests of particular social groups are manifested in literature, rather than theories of literature *per se*. As such they construct the object of their study in such a way that it is essentially distinct from those of other theories. This means that they may lay claim to a unique perspective on, for example, the representation of women in the nineteenth-century novel, yet not to the exclusion of other theoretical approaches to the same novels. Although they are therefore distinct approaches, literary theories can nonetheless use aesthetics both to defend their own approach and criticize the work of others. Aesthetics is not a general theory of the characteristics shared by all works of art, but a way of ensuring that the methodologies by which each theory goes about constructing its own objects and drawing conclusions from them are consistent and appropriate.

Wayne C. Booth uses an analogy which graphically illustrates this situation: he compares literature with a cone which is contemplated by a number of observers, each with a different point of view. To the observer directly underneath the cone it is accurate to say that the object is circular. To those elsewhere the cone might appear triangular. The point that Booth makes is that each observer is correct in his/her description, despite his/her different conclusions. In this case geometry is analogous to aesthetics in that geometry is the methodology of describing and possibly correcting observations from any viewpoint (Booth 1979: 35). Different perspectives such as this can always co-exist; they cannot eliminate their rivals, yet they can eliminate positions which have no foundations in the appropriate methodology at all. This leads to what Booth calls a 'limited pluralism', whereby entry to the literary fold is regulated by theoretical consider-ations. Pluralism in criticism is not a condition that leads to anarchy; it is simply a feature of the humanities as opposed to the sciences that there can be no unanimous agreement on the purpose of the enquiry. Human life is too varied to describe an absolute set of human interests that pertain to everyone.

What at present passes as literary theory is therefore a combination of theories (in the Popperian sense) together with a range of disparate methodologies. Feminism is an example of a theory which has on occasions used deconstruction as its methodology. For every interested theoretical position there are three elements: an interest group, an object and a methodology for uniting the two. Criticism of other theories is possible where these three elements do not properly cohere in practice. Derrida, for example, has recently suggested that in his view Marxist theory is still 'heavily loaded with metaphysical assumptions' (Fabb *et al.* 1987: 254), the very burden which Marxists have been explicitly seeking to throw off.

It is possible to illustrate the process by which aesthetic considerations can inform a methodology and have reper-cussions for the discipline itself by compelling a reconsideration of its ultimate object. Linguistics does not speak for a particular social group, yet it does select a particular aspect of literature as the focus of its attention. It is a 'selective viewpoint' in Popper's terms. Geoffrey Leech proposes that Jakobson's famous but dated definition of the poetic function, the 'set to the message', should now be abandoned in favour of what he calls 'the set towards the discourse' (Fabb *et al.* 1987: 85). Rather than arguing that literature can be defined as self-reflexive communication, Leech advances the view that it is writing which compels us to consider the functional elements which bind the separate sentences together into a poetic whole as discourse. This, of course, has implications for methodology in literature: it suggests where we should begin to carry out a literary study. Furthermore, Leech uses this to defend an aesthetic opinion, namely that the text is autotelic or self-contained. Quoting H.G. Widdowson, Leech describes the literary message as 'arising from no previous situation and requiring no response, it does not serve as a link between people or as a means of furthering the business of ordinary social life' (Fabb *et al.* 1987: 86). The discourse can be understood without reference to events outside the poem, in other words; it is an entirely separate and novel 'game' with its own rules. It is possible to refer to the world of everyday events, of course, but only by virtue of the relationships between the constituents of the poem. Orwell's *Animal Farm* may be able to refer us to the Russian Revolution, yet only because of the relationships between the internal characters which we notice first.

Discourse is always, by definition, incomplete, since it consists of elements of a linguistic whole which show no immediate signs of coherence, yet there are occasions when discourse structure cannot be decided by reference to purely internal principles. Seamus Heaney's poem 'The Ministry of Fear' is addressed to his fellow poet, Seamus Deane, and relates the following exchange between the young Heaney and the police at a check-point:

'What's your name, driver?'
    'Seamus . . .'
        Seamus?

                (1975: 64)

Here it may be necessary for the uninitiated to know that the name 'Seamus' identifies him as a Catholic, and thereby makes him suspicious to the police. It is therefore arguable that this fact, which is not remotely suggested by the poem itself, needs to be discovered in external sources before the discourse can be made coherent. This exchange illustrates what the Russian Formalist Bakhtin calls an 'utterance', a dialogue which cannot be fully understood by reference to its syntax or semantics, but only by reference to the context in which it takes place. Leech's methodology, therefore, cannot always be used successfully: the aesthetic challenge to it from sociolinguistics forces a reappraisal of the object of linguistic criticism – the language itself. Language cannot be a formal system of rules, a 'calculus'; it must be a formal system embedded in a social practice of some kind.

The fundamental objection to the notion of an autotelic text, however, dates from an earlier debate about Kant's aesthetics. In *The Critique of Judgment*, he proposed the view that the essential characteristic of the work of art was its disinterestedness, its total lack of utilitarian value. The objections to this theory are numerous and, ironically, they can be applied to some attempts to defend the aesthetic attitude as well. In order to describe the state of attention which characterizes the aesthetic attitude, some theorists have claimed that it is a state in which the audience contemplate the work for no purpose other than to enjoy its intrinsic qualities. As some aestheticians have pointed out, however, it is very difficult to disengage interested and disinterested attention (Dickie 1964). The example of a professional critic watching a play in order to review it would be a case in point.

In *Literary Theory* (1983), Terry Eagleton clearly skirts the issue of how to define the aesthetic attitude. He mentions the possibility that literature could be defined as 'non-pragmatic discourse', yet he is cautious not to seize on this theory, conscious, no doubt, of the many arguments against it. One reason why any such definition is bound to fail is that it offers an objective criterion for an object – art or literature – which is constituted subjectively. If non-pragmatic discourse could be defined independently, then we would have a fixed set of characteristics which would determine what could and could not be literature. The aesthetic attitude, however, can transform an illimitable range of things.

It is rather surprising, therefore, that Eagleton rejects the Russian Formalist concept of defamiliarization or estrangement as the defining function of literature on the grounds that 'there is no kind of writing which cannot, given sufficient ingenuity be read as estranging' (1983: 6). The aesthetic theory which Eagleton adopts maintains precisely this point: the characteristics of the literary can potentially be seen anywhere. The essential characteristic is not, as it is perhaps customary to think, an exclusive feature of literature. After all, an experience such as a conversion to a religion may contain all the elements of literary experience. Perhaps the most accurate way to describe literature is that it is the process of defamiliarization through writing, and that the same goal can be approached through other media such as images.

The expression theory of art offers an explanation of the way that literature conveys emotions to an audience, but not how these emotions are modulated in any way. Defamiliarization promises to account for the necessity of what used to be called an 'ironic counterpoint' in literature, a means of seeing a recognizable emotion in a new, unsuspected light. It is not enough to express sadness with which we are all wholly familiar. Furthermore, the question of whether literature defamiliarizes such experiences is a personal one: whether it does so or not will depend on what we are already familiar with. The precise state of knowledge of the individual will determine how 'literary' a particular example of writing appears. Defamiliarization therefore explains how we can have both popular and highbrow writing, adult and children's literature. The term is more descriptive of current usage than prescriptive with regard to moral or artistic values. As we learn more, of course, it becomes increasingly difficult to surprise us; hence the concept of literature becomes increasingly narrow for many highly educated people. This is not to say, however, that the views of highly educated people who are steeped in the classics necessarily hold sway. Popular literary forms can achieve a radical shift of perception on the part of their audience even if they are not implicitly conscious of the literary conventions which have shaped traditional movements. In the case of women, it is now becoming clear that a great many writers who were able to defamiliarize the lives of other women were nonetheless not recognized by the male establishment in their own time. If the object of women's writing is women's lives, then it is not surprizing that male critics have often failed to notice those who were particularly skilled at illuminating it from a different perspective.

The answer to the question of the precise relationship between aesthetics and literary theory is, therefore, that aesthetics is the discipline of constructing the object of any literary study in a coherent and feasible manner which is in accord with the principles of the literary theory in question. In *The Ideology of the Aesthetic* (1990), Terry Eagleton shows how various aesthetic arguments are appropriated for political purposes throughout the ages. Aesthetic arguments are not implicitly ideological, but can be harnessed in the service of ideological interests; they cannot be reduced to particular ideologies by zealous Marxists.

There is, however, no use of aesthetics which is not in some way ideological. In this work, however, Eagleton sounds as if he sometimes has little relish for the task he has set himself:

> With the birth of the aesthetic, then, the sphere of art begins to suffer something of the abstraction and formalisation characteristic of modern theory in general; yet the aesthetic is nevertheless thought to retain a charge of irreducible particularity, providing us with a kind of paradigm of what a non-alienated mode of cognition might look like. Aesthetics is thus always a contradictory, self-undoing sort of project, which in promoting the theoretical value of its object risks emptying it of exactly that specificity or ineffability which was thought to rank amongst its most precious features. (1990: 2)

The theory of defamiliarization would also lead inevitably to this conclusion. It is clearly not possible to expose and examine the sources of our sudden recognition of new ways of seeing without making those ways familiar and expected. The formalist Viktor Shklovsky described the aim of art as to 'increase the difficulty and length of perception', whereas theory aims to make us familiar with its devices. The failure of theory has been its failure to describe how to produce such defamiliarizing experiences; it has concentrated on describing those already in circulation. Nonetheless, if the concept of defamiliarization can be recuperated to encourage a fresh, more receptive concept of literature, it can also perhaps reinstate literature as a radical human practice which has, as its very *raison d'être*, the revolutionizing of our ossified, habitual perception. In order to develop such a concept of literature, we perhaps need a 'socio-poetics' of literature which will consider its function relative to particular social groups and other cultures, rather than an aesthetics of art in general (Swingewood 1986).

An obvious response to the concept of defamiliarization is that it permits anyone to create literature by some kind of imaginative fiat, which reduces the concept to a triviality. Although estrangement is a personal response, it is not, however, one which can be applied indiscriminately at the whims of any reader. Seamus Heaney has described the literary effects of Craig Raine as examples of defamiliarization (Heaney 1988: 40), and if this is so, then it shows that objects can be made to seem strange, yet the experience may also appear curiously unfulfilling and leave us none the wiser. The critical controversy which was engendered by Craig Raine's poetry can be interpreted as raising the question of whether estrangement alone is sufficient to merit the description 'literary'. The further element in the concept is that, as Shklovsky writes, the aim of literary devices is to 'make the stone stony', to enable us to know the object better. The paradox of defamiliarization is that, where it succeeds, the more it estranges the object, the more we feel that we know the object in question. There is therefore a sense in which the claim that a text has the potential to defamiliarize is not uncontestable: a literary representation must not merely seem strange, but it is also necessary to argue just how it does represent a significant advance in one's familiar knowledge and belief. The reader does not have an absolute right to employ this concept as he or she chooses, yet it is nonetheless relative.

Roger Fowler recognizes the importance of the concept of defamiliarization and uses it to describe the typical effects of literary writing. He defines defamiliarization as the occasions when 'the context of reference introduces elements which in any way deviate from the expected cultural context' (Fowler 1986: 89). The problem with this definition, however, is that it suggests that the context of culture is somehow homogeneous and can be safely assumed to exist in the same form for all readers. This is rather like assuming that all readers share common characteristics, an assumption which has long been denounced in reader-response theory. The expectations of readers will differ according to their precise cultural situation, and it is possible to argue that there are as many cultural contexts as readers.

The fundamental approach taken by linguists such as Fowler is to attempt to identify the literary devices which give rise to certain literary effects. Although much of this work succeeds in its aim, it can give the impression that language is a mechanism which automatically causes effects irrespective of the age, education, class, gender or race of the reader. Not since Wordsworth has any serious attempt been made to found an aesthetic theory on reactions which can be presupposed of all men, simply by virtue of their human nature. Another example of this linguistic approach is David Lodge's argument in *The Modes of Modern Writing* (1977) where he differentiates between Orwell's description of a hanging and a newspaper account. The argument that Orwell's work is literary because it employs certain devices recognized by the Russian Formalists fails when the same devices can be found in a number of texts which have no pretensions to literary status. The theory of defamiliarization can be developed into an aesthetic theory which defines literary writing by its function in society, and this involves examining the uses to which it is put and the reactions of readers. There is no need to define the concept so closely that we can predict with accuracy where it will occur. As with a concept such as humour, we cannot dictate what will amuse people, but instead we have to derive our definition from their reactions at various stages in history. If a particular type of writing succeeds in making experiences unfamiliar for a major section of society, and this expands their perceptions, then the concept of 'the literary' should be expanded to accommodate it. As Fowler notes, defamiliarization is a concept which changes with history, and what can be so described in one age does not necessarily achieve the same effects in a later period. It also follows that the same effects do not occur to all people when their experience of contemporaneous culture is radically different.

Craig Raine quotes from James Joyce in the Preface to *A Martian Sends a Postcard Home* and creates the impression that he will be using Shklovsky's defamiliarizing devices:

> When travelling you get into those wagons called railway coaches which are behind the locomotive. This is done by opening a door and gently projecting into the compartment yourself and your valise. A man in an office will give you a piece of cardboard in return for some money. By looking at it attentively you will see the word Paris printed on it which is the name of this stop (Raine 1986: Preface).

Shklovsky comments on various uses of defamiliarization in literature to depict the sexual act, and Raine offers his own version of this in his poem, 'Sexual Couplets':

> Here we are without our clothes,
> one excited watering can, one peculiar rose . . .
>
> (Raine 1986: 6)

The rose is a familiar emblem of female sexuality in literature, yet here it is deliberately juxtaposed with the conveniently phallic angle of the watering can. By extending a traditional metaphor, Raine brings the poetic into close liaison with the banal, and no doubt amuses many readers. It is, of course, crucial, however, that the banal image comes first in order to surprise the reader who might suspect that it has no literary origin. If we ask of this couplet 'For whom is Raine writing?', the debate would undoubtedly focus on whether he is here attempting, like John Donne, to please only those university wits who are capable of fully appreciating the irony of this contribution to literary history.

In successive couplets Raine's imagery is less esoteric, and corresponds more to what Shklovsky describes as 'riddles', where the task is to identify the sexual euphemisms used:

I am wearing a shiny souwester;
You are coxcombed like a jester. . . .

This could hardly be accused of appealing to esoteric knowledge on the reader's part, yet as an example of defamiliarization it has lesser impact. The reader's energy is devoted to recognizing the precise comparisons here, and once the 'riddle' is solved, there is no motivation to pursue the analogy to any great lengths. An obvious justification for the poem is that it allows us to see the sexual act as a comical experience, and lessens the effect of generations of romantic description. In this sense it is defamiliarizing, yet not to the extent that we could be said to view the sexual act between men and women in an entirely new light. The overwhelming feeling once the riddle is understood is of familiarity rather than a radical shift of perception. The context of reference makes little change to the context of culture, and this might be used to evaluate the worth of literature for particular groups of people.

Shklovsky's description of defamiliarization is not abundantly clear, and even seems contradictory at times. He remarks that the intention of the device is 'to make the stone stony', yet he also asserts that 'Art is a way of experiencing the artfulness of an object; the object is not important'. The former remark suggests that art is a play of formal devices and has no bearing on the real world. In this sense Raine's poetry conforms to the definition. On the other hand, it may simply be stating that a radical shift of perception of things as they are need not be achieved by supplying knowledge of the world. A full-blooded concept of defamiliarization would account for the way that the formal devices of art in the context of reference can impinge on our understanding of the context of culture (Bennett 1979).

Seamus Heaney also uses the image of the sexual act in his

poem 'Act of Union', where he addresses Ireland as a woman whose body is represented as the landscape:

Your back is a line of eastern coast
And arms and legs are thrown
Beyond your gradual hills. I caress
The heaving province where our past has grown.
(Heaney 1976: 19)

The lyrical speaker is the male whose 'act of union' has left the woman to bear his offspring. The product of the union is a 'fifth column whose stance is growing unilateral' and now is beyond control. The 'child' of the union is a figure of disunity. The male participant watches the continuing agonies of the 'stretchmarked body', which now has an open wound which no treaty can heal. Here the poem achieves more than the defamiliarization of formal elements. At its most effective, Shklovsky argues that defamiliarization can cause 'semantic modification', in other words it can permanently alter the meaning which the words used have for us. By permanently enlarging the metaphorical possibilities of the expression 'act of union', Heaney reveals ironies in the semantics of the phrase which bring about an interesting new vision of this relationship in Irish history. The anticipated reader of this poem need not possess any unusual cultural background except perhaps an understanding of the coincidence between this poem and the classical metaphor of Ireland as an old woman. Heaney's poem deserves more praise for the manner in which the context of reference elaborates a new perspective on a vitally important context of culture without making any claims to fresh knowledge.

Traditionally aesthetics has searched for a concept of art which is *a priori* and sets limits to the use of the term rather than attempting to observe and describe actual cultural practices. By defining literary art in English Studies in accordance with its social functions, there is hope that literature will eventually escape those narrow definitions which exclude so much work of value.

References

Belsey, C. (1980). *Critical Practice*. London, Methuen.
Bennett, T. (1979). *Marxism and Formalism*. London, Methuen.
Booth, W.C. (1979). *Critical Understanding: The Powers and Limits of Pluralism*. Chicago and London, Chicago University Press.

Dickie, G. (1964). 'All Aesthetic Attitude Theories Fail: The Myth of the Aesthetic Attitude'. *American Philosophical Quarterly*, Vol, No. 1.

Eagleton, T. (1976). *Marxism and Literary Criticism*. London, Methuen.

—— (1983). *Literary Theory*. Oxford, Blackwell.

—— (1990a). *The Ideology of the Aesthetic*. Oxford, Blackwell.

Eliot, T.S. (1933). *The Use of Poetry and The Use of Criticism*. London, Faber and Faber.

Fabb, *et al.* (1987). *The Linguistics of Writing: Arguments Between Language and Literature*. Manchester, Manchester University Press.

Fowler, R. (1986). *Linguistic Criticism*. Oxford, Oxford University Press.

Golding, W. (1982). *A Moving Target*. London, Faber and Faber.

Heaney, S. (1975). *North*. London, Faber and Faber.

Mandelbaum, M. (1965). 'Family Resemblances and Generalizations Concerning the Arts'. *American Philosophical Quarterly*, Vol. 2, no 3.

Parrinder, P. (1987). *The Failure of Theory*. Brighton, Harvester.

Popper, K. (1957). *The Poverty of Historicism*. London, Methuen.

Raine, C. (1980). *A Martian Sends A Postcard Home*. London, Faber and Faber.

Small, Ian and Guy, Josephine (1990). 'English in Crisis?'. *Essays in Criticism*, 40, 185–197.

Stolnitz, J. (1960). *Aesthetics and the Philosophy of Art Criticism*. Boston, Houghton.

Swingewood, A. (1986). *Sociological Poetics and Aesthetic Theory*. London, Macmillan.

Todorov, T. (1981). *Introduction to Poetics*. Brighton, Harvester.

Christian Cook

9

Stalemates? feminists, postmodernists and unfinished issues in modern aesthetics

Patricia Waugh

George Eliot's Mr Brooke could not have known, as he reflected upon the perils of reading Adam Smith, that his reservations about the benefits of a little theory would become central to many of the aesthetic debates of the late twentieth century: 'The fact is, human reason may carry you a little too far – over the hedge in fact. It carried me a good way at one time; but I saw it would not do. I pulled up; I pulled up in time. But not too hard.' Gentle deceleration is preferred, as he goes on to explain, because 'we must have Thought, else we shall be landed back in the dark ages' (Eliot 1965: 39). However, reading much of the aesthetic theory arising out of the so-called 'postmodern debate', it is difficult to avoid feeling that not only are we landed back in the dark ages but that it is the rationalisms of Enlightenment thought that have marooned us there in the first place.

Modernity, we are told, is coming to an end, strangled by its own contradictory logic, born astride of the grave which has become its own abyss. Just as Greek civilization or the feudal age had come to an end and just as Nietzsche had announced the death of God a century earlier, so contemporary theorists like Michel Foucault have announced the end of modern Western man, a face in the sand eroded by an ever-encroaching sea. Yet while postmodernist thinkers (dare one say it – largely male) were proclaiming their own death (the end of humanism), feminists were in their most optimistic vein. For postmodernists, modernity might be exhausted, but for feminists it was clearly unfinished, needing to be renovated perhaps, but not abandoned.

Postmodernism was first used as a period term in the early 'fifties by Arnold Toynbee who announced that we were entering the fourth and final phase of Western history: one of irrationalism, anxiety, and helplessness. If modernism had tried to anchor in consciousness a centre which could no longer hold – the conscience of the heroic, socially alienated artist – postmodernism had shown us an even darker side of modernity and the aporias of its aesthetic. It had shown that there is nothing for consciousness to be anchored to: no universal ground of truth, justice, or reason, so that consciousness itself is thus 'decentred', no longer origin, author, location of intentional agency but a function through which impersonal forces pass and intersect – Dover beach displaced by an international airport lounge. In this context art seems to have no special role. In a world where truth is only the effect of power or rhetoric, where all interpretative models are provisional and contingent, neither the Romantic concept of poets as the unacknowledged legislators of mankind, nor the late Romantic (Freudian) concept of universal mind as a poeticizing instrument, seem to carry any validity. Both concepts seemed to have been turned back on themselves in a bleak parody: if everything is fictional or textual then there can be no 'outside', no 'real', no way of saying that one act or text is better than another; no ethics, no aesthetics because existence is itself aestheticized and no ideology because no 'truth': at best only provisional consensus, pragmatism, interpretative communities.

Such is the generally apocalyptic vision of much postmodern thought. But, as Frank Kermode had reminded us in the late 'sixties, if we do not have a sense of an ending, we invent one: concordances are reassuring, they produce the illusion of retrospective significance. Endings confer meaning and for all human beings, 'the End they imagine will reflect their irreducibly intermediary preoccupations . . . we thrive on epochs' (Kermode 1967: 7).

Could it be that postmodernism is the ending invented by its theorists searching for their own significance? Of what will that significance consist? Why have feminists on the whole, though registering the transitionality of the current epoch, not represented it through the same sense of an ending? Redemption through retrospective narrative significance is in itself, of course, also central to the modernist aesthetic. In that key text for modernism, *Heart of Darkness*, when Marlow chooses to interpret Kurtz's acknowledgement of 'the horror' as an heroic act, one can see in Marlow's eloquence a mirror of Kurtz's own: it is the retrospective narrative rather than the experiential act which 'redeems'. But, despite the heroic adventure story quest form, redemption can, in the end, only be offered through the rhetorical structures of that same Enlightenment vocabulary which Conrad's text has exposed as corrupt and fraudulent. Nevertheless, to read this text is to feel that one remains in a state of hesitation about whether it is art or experience which redeems. Not so with postmodernism. Here, the sense of an ending has to be *continuously* revised through the endless deferral of repeated narrative reconstruction. There can be no experience outside text. History is narrative. The end is the insight that there can be no ending, no beginning, no ground, and no telos. Again, however, in this world of hyperinflated discourse (Newman 1985), one may begin to feel, indeed, that it is not the worst so long as we can say it is the worst, and thus to begin to question *whose* apocalypse is being represented.

Which brings me to silence. And at last to feminism. Nietzsche's critique of Enlightenment modernity was basically that it had not been modern enough. He saw all its major institutions and categories of thought as redescriptions of Christianity: a slave mentality which could not confront the existence of the 'will to truth' as a form of the 'will to power'. Postmodernism seems, in its renunciation of modernity, to have embraced an insistent secularism. It seems to me, though, that its rhetoric of apocalypse is just as insistently religious as the modernist search for redemption through art. Just as the narratives of modernism search for their own self-grounded formal redemption, so too the narratives of postmodern theory seek a self-overcoming, though one outside the ultimately Aristotelian notion of form which underlies the modernist concept of formal autonomy. What alarms me as a feminist, however, is the pervasive redescription of this possibility of redemption, this space of the sacred beyond the linearity of Aristotelian form, as the space of the feminine. Kurtz's Intended continues to be used as the justification for that necessary Lie which seems to offer us a paradise regained outside the logic of modernity. Before this tendency is examined more closely, however, I wish to look briefly and more generally at the history of the relations between feminism and postmodernism.

Modernity, postmodernism and feminism

Feminism as a discourse clearly arises out of modernity and its models of reason, justice and subjectivity. Feminism, however, has also been one of the discourses which has with similar clarity revealed some of the most entrenched and disguised contradictions and limitations of Enlightenment thought. To this extent, it can be seen as intrinsically post-modern, if problematically so. Yet, until very recently, the debates within postmodernism have tended to ignore those taking place within feminist discourse, and vice versa. Things have begun to change. Feminist theory has developed a self-conscious awareness of its own hermeneutic perspectivism based on the recognition of a central contradiction in its attempts to define an epistemology: that women seek equality and valorization for a gendered identity which has been constructed through the very culture and ideology that feminism seeks to challenge. In fact, one can see such contradictions manifesting themselves as early as 1971 in Julia Kristeva's essay 'Women's Time'. The concept of a 'women's identity' functions in terms both of affirmation and negation, even within feminism itself. There can be no simple legitimation for feminists in throwing off a 'false consciousness' and revealing a true 'female self'. To embrace 'difference' in essentialist terms is to come dangerously close to reproducing that very patriarchal construction of gender which feminists have set out to contest.

Feminism of late, therefore, has developed a self-reflexive mode: questioning its own legitimating procedures in a manner which seems to bring it close to a postmodernism which has absorbed the lessons of poststructuralism and consists at the most general level of a crisis of legitimation across culture, politics and aesthetic theory and practice. The slogan 'Let us wage war on totality', however, could be seen as postmodernism's response to that earlier slogan of the feminist movement, 'The personal is the political'. But if the latter can be seen as a rallying cry, the former implies a hostile attitude towards its implicit ideals of collectivism and community. In fact the feminist cry situated its politics firmly within what Jean-François Lyotard wishes to denounce and what Jürgen Habermas calls the 'project of modernity'(1987). It will be my argument that even if feminists have come to recognize in their own discourses some of the epistemological doubt and perspectivism that afflicts postmodernism, feminism must still continue to define itself as an emancipatory movement broadly within the terms of the aforementioned project. Is it possible for feminists to draw on the aesthetics of postmodernism as strategies for narrative disruption without embracing its nihilistic pragmatism? Surely to assume otherwise is in itself to embrace a naively reflectionist aesthetic which sees representation as necessarily reflective of prior structures or ideologies? Can feminists occupy a position of hermeneutic perspectivism which questions epistemology without, therefore, relinquishing ethics in an embrace of hermeneutic anarchism where no discourse is seen as more valid than any other, but simply more useful at a particular time or place? Can feminism remain opposed to postmodernism's circular tendency to project itself onto the contemporary world and thus, not surprisingly, to find in that world an affirmation of its own theoretical presuppostions? Can it, in other words, continue to resist the implicitly religious terminology of the postmodern sense of an ending while recognizing the force of its critique of epistemology?

One way of approaching these issues is to think about the implications of the various models of subjectivity with which feminists and postmodernists have worked. What the preceding discussion has suggested is that the epistemological and ethical contradictions now confronting both of them are fundamentally issues about identity and difference. Subjective transformation has been central to feminist agendas for political change. Similarly, over the last thirty years, the deconstruction of liberal individualism and the dissolution of traditional aesthetic conceptualizations of character have been central to postmodern art and theory. Like feminism, postmodernism has been engaged in a re-examination of the Enlightenment concepts of subjectivity, truth and reason enshrined in the belief that human beings are collectively engaged in a progressive movement towards moral and intellectual self-realization through the application to their situation of a universal rational faculty.

Personal freedom or autonomy in these terms has been defined as freedom from the irrational forces within and the social forces without. The work of Freud has been seen as axiomatic for the former and the work of Marx for the latter. The focus of much postmodern theory has been to dismantle the basic assumptions of their writing, laying bare an epistemology and methodology which, it is argued, is at one with an oppressive and authoritarian rationalism which has produced terror in place of emancipation and disguised its will to power as a disinterested 'scientific' desire for truth. The self-determining subject has had a similarly difficult time of it in postmodern fiction. Such fictions are often enactments of the frustration of attempting to find correspondences to their linguistic condition outside of language itself. Robert Coover's 'Panel Game' parodies the attempt to find an all-encompassing truth in language by showing the narrator caught up in a maze of the myriad possibilities of meaning, of *paroles* with no discoverable *langues*, while all the possible formal functions of language – emotive, referential, poetic, conative, phatic, and finally, metalingual – whirl about him: 'So think. Stickleback. Freshwaterfish. Freshwaterfish: green seaman. Seaman: semen. Yes, but green: raw? spoiled? vigorous? Stickle: stubble. Or maybe scruple. Back: Bach: Bachus: Bachate: berry. Rawberry? Strawberry.' (1969: 63). Through the emphasis on the arbitrary associations of sound, rhyme and image, attention is drawn to the formal organization of language and away from its referential potential. The quotation could almost be an exercise in Jakobsonian linguistics as the internal operations of language produce that poetic equivalence which endlessly substitutes one arbitrary phoneme for another: Stickleback. Freshwaterfish (metonymic). Freshwaterfish: green seaman (metonymic/metaphoric) seaman: semen (metaphoric).

In Donald Barthelme's fictions abstract nouns and passive constructions almost entirely replace personal assertion or human agency. The story 'Brain Damage' (1971) begins: 'At the restaurant, sadness was expressed'; moods are reflexes of disembodied signifiers rather than of personal feeling. Endless lists, catalogues, insistent stylization flaunting the materiality of writing as depthlessness, again seem to present a self-conscious articulation of the rules of selection and combination in grammar, an endless play of linguistic substitution for its own sake; metaphors proliferate, syntax continuously breaks down. The reader is offered sentences such as this: 'The world is sagging, snagging, scaling, spalling, pulling, pinging, pitting, warping, checking, fading, chipping, cracking, yellowing, leaking, staling, shrinking and in dynamic unbalance' (1974: 6). Certainly this sentence enacts these actions, for as the material world shrinks, the linguistic one expands and it is the materiality of language again, what Fredric Jameson (1985) has characterized as the schizophrenic present of postmodernism, which is obsessively foregrounded.

Barthelme's sentence, of course, enacts entropy, another postmodern image of Apocalypse. I think Jameson is quite correct, however, in the essay mentioned above, to connect the 'schizophrenic' tendency in postmodernism with a pervasive nostalgia. It is worth thinking about this in relation to feminism. It seems to me that much postmodernist writing is pervaded by a nihilism produced through nostalgia – Nietzsche is one of several thinkers who have connected these impulses. Often in such texts the possibility of humanist affirmation is destroyed by an insistent and excessive but familiar enough Romantic desire to rediscover a transcendent metaphysical truth, an essence of Being, whose impossible realization produces the urge to render absurd or to destroy altogether what can be: the human subject as an ethical, affective and effective historical agent.

In Thomas Pynchon's V, for example, V functions as both goal and negation of Stencil's quest for transcendent meaning and is pictured thus:

> skin radiant with the bloom of some new plastic; both eyes glass but now containing some photoelectric cells, connected by silver electrodes to optic nerves of purest copper wire leading to a brain exquisitely wrought as a diode matrix ever could be. Soleroid relays would be her ganglia, serio-actuators move her flawless nylon limbs, hydraulic fluid be sent by a platinum heart-pump through buthyrane veins and arteries.
>
> (1979: 406)

For those who wish to equate 'totality' with totalitarianism (as Lyotard does at times), or to conflate linguistic or textual with political subversion, then such postmodern strategies, which appear to dissolve humanist subjectivity into textual play, have been hailed as the only means of resisting the oppressive structures of global capitalism, of patriarchal surveillance and control of the pleasure principle. They are seen as part of the assault on the bondage of thought to regulative ideals such as 'truth' and 'goodness'. In response, one might point out some obvious difficulties here: why is V a woman? And surely it matters that Nietzsche insisted that such regulative ideals were tied to what he saw as phallic castration, an emasculation of the intellect he associated with all emancipatory movements, particularly feminism? The idea of truth as untruth has repeatedly been articulated through the image of the seductive woman, a Salome who is only her veils, whose adornments disguise a gaping absence. She continues to appear with monotonous frequency in the metaphorical femininity of postmodern writing. This grotesque version of the wearisome metaphor, for example, appears in Nietzsche's *My Sister and I:* 'Truth is still elusive. However, she is no longer a young girl but an old bitch with all her front teeth missing' (1990: 114). Before examining in more depth what such rhetoric means for actual women – whether, indeed, Pynchon's *V* assaults the oppressive structures of late capitalism for women, in particular – we need first to look at the historical and philosophical foundations of postmodernist and feminist aesthetics and to see whether it is indeed possible to move beyond the position of stalemate.

Founding assumptions: feminism and postmodernism

Fredric Jameson has suggested that postmodernism's most radical insight may be seen as the view that the bourgeois individual subject is not only a thing of the past but also a myth. We have never possessed this sort of autonomy: 'Rather this construct is merely a philosophical and cultural mystification which sought to persuade people that they "had" individual subjects and possessed this unique personal identity' (1985: 115). If the subject is a myth and if narrative as the reflection of the grand 'master plot' of history is a redundant illusion, why should I have the feeling, as I read much postmodernist writing, that its apocalyptic nihilism about the possibility of ethical and imaginative subjective existence is grounded in that very nostalgia of which I spoke earlier, a nostalgia for an ideal autonomous self? Nostalgia involves the projection of the self onto history through identification. It rewrites history in the terms of desire, for to see the past as past is to recognize one's own mortality and temporality, fundamentally to disturb one's sense of presence. Nostalgia is the desire to recover the past as paradise, as a myth of origins. Identification, however, necessitates ideal images with which to identify. It seems to me that feminists are highly unlikely to bear this sort of relationship to history or to the ideal autonomous self which is central to the discourses of modernity. Those who have been excluded from the constitution of that so-called 'universal subject' – whether for reasons of gender, class, race, sexuality – are unlikely either to long nostalgically for what they have never experienced or possessed, or to revel in the 'jouissance' of its disintegration. Never having experienced it as an ethical ideal which might be materially realized, they are unlikely therefore to fall into nihilistic apocalypticism at the recognition that it may simply not be realizable at all in its pure or original form.

They will surely be more likely to want to occupy its position and to be able to offer a critique from both within and outside of it. In my view, the decentred and fragmented subject of much postmodernist writing is one whose existence is premised upon the disintegration of a pre-existing belief in the possibility of realizing the full autonomous subject of Enlightenment rhetoric, of German idealist philosophy and Kantian aesthetics. It is present at least as a structure of feeling if not fully articulated. It is clear from recent feminist scholarship that most women are unlikely to have experienced history in this way. Thus the goals of agency, autonomy and self-determination are not ones which feminists have taken for granted or glibly seen as exhausted. They are ideals which feminism has helped to re-formulate, modify and challenge. Feminism needs a subject and it seems to me it has found a means of articulating it which both avoids the fetishization of pure reason as the locus of sub-jecthood and the irrationalism born out of the perceived failure of this ideal.

Alternative histories

As part of our current dilemma of the ultimate impossibility of separating knowledge from experience, it is difficult to talk about 'origins' in relation to either postmodernism or feminism. Postmodernism is a notoriously unstable concept, whether used in the more narrow aesthetic sense or the wider philosophical or sociological one. It entered American criticism in the 'fifties in Charles Olson's attempt to define the existence of a new non-anthropocentric poetry whose Heideggerian anti-human-ism was directed at seeing 'man' as in the world, an object among objects. The same tendency can be detected at around the same time in the French New Novel and its theorization in the writings of Robbe-Grillet and in Susan Sontag's rejection of a hermeneutic depth/surface model of interpretation for a return to the sensual surface, an 'erotics' of literature. John Barth talked of abandoning the literature of exhaustion for the essentially parodic literature of replenishment, Leslie Fiedler of a new art which would bridge the gap between high and mass culture. For both Sontag and Ihab Hassan, in particular, postmodernism, an art of the surface, was the contemporary period's answer to Adorno's 'negative aesthetics' of modernism: an art which in making itself opaque and difficult would refuse consumption even as it partook of a culture of consumption. By the early 'eighties, however, the term shifts from one used to describe a range of aesthetic practices involving playful irony, parody, self-consciousness, and fragmentation, to one which encompasses a more general shift in thought and seems to register a pervasive cynicism about the progressivist ideals of modernity and a sense of a new cultural epoch. In this later definition distinctions between critical and functional knowledge break down and capitalism in its last and most insidious phase invades everything, leaving no oppositional space outside itself. Just as many novels of the 'seventies had displayed the hidden processes of artistic production, so too poststructuralist thought now proceeded by exposing the concealed rhetorical mechanisms which both produce and subvert conceptual meaning. Both postmodernism and poststructuralism undermine classical conceptions of representation in which truth precedes or determines the representations which either communicate it directly or mediate it indirectly. Postmodernism had gradually become a phrase describing a whole new 'episteme' of Western culture.

None of this says or said much about gender or feminism. In fact, although postmodern theory increasingly draws on a highly idealized and generalized notion of femininity as 'other' in its search for a space outside of the disintegrating logic of modernity, it rarely talks about (or to, one suspects) actual women or about feminism as a political practice. Yet there are obvious historical points of contact between feminism and postmodernism: both attacked the romantic-modernist cultivation of the aesthetic as an autonomous realm, both assault Enlightenment discourses which universalize white, Western, middle-class male experience. Both recognize the need for a new ethics. Fundamentally each has offered critiques of foundationalist thinking to produce the recognition that gender is not a consequence of anatomy just as social institutions do not so much reflect universal truths as construct historical and provisional ones. Postmodernism is 'grounded' in the epistemological problematization of grounding itself, in the idea of identity as absolute, or truth as essential. In terms of aesthetic practice, writers like John Barth or Jorge Luis Borges foreground epistemological and ontological questions about the construction of the 'real' and the 'self' by playing metafictionally on the textual paradox of the book as artefact and the book as world. Others, such as Salman Rushdie, foreground the paradox of history as both a series of events which happened and also the imposition of a retrospective, paradigmatic and provisional linguistic structure which is itself the product of its own historical situation conceived of as an interplay of textual paradigms *ad infinitum*. Postmodern writing may, indeed, proceed from this critique of foundationalism to social or political critique. In Salman Rushdie's *Shame*, for example, the intervention of alternative narrative voices is used as part of a critique of regimes of 'truth' presented as effects of power. As a strategy for dismantling oppressive concepts of truth, such narrative perspectivism is highly effective, but in a text where all positions are seen to be effects of rhetoric, the possibility of an oppositional space is also dismantled.

Feminism has also, of course, provided its own critique of essentialist and foundationalist assumptions. But however it draws upon postmodern narrative strategies, it cannot repudiate entirely the framework of enlightened modernity without perhaps fatally undermining itself as an emancipatory politics. In proceeding through the demands of political practice, feminism must posit some belief in the notion of effective human agency, the necessity for historical continuity in formulating identity and a belief in historical progress. Even if people are shaped by historical forces, they are not simply reflexive epiphenomena of impersonal deep structures or of a global agonistics of circulating and competing language games. Feminism must believe in the possibility of a community of address situated in an oppositional space which can allow for the connection of the 'small personal voice' (Doris Lessing's term) of one feminist to another and to other liberationist movements. One writer producing personal confessional novels about 'women's identity' can then be seen to connect with the activity of another woman rewriting the history of slavery or one camped on the mud of Greenham Common, even as they accept and recognize each other's differences.

Glancing through the various postmodernisms, in fact, one can see how the range of conceptualizations of difference has entered feminist theory and aesthetic practice. An invigorating, imaginative playfulness has appeared in recent feminist writing. Too often however political claims are made for avant-garde formal disruption which are difficult to justify. Ironically one can again see a reflectionist aesthetics at work here which sees one form of disruption simply reflecting another. Concepts are transferred unproblematically from the context of aesthetic to political practice with no analysis of the sort of problems mentioned above. Surely feminists should keep in mind the centrality to his work of Lyotard's assertion (1984) that emancipatory discourses are no longer possible because there can no longer be a belief in privileged metadiscourses which transcend local and contingent conditions in order to ground the 'truths' of all first-order discourses. According to this view, gender can only be seen as positional, shifting, and cannot be used cross-culturally to explain the practices of human societies. In one sense this is the state of affairs feminism is aiming for in the ideal society which it imagines to be possible. It should not, however, mean that feminists should abandon their struggle against sexual oppression because 'gender' as a metanarrative is necessarily a repressive enactment of metaphysical authority. Lyotard unnecessarily conflates the concept of totality with that of totalitarianism. Feminists should remember that 'totalities', including political unity, need not mean uniformity, that they can be enabling and liberating.

The postmodern concept of language games, dissensus and dispersal, developed in Lyotard's reading of Wittgenstein, has again often been naively appropriated by an avant-garde desire to conflate linguistic or textual disruption with political subversion and to claim a massive political significance for formally innovative writing, modernist and postmodernist. Feminists such as Kristeva have done as much as postmodernists like Lyotard to popularize this concept. It is here that the dangerous metaphor of 'femininity' as 'otherness' is most apparent in what seems to me to be the reproduction of a masculine space of the sacred which continues to be dependent upon concepts which deny the *material* existence of actual women. From Nietzsche through Ihab Hassan and Jacques Lacan, femininity has been used to signify an 'otherness' which has effectively been essentialized as the disruption of the legitimate (viewed as everything from the logic of the Law of the Father – the psychoanalytic version of God – to the Logocentric). This 'otherness' has itself been variously expressed as the repressed other, the hysterical body, the semiotic, the pre-oedipal, ecstatic, fluid, the maternal body. Women, however, have no privileged access to it, though several male avant-garde writers can speak it. In fact, as often as not this celebration of 'difference' goes hand in hand with an amazing indifference to the material and psychological circumstances of actual women. The postmodern espousal of psychotextual 'decentring' as liberatory says little about women as beings in the world who continue to find themselves displaced and invisible even within a critique of epistemology which has supposedly, in deconstructing the centre, therefore done away with the margins. The idea of alterity as feminine can be seen as the attempt to name a space outside the rationalizing logic of modernity – a new space of the sacred. As in most religious discourses, it promises a non-linear space outside the sense of ending, a space of redemption beyond time, language, fixity. Within postmodern psychoanalytic theory it has been described as 'the body without organs' (the small boy's view of the mother?), 'becoming woman' (the male fantasy of plenitude) and the 'hysterical body' (the female object through which psychoanalysis first arrived at its definition of the implicitly masculine subject: see Jardine 1985). It seems that as postmodernists obsessively register their sense of the collapsing legitimacy of the frameworks of Western knowledge, they are also registering unconsciously and metaphorically a fear specifically of the loss of the legitimacy of Western *patriarchal* grand narratives, a new form of fear of women, in effect. As always, appropriation becomes one of the means of dealing with this. Is it a coincidence that at the very historical moment when (male) postmodernists intensify their interest in (and master through their own discourses) a (religious) space described as the 'feminine' and nothing to do with actual women, feminists are establishing an (Enlightened modern) sense of their coherent identity as women through the very categories and discourses which postmodernists claim to have dismantled and done away with in the name of this 'femininity'? Surely this has an ominously familiar ring to it? Could one see the oppressed (women) returning in the form of the repressed (femininity) in postmodern discourse only to be worked through and mastered yet again in the language of theory?

If femininity has become, once more, a metaphor for a state

beyond metaphysics, feminists should be certain that its tenor is not simply the contemporary theoretical counterpart to the Victorian parlour. If they have any suspicions then they should continue to hammer through its boundaries, those between public and private, in an assertion of their continued belief in their own capacity for agency and historical reconstruction. If Roland Barthes writes a pseudo-autobiography to articulate the idea that 'to write an essay on oneself may seem a pretentious idea, but it is a simple idea, simple as the idea of suicide' (1977: 56), feminists should remind themselves that the shelves of books by Barthes in libraries all over the world proclaim a confidence in his authorship even as he disclaims it. They should not be surprised then that so many women writers in the 'seventies articulated a desire to become 'authors of their own lives' at precisely the moment that Barthes was announcing the death of that concept.

Jean Baudrillard's work, it seems to me, is even more problematic for feminism. For him postmodernity signifies the state of contemporary culture which exists as a simulacrum of signs where the information age has utterly dissolved identity. In this perspective all that literature can do is to play off 'alternative worlds' in a state of pluralistic anarchy where the subject is simply a simulating machine of commercial images, the mass a silent majority, and the very idea of resistance an absurdity. Simulation replaces imagination and human beings are left with no capacity to reshape their world even in their own heads. They act like the characters in Robert Coover's novel *Gerald's Party* (1986), as dense points of transmission for all the cop and thriller and porn movies which construct their desires and which churn out incessantly throughout this text in an orgy of hedonistic sensationalism. It may be that Coover is using the parodic mode of the postmodern to offer a critique of postmodernity from within its own codes, but again one is left with the claustrophobic sense that there can be no real opposition to it because there is no place outside. In most versions of the postmodern, in fact, any claim to a substantive reality outside representation is discredited: if signs determine reality, there can be no opposition because there is no space which is not already reproduced.

One difficulty in discussing postmodernism is that the apocalypticism of the theory may have unduly affected our response to the fictional artefacts – if I may be so old-fashioned as to hang on to such a distinction. It seems to me this is an important distinction, because it is evident that many women writers are using postmodern aesthetic strategies of disruption to re-imagine the world in which we live, while resisting the nihilistic implications of the theory. Certainly one can see the writing of Angela Carter, Jeanette Winterson, Margaret Atwood, Maggie Gee, and Fay Weldon, to name but a few, in this way. This is perhaps not so very surprising since women have always experienced themselves in a 'postmodern' fashion – decentred, lacking agency, defined through others. Which is why, it seems to me, they had to attempt to occupy the centre in the early 'seventies. It is why women began to seek a subjective sense of agency and collective identity within the terms of the discourses of modernity at precisely the moment when postmodernists were engaged in the repudiation of such discourses, proclaiming the 'death of the author' and the end of humanism. Much feminist fiction of this period, therefore, was either confessional or concerned with the idea of discovering an authentic identity. If its philosophical roots are to be found anywhere it is in existentialism rather than poststructuralism. It may now appear to be philosophically naive and formally unadventurous, espousing an uncontested aesthetics of expressive realism or a simple reversal of the romance quest plot which did little to problematize ideologies of romantic love or essential identity. I have argued that perhaps feminist writers needed to formulate a sense of identity, history, and agency within these terms before they could begin to deconstruct them. However, feminist writers did not subsequently rush off to embrace the postmodern – indeed they have largely maintained a cautious distance, certainly from much of the theory. This is where I shall declare my own distance as a feminist in offering some 'grand and totalizing' narratives which allow us to think of subjectivity in ways which neither simply repeat the Enlightenment concept of modernity nor repudiate it in an embrace of anarchic dispersal.

Rethinking subjectivity and aesthetics: alternative feminist positions

I want to suggest, somewhat tentatively, that despite differences in the theoretical construction of modernity and postmodernity, common to them both is the inheritance of a particular ideal of subjectivity defined in terms of transcendence and pure rationality. Postmodernism can be seen as a response to the perceived

failure of this ideal. This notion of subjectivity, whether expressed through Descartes' rational 'I' and refined into Kant's
categorical imperatives, or through Nietzsche's *Übermensch* or
Lacan's phallogocentric symbolic order, has not only excluded
women but has made their exclusion on the grounds of emotionality, failure of abstract intellect, or whatever, the basis of its own
identity. This position has been reproduced across philosophy,
psychoanalysis, and literature. In viewing this situation as
fundamentally unchanged, I am, in effect, repudiating the
postmodern notion that there are no longer any generally
legitimated metanarratives. What I am saying is that patriarchal
metanarratives function just as effectively within our so-called
'postmodern age' as in any other age and in its metaphorical play
on notions of the feminine they continue insidiously to function
powerfully within postmodern theory itself.

Jameson has diagnosed postmodernism as the schizophrenic
condition of late capitalism, but I would argue that the autonomous transcendent self of German idealism, Enlightenment
humanism, European Romanticism and realist aesthetics, and
the impersonally fragmented self of postmodernism are a product of the same cultural tradition. Schizophrenia is clinically
defined as a splitting of thought and feeling: the 'schizophrenia'
of postmodernism can be seen as a fin-de-siècle parody or
caricature of a dualism inherent in the Western tradition of
thought where the self is defined as a transcendent rationality
which necessitates splitting off what is considered to be the
irrational, and projecting it as the 'feminine' on to actual women.
It is to see T.S. Eliot's 'dissociation of sensibility' from a feminist
rather than a high tory position. Freud, of course, has taught us
that reason and feeling are inextricably bound up with each
other, but even he believed that ego could and should master id,
that impersonal reason is the basis of personal autonomy.
Increasingly in this century, such a contracted 'rational' self
cannot make sense of the world; whether in the fictions of Franz
Kafka or Saul Bellow, for example, or in the aetiolated dramas of
Samuel Beckett. When transcendence fails, however, the threat
of disorder is seen to come from the split-off (and therefore
uncontrollable) aspects of the psyche. The non-rational is projected on to, and thus defines women, racial minorities, so-called
'sexual deviants' or even 'the masses'.

Postmodernism may seek to locate the possibility of disruption
or *jouissance* in this space, but in continuing to regard it as

'feminine', whether it speaks of actual women or not, it simply continues the process of projection and does little to overcome the dualism and psychological defensiveness inherent in it. Often in postmodernist fiction, for example, traditional images of the castrating female, the unknown and therefore uncontrollable woman, are overlaid in a technological age with their representation as machines which have outstripped the controlled and rational dominance of the male (one thinks of V again). The 'emotionality' thus projected onto the feminine or onto women in order to retain rationality and autonomy as the core of masculine identity produces both images of woman as the 'other' of romantic desire and woman who, thus beyond control, threatens annihilation or incorporation. If feminists wish to argue a politics of femininity as avant-garde disruptive desire they should first think about some of the meanings of, for example, V or Nurse Ratchett in Ken Kesey's novel, *One Flew Over the Cuckoo's Nest* (1962).

In fact, in both modernist and postmodernist writing, when order conceived as a circumscribed rationality seems no longer to cohere in either the self or in history, then it is projected onto the impersonal structures of language or of history conceived as myth, a static and synchronic space. Despite the new 'perspectivism' which enters literary history in the early part of the twentieth century, the potential for the re-evaluation of the relations between subjectivity and objectivity, so many of the aesthetic manifestoes of the time and later critical accounts of the period emphasise 'impersonality', 'autonomy', 'objectivity', universal 'significant form', 'spatial form', 'objective correlative' – even when some of the artefacts, such as *Ulysses*, clearly problematize such notions. The New Critical theorization of literature, in particular the modernist text, as an autonomous linguistic structure, reinforced this. Since then the increasing professionalization of literature has extended this: defamiliarization, systems of signs, the death of the author, the free play of the signifier, simulations. . . .

One can see in much modernist literature both the attempted assertion and the failure of Enlightened modernity's ideal of autonomy. The belief in absolute self-determination, whether that of Stephen Dedalus or Mr Ramsay, is always discovered to be dependent on the desires of others. Whereas a transcendent being could anchor desire as absolute, to express it in relation to others is always seen to produce delusion, deception, jealousy, a whole variety of epistemological crises which modernist texts offer. The possibility of art itself as an absolute autonomous realm, however, often comes to take the place of the sacred here. Art, as religion, seems to offer precisely that illusion of utter self-determination and transcendence which relations with other mortals must always shatter. It is interesting to note how many of the male heroes of modernist literature achieve an apparent self-determination in aesthetic terms through a refusal of social relationship. Hence the figure of the alienated artist who affirms his own autonomy, his independence from the mediation of others at the price of the cessation of human relationship and desire: Marcel writing in his room, Ralph Touchett vicariously living through Isabel, Malone talking to himself, Mann's Leverkühn, Hesse's Steppenwolf. Art as the impersonal focus for desire displaces the possibility of human relationship because it involves no mediation through the desire of the other. Hovering behind these texts is Nietzsche's self-creating and self-affirming artist for whom to recognize the other would be to fall into a slave mentality.

In my view it is the identification of self with an impossible ideal of autonomy which can be seen to produce the failure of love and relationship in so many texts by male modernist and postmodernist writers. Can one rethink the self outside of this concept without abandoning subjectivity to dispersal and language games? Not only do I believe that one can, I also believe that many feminist writers have done so. This is the really 'grand and totalizing' part of my argument. It seems to me that autonomy defined as transcendence, impersonality and absolute independence, whether an idealized goal or a nostalgic nihilism, whether informing the aesthetics of modernism or those of postmodernism, is not a mode with which most feminists, nor indeed, most women, can very easily identify. Feminist theory, though drawing on anti-humanist discourses to sharpen its understanding of social processes, has emphasized that 'impersonal' historical determinants are lived out through experience. This distance from anti-humanist discourse has allowed feminist academics to connect with grass-roots activists outside the academy. Their own historical experience has tended to develop in women strongly 'humanist' qualities in the broader sense of the term and feminism has always been rooted in women's subjective experience of the conflicting demands of home and work, family and domestic ties, and the wider society.

Psychoanalysis, gender and aesthetics

Jürgen Habermas has recently suggested that modernity is not exhausted, simply unfinished. His view of this is not incompatible with some of the ideas I am trying to develop here. What he has argued is that instead of abandoning its ideals we need to modify them by redefining the model of Reason which underlies them. His work is part of a tradition of critical thinking which sees Enlightenment reason failing because defined too narrowly in the terms of an instrumental, purposive, or utilitarian epistemology. He proposes instead a model of what he calls 'communicative reason', based on speech act theory and emphasizing not individual autonomy but intersubjectivity (1987). Like so many theorists within the postmodern debate, however, he seems singularly unaware of many of the developments in feminist thinking over the last twenty years. It seems to me that many feminists have been working for some time with models which are not fundamentally incompatible with that of Habermas whether or not they have used them in specifically theoretical ways. I will now examine some of these ideas and suggest that through them it is possible to arrive not only at an alternative definition of the aesthetic but also of subjectivity itself.

According to most psychoanalytic theories and their popularly disseminated forms, subjecthood is understood as the achievement of separation. Maturity is seen to be reached when the dependent infant comes to regard its primary caretaker (nearly always a woman) as simply an object through which it defines its own identity and position in the world. This is then maintained through the defensive patrolling of boundaries. Implicit in most theories of identity is the assumption that the 'otherness' analysed by feminists from de Beauvoir on, is the necessary condition of women – certainly as long as women mother. Separation and objectivity rather than relationship and connection become the markers of identity. Freudian theory has been used to support this view. Both the liberal self and the postmodern 'decentred subject' can be articulated through Freud's notion of the unconscious, dominated by instinctual and universal drives seeking impossible gratification. In the liberal version, ego as rationality can master the drives either intrapsychically or with the help of the silent, impersonal and objective analyst who will be uncontaminated by counter-transference. In the postmodern version, rationality breaks down and the anarchy of desire as impersonal and unconscious energy is unleashed either in the freeplay of the signifier of the avant-garde text or that of the marketplace of late capitalism. Freud's infant hovers behind both: an autoerotic isolate, inherently aggressive and competitive, its sexuality and identity oedipally resolved only by fear, seeking to discharge libidinal energy which is necessarily in conflict with 'rational' and 'enlightened' concern for others and for society as a whole.

Can we imagine alternative models of subjectivity? If knowledge is inextricably bound up with experience then it seems that we certainly can, for this is not a description of universal experience. In fact Freud himself hints at other possibilities in less familiar parts of his writings. In the paper 'On Narcissism' (1914), for example, he says, 'A strong egotism is a protection against falling ill, but in the last resort we must begin to love in order not to fall ill and we are bound to fall ill if in consequence of frustration, we are unable to love' (1957: 85). In fact, in the development of selfhood, the ability to conceive of oneself as separate from and mutually independent of the parent develops with the ability to accept one's dependency and to feel secure enough to relax the boundaries between self and other without feeling one's identity to be threatened. Why, then, is autonomy always emphasized as the goal of maturity? Why not emphasize equally the importance of maintaining connection and intersubjectivity? As Joan Riviere has argued, 'There is no such thing as a single human being pure and simple, unmixed with other human beings . . . we are members one of another' (1986). Parts of other people, the parts we have had relationships with, are parts of us, so the self is both constant and fluid, ever in exchange, ever redescribing itself through its encounters with others. It seems to be this recognition of mediation as that which renders total self-determination impossible which so many male modernist and postmodernist writers find unacceptable. Yet much women's, particularly feminist, writing has been different in that it has neither attempted to transcend relationship through the impersonal embrace of art as formal autonomy or sacred space, nor through rewriting its own apocalyptic sense of an ending.

Returning to psychoanalysis, however, one can see some of the reasons why the definition of subjectivity as transcendence and autonomy has been so powerful and why it has come to be seen not as a description of the experience of most white,

Western males, but of universal structures of subjectivity. In psychoanalytic terms, if subjectivity is defined as separateness, its acquisition will involve radical disidentification with women in a society where women are normally the exclusive caretakers of children. This will be true even for girls who, at the level of gender, will also seek to identify with the mother. Fathers are not perceived as threatening non-identity for in classical analysis they are seen as outside the pre-oedipal world of primary socialization with its intense ambivalences and powerful Imagos. They are from the start associated with the clear, rational world of work and secondary socialization. Object-relations theorists like Nancy Chodorow (1978) have pointed out that the desire for radical disidentification with the mother will be more acute for boys, for the perception of women-as-mothers will be bound up with pre-oedipal issues of mergence and potential loss of identity requiring a culturally reinforced masculine investment in denial and separation. The world of secondary socialization associated with the father comes to be seen as superior and as inherently male. Subjectivity thus comes to be seen as autonomy or as role-definition through work. Truth is defined as objectivity and transcendence. Science in the form of an instrumental technology will be overvalued and defined in terms of objectivity; philosophy comes to deal only with universal and metaphysical truths (whatever the theoretical challenges to these notions). Women (or the 'feminine') come to be identified in Cartesian or poststructuralist philosophy with all that cannot be rationally controlled and thus threaten dissolution or non-identity: mortality, the body, desire, emotionality, nature. Poststructuralist 'femininity' is simply another way of making actual femininity safe, of controlling through a process of naming which in poststructuralist fashion utterly prises the term away from the anatomical body of woman.

If the female sex thus represents, in Sartre's words 'the obscenity . . . of everything which gapes open' (1958), then men seem to be justified in their instrumental attitude to women and to everything, including nature, which has been 'feminized' and which must therefore be distanced, controlled, aestheticized, subdued; one might call this the Gilbert Osmond syndrome. Women appear threatening in this way because they carry the culture's more widespread fear of the loss of boundaries, of the uncontrollable, more threatening because unconsciously split off in order to retain the purity of a subjectivity, a human-ness defined as autonomy, pure reason and transcendence. Cartesian dualism thus persists along with strict empiricism in science and impersonality and formalism in literary theory and criticism.

If women's identity is broadly speaking, and allowing for a range of differences, experienced in terms which do not necessarily valorize separation at the expense of connection, one would expect some expression of this in fictional writing as well as in theory. Women's sense of ego is more likely, for psychological and cultural reasons, to consist of a more diffuse sense of the boundaries of self and their notion of identity understood in relational and intersubjective terms. Virginia Woolf has been so important for feminist literary criticism because both formally and thematically her work articulates a critique of patriarchal institutions through its exploration of the relatedness of subjects and of subjects and objects. Beyond this, however, she simultaneously offers a critique of the exclusive identification of women with relationality through an exploration of its negative effects in characters like Mrs Dalloway and Mrs Ramsay. For relationality as the basis of identity in a society where women are perceived as culturally inferior, has often functioned to reinforce their desire to please, to serve others and seek definition through them, masochistically internalizing any anger about this as a failure of 'essential' femininity. We are back, therefore, to the contradiction at the heart of feminism expressed at the beginning of this essay: that women have sought recognition for a concept of identity which they simultaneously attempt to change, viewing it as a construction of patriarchy. The formal and thematic expression of identity as mutually defined, the centrality of primary affectional relationships need not, however, be experienced in pathological ways, and indeed, as writers like Alice Walker, Doris Lessing and Toni Morrison have recently shown us, are essential for the survival of the human race. Freud emphasized that the development of the ego is the work of culture. If that culture's ideal of selfhood is that of an impersonal, contained rationality, then it seems to me that culture can only produce incomplete and divided human beings, postmodern beings.

Much feminist writing has, over the last thirty years, explored modes of relational identity, often, indeed, also drawing on postmodern ideas about 'situatedness' or using its techniques of parody, irony, playfulness. Such a relational understanding of identity makes possible, ethically and imaginatively, a new negative capability which can transform both the Enlightened discourses of emancipation as well as those of subjectivity. A writer whose work is particularly important in this respect, for example, is Doris Lessing. In her novel *Memoirs of a Survivor* (1976), she explores how utopian impulses fail because they are still tied to a model of human subjectivity based on autonomy, separateness and overvaluation of a particular definition of rationality. The narrator, struggling to preserve an order within her psyche which has disappeared from the world outside, finds herself drawn towards a perception of the fundamental inter-dependence of human beings, of the persistence in us of an elemental hunger, the need to be fed – the novel abounds with images of eating and orality – to give food and to receive it, which binds us physically and psychologically to one another. She reflects:

> As for our thoughts, our intellectual apparatus, our rational-isms and our deductions, our logics and so on, it can be said with absolute certainty that dogs and cats and monkeys cannot make a rocket or fly to the moon or weave artificial dress materials out of the by-products of petroleum, but as we sit in the ruins of this variety of intelligence it is hard to give it much value.
>
> (74)

The most frightening aspect of the 'now' of this novel is that its children of violence, the wild, anarchic, semi-humans born out of upheaval and brutality, out of the failures of over-rationalized logic and the denial of human relational need, can no longer recognize their own or other's needs, cannot nurture each other and have, literally, turned cannibal and are consuming each other. For Lessing, salvation can only come through a profound and full recognition of our relational being, which means trying to imagine a world not constructed as an extension of a model of self as isolated, competitive ego nor one where ethics is reduced to nihilistic performance. She may use the formal modes of postmodern art but to articulate an imaginative world which is very far from those which emerge in most postmodern theory. Lessing's novel is apocalyptic in the sense that it is set after a holocaust, but it does not proclaim either the end of modernity or the end of hope. We can compare this with, for example, Arthur Kroker's vision of postmodernity as a 'dead space which will be marked by increasing and random outbursts of political violence, schizoid behaviour and the implosion of all signs of communication, as Western culture runs down toward the brilliant illumination of a final burn out' (1988: xvii). If Lessing's 'small personal voice' is heard only as a whisper, it seems to me it can, drawing on postmodern *aesthetic* forms, speak to more people, women and men, but in ways which resist the theoretically ubiquitous postmodern Big-Bang.

References

Barth, John (1980). 'The Literature of Replenishment'. *The Atlantic*, 65–71.

Barthelme, Donald (1971). *City Life*. London, Jonathan Cape.

—— (1974). *Guilty Pleasures*. New York, Farrar, Straus & Giroux.

Baudrillard, Jean (1983). *Simulations*, trans. Paul Foss, Paul Patton and Philip Beitchman. New York, Semiotext(e).

Barthes, Roland (1977). *Roland Barthes by Roland Barthes*, trans. Richard Howard. New York, Farrar, Straus & Giroux.

Chodorow, Nancy (1978). *The Reproduction of Mothering: Psychoanalysis and the Sociology of Gender*. Berkeley and London, University of California Press.

Coover, Robert (1969). *Pricksongs and Descants*. New York, Dutton.

Eliot, George (1965). *Middlemarch*. Harmondsworth, Penguin.

Fiedler, Leslie (1975). 'Cross the Border – Close that Gap: Postmodernism', *Sphere History of Literature* 9, ed. Marcus Cunliffe. London, Sphere.

Freud, Sigmund (1957) 'On Narcissism: an Introduction', *S.E.* 14, ed. James Strachey. London.

Habermas, Jürgen (1985). 'Modernity – an Incomplete Project', in *Postmodern Culture*, ed. Hal Foster. London and Sydney, Pluto.

—— (1987). *The Philosophical Discourse of Modernity*, trans. F.G. Lawrence. Oxford, Polity.

Jameson, Fredric (1985). 'Postmodernism and Consumer Society', in the *Postmodern Culture*, ed. Hal Foster. London and Sydney, Pluto Press.

Jardine, Alice A. (1985). *Gynesis: Configurations of Women and Modernity*. Ithaca and London, Cornell University Press.

Kermode, Frank (1967). *The Sense of an Ending*. Oxford, Oxford University Press.

Kristeva, Julia (1982). 'Women's Time', *Feminist Theory: A Critique of Ideology*, ed. Nannerl O. Keohane et al. Brighton, Harvester.

Kroker, Arthur and Cook, David (1988). *The Postmodern Scene: Excremental Culture and Hyper-Aesthetics*. London, Macmillan.

Lessing, Doris (1976). *Memoirs of a Survivor*. London, Vintage.

Lyotard, Jean-François (1984). *The Postmodern Condition: A Report on Knowledge*, trans. Bennington and Massumi. Manchester, Manchester University Press.

Newman, Charles (1985). *The Postmodern Aura*. Evanston, Northwestern University Press.

Nietzsche, Friedrich (1990). *Twilight of the Idols / The Antichrist*, trans. R. J. Hollingdale. Harmondsworth, Penguin.

—— (1990). *My Sister and I*, trans. Oscar Levy. Los Angeles, Amok.

Pynchon, Thomas (1979) *V*. Harmondsworth, Penguin.

Riviere, Joan (1977). 'The Unconscious Phantasy of an Inner World Reflected in Examples from Literature', *New Directions in Psychoanalysis*, ed. Melanie Klein. London, Karnac Books & the Institute of Psychoanalysis.

Sartre, Jean-Paul (1958). *Being and Nothingness*, trans. H.E. Barnes. London, Methuen.

Sontag, Susan (1966). *Against Interpretation*. New York, Farrar, Straus & Giroux.

Gareth Watkins

10

Aesthetics, pleasure and value

Steven Connor

The various attempts through the nineteenth and twentieth centuries to construe the objective and universal conditions of aesthetic value always involve the difficult problem of pleasure. For Kant, if the aesthetic were to be characterized entirely and exclusively in terms of pleasure, then this would inevitably be to reduce it to a matter of purely private interest or indulgence. For aesthetic pleasure to be valuable, therefore, it must be disinterested, and consequently, universal pleasure; this is to say pleasure without individual profit, advantage or gratification. One contemporary current of antiKantian thought would view this account of aesthetic pleasure as a simple denial or abolition of sensual pleasure in favour of an aesthetic 'pleasure purified of pleasure', as Pierre Bourdieu puts it, that is no longer really pleasure at all (1984: 6). Another, perhaps more nuanced view is that suggested by Terry Eagleton (1990), who sees the emergence of the self-legitimating realm of the aesthetic after Kant as instructed by the political necessity of mediating experience and authority; the self-governing artefact, which blends together desire and law, sensuous pleasure and abstract structure, submits to no external principle of restraint or regulation, but is all the more effective for that as a model of the interiorization of authority in bourgeois society.

Eagleton suggests valuably the doubleness of autotelic aesthetic pleasure, the fact that it can represent a challenge to dominative and instrumentalist modes of thinking even as it brings about a soothing and reactionary resolution of political tensions and problems. In holding to this duality, Eagleton's work is unusual. Accounts of the issue of pleasure in nineteenth-

and twentieth-century aesthetic theory tend to be more strictly bifurcated, between the disapproval of pleasure on the one hand and the assertion that pleasure is all on the other. This bifurcation is related to a more fundamental division regarding the relation of pleasure and value: the division between a hedonist or utilitarian view that, in the end, every form of value must be grounded in and reflect human needs and desires (which is to say, must give pleasure), and the moralist view that, even though pleasure can or should conduce to or be brought to coincide with moral or ethical value, the pleasure attaching to an object or behaviour can never of itself constitute that value. Put simply, for the hedonist, pleasure and value are identical; for the moralist, they are distinct. Where the moralist will characteristically attempt to measure the value of pleasure by exchanging it for some other currency, such as 'good' or 'justice', the hedonist takes pleasure to be the very medium of exchange, as it were, the money form of value; the moralist aims to convert pleasure into value, the hedonist to convert all value back into pleasure.

Most attempts in this century to account for aesthetic pleasure adopt one or other of these alternatives, arguing either the moralist position that pleasure and value are distinct, or the hedonist position that they are identical. But this binarity constitutes a ruthless logical shrinkage. In most cases, the very enquiry into the relationship of pleasure and value induces splittings, displacements and reformulations in the respective meanings of these terms; such that, for example, attempts to distinguish value from pleasure tend to end up generating a distinction between fundamentally different forms of pleasure, while attempts to identify value and pleasure may depend on a similar distinction between different forms of value in pleasure. In most cases, too, the move to concentrate, generalize and hypostatize the alternatives of value and pleasure will be undercut by the very mobility of the terms as employed in the argument. Nowhere is this more the case than in political versions of aesthetic theory, which bring about a particularly intense conjunction of questions of pleasure with questions of value; and, as a consequence, nowhere is it more important to resist the reductive binarity of pleasure or value.

Sublimation: value against pleasure

Most people would agree, wrote Roger Fry confidently in 1909,

'that the pleasures derived from art were of an altogether different character and more fundamental than merely sensual pleasure' (1982: 81). The separation of different forms of pleasure
effected here is in fact the commonest form in which pleasure is
distinguished from value. According to this view, pleasure can
only be valuable, or lead to value as a result of being concentrated, purified, sublimated or otherwise transformed from itself.

It might seem odd to associate I. A. Richards with this separation of pleasure and value, since, in his *Principles of Literary
Criticism* (1924), he argues against the aestheticist view, held by
Fry and others, that the experience of art is utterly *sui generis* and
distinct from any other kind of experience. Arguing, as he does,
for the identity of pleasure and value – 'anything is valuable
which will satisfy an appetency without involving the frustration
of some equal or *more important* appetency' – Richards is therefore
opposed to any objectification or universalization of principles of
value, the consequence of this view being 'that morals become
purely prudential, and ethical codes merely the expression of the
most general scheme of expediency to which an individual or a
race has attained' (1983: 36). So Richards identifies value, not
with individual desires which are to be satisfied at the expense of
others, but with the systems by which competing desires are balanced, coordinated and organized to yield the most productive
results, which is to say, the most satisfaction. The work of art is
life-giving and valuable insofar as it produces such states of 'intricately wrought composure' and the 'equilibrium of opposed impulses' (1983: 197). Literature and the arts are justified on these
economic grounds, as the organizing of tensions and the maintaining of civilization, which Richards glosses as 'free, varied and
unwasteful life' (1983: 43).

But if Richards's argument suggests an unbroken continuum
between disorganized and organized pleasure (or value), it also
tends to concentrate dualistically on the two extremes of that continuum, producing in effect a sharp division between pleasure
and value. Bad art, says Richards, is characterized by its tendency
to provide instant gratification and to encourage fixation upon
stock responses and received ideas, rather than to encourage the
ironic, impersonal play of judgement. In the way of such arguments, Richards's relative scale of evaluation for good and bad art
quickly turns into a way of distinguishing art from non-art; this
latter is identified paranoically in the forms of mass-culture and
especially the cinema. The distinctions between immediacy and

complexity, childishness and maturity, and culture and art, all enforce an absolute distinction between pleasure and value:

> At present bad literature, bad art, the cinema, etc. are an influence of the first importance in fixing immature and actually inapplicable attitudes to most things. . . . The losses incurred by these artificial fixations of attitude are evident. Through them the average adult is worse, not better adjusted to the possibilities of his existence than the child.
>
> (1983: 159)

When adapted to the purposes of the New Criticism, the model of value that Richards here proposes will have hardened into a critical technology of tensions, ambiguities and resolutions, having apparently purged itself of the rather awkward questions of affectivity and response that here bulk so large. But, awkward as it is, the synthesis that Richards offers between the aesthetic, the subjective and the social is revealing. For it is plain that his stress on the ironic equilibrium of contending forces provides a model not only of the well-adjusted person, but also of the well-balanced liberal state. But it is equally plain that the model is also contradicted by the implicit social divide between those who have access to the affective complexity of the cultured classes and those who are abandoned to the cretinous gratifications of mass culture. There seems to be no way of effecting an aesthetic resolution of the contradiction between different forms of aesthetic response, of imagining a socio-cultural coordination of those who are coordinated and those who are not. By allowing pleasure to precipitate into brutish gratification and determining value as the transcendence of such gratification, Richards's model here settles into the kind of fixation that it condemns.

Richards's argument has proved adaptable to many forms of twentieth-century aesthetic and cultural theory. An essay by Leonard B. Meyer from 1959, entitled 'Some Remarks on Value and Greatness in Music', shows just how easily this account of pleasure, along with its neurotic politics, can be transferred to another cultural realm. Here, as in Richards, the establishment of a criterion of aesthetic value depends upon a differentiation of pleasures that hardens into a duality between pleasure and value. Meyer distinguishes the pleasure experienced in listening to 'primitive' music (by which he means, mostly, not non-Western native music but pop music), which 'operates with such conventional clichés that gratification is almost immediate', and the more complex pleasure offered by sophisticated music (by which he means classical music and modern jazz), which 'consists in the willingness to forgo immediate, and perhaps lesser gratification, for the sake of future ultimate gratification' (1980: 277). Where primitive listeners must be content with 'sensuous-associative pleasure', sophisticated listeners, who are able to tolerate the uncertainties and formal resistances proposed by musical works, harvest the rewards of 'syntactical-associative' pleasure. Like Richards, Meyer seems to acknowledge that both of these are indeed forms of pleasure and, as such, are both valuable (though to different degrees). Nevertheless, Meyer surrenders progressively to the urge to reify and, more importantly, to personify the extremes of aesthetic response. It never occurs to him, for example, to wonder whether the listener to primitive music must always and necessarily be a 'primitive listener'. This produces something like an absolute distinction between, on the one hand, the primitive or mass-cultural response, which leads to 'the degradation and dissolution of the self' in its merging, violent and inert at once, with 'the primordial impulses of the group which, as Freud has pointed out, "cannot tolerate any delay between its desires and the fulfillment of what it desires"', and, on the other hand, that mature, civilized self, which has achieved individuation through its assimilation and tempering of opposed impulses and resistances to gratification (Meyer 1980: 283). The cultured adult knows what the tantrum-prone consumer of mass culture does not – that you can't have your pudding before you've eaten your greens.

Meyer's moral-political split between mass and individual pleasures seems to derive quite closely from Richards. For Richards, too, mass culture is life-denying because its instantaneous gratifications, its immediate discharges of unpleasurable tension, seem to produce a kind of entropy, a running down towards death. High culture is life-affirming, on the other hand, because the forms of equilibrium it achieves take longer, and involve more delay and resistance. For Theodor Adorno and Max Horkheimer, pleasure is also associated unequivocally with the deathliness of mass culture, or, as they gloss it repeatedly, the 'pleasure industry'. Their *Dialectic of Enlightenment* (1944) presents the pleasures of popular music, of the radio and that 'bloated pleasure apparatus', the cinema, as simply the extension of the rhythms and structures of work, for both work and popular culture consist of nothing more than 'the automatic succession of standardized operations' (Adorno and Horkheimer 1986: 137). Like Richards, Adorno and Horkheimer inherit from Freud a notion of pleasure which is related closely to the idea of resistance. The mass pleasure induced by the culture industry 'hardens into boredom because, if it is to remain pleasure, it must not demand any effort and therefore moves rigorously in the worn grooves of association' (Adorno and Horkheimer 1986: 137). The terms of this metaphor are striking. Mass pleasure is both soft and hard: soft, because it involves no resistance from the reality principle, no effort of self-distantiation, so that even the grooves it runs along are softened and worn; hard, precisely because, encountering no resistance on its path, pleasure is set into fixed and invariable patterns. A similar idea recurs a little later on when Adorno and Horkheimer are discussing the omnipresence of laughter in mass culture as 'the instrument of the fraud practised on happiness' (1986: 140). Where Bergson had conceived of laughter as life bursting through the rigid carapace of the inorganic or the mechanical, Adorno and Horkheimer see the laughter induced by the culture industry as an 'invading barbaric life, self-assertion prepared to parade its liberation from every scruple' (1986: 141). Meeting no resistance from anything, the 'life which . . . breaks through the barrier' (1986: 141) here is inhumanly liberated from any constraint, a pure and unopposable gratification which therefore hardens into a kind of mechanization or barrier to flexible response.

For Adorno and Horkheimer, mass pleasure displays a strange blending of vigour and inertness. For mass pleasure is a peculiarly exacting sort of dissipation, an absolute relaxation of attention which, because it is routinized and disciplinary, actually requires a continued effort of attention. Distraction becomes exertion in the watching of cartoon films in which

> nothing that the experts have devised as a stimulant must escape the weary eye; no stupidity is allowed in the face of all the trickery; one has to follow everything and even display the smart responses shown and recommended in the film.
>
> (Adorno and Horkheimer 1986: 139)

There are two alternatives to this regularized distraction. One is the 'pure nonsense' of popular art, of clowning, farce and the circus, whose traces are to be seen in Charlie Chaplin and the Marx Brothers (Adorno and Horkheimer 1986: 137), and the other is the authentic work of art. Adorno and Horkheimer follow a dominant tradition in setting the sublimated pleasures of art against the unsublimated pleasures of the popular. But the sublimation they imagine is of an extreme kind. In the model employed by Richards, the negativity of art, its more or less complex deferral of pleasure, is in the interests of a higher pleasure, a more abundant form of satisfaction in the long run. For Adorno and Horkheimer, the value of the aesthetic lies precisely in its refusal or permanent deferral of pleasure and its stimulation of suspicion as to every form of gratification: 'The secret of aesthetic sublimation is its representation of fulfillment as a broken promise' (1986: 140). But there turns out to be no absolute distinction between authentic art and mass culture here, because, by refusing to gratify desire, authentic art draws attention to that failure of gratification which in fact also characterizes mass culture. Like most severe moralists of pleasure, Adorno and Horkheimer see the lower pleasures as both dangerously intense and indifferently vacuous; the unsublimated or desublimated energies of mass pleasure are in fact insubstantial and unsatisfying:

> The culture industry perpetually cheats its consumers of what it perpetually promises. The promissory note which, with its plots and staging, it draws on pleasure is endlessly prolonged; the promise which is actually all the spectacle consists of, is illusory: all it actually confirms is that the real point will never be reached, that the diner must be satisfied with the menu.
>
> (1986: 139)

Strikingly, then, art and mass culture are here distinguished not in terms of value as opposed to pleasure, or even as sublimated pleasure as opposed to brute gratification, but in terms of a higher as opposed to a lower form of frustration. This goes further than most in the imposition of a split between pleasure and value, suggesting that under the debased conditions of modern capitalism, value inheres only in the more or less intense refusal or negation of pleasure. Where mass culture produces a state of addiction, a desire for more and more of the pleasure that brings no satisfaction, authentic art provides a higher form of disappointment altogether, which points to the emptiness of all corrupted pleasures. Though the negations of authentic art allow the reconstitution of a certain masochistic pleasure in the severe rapture of the mystic ('Delight is austere:

res severa verum gaudium' write Adorno and Horkheimer [1986: 141]), their real value lies in their very refusal of the possibility of pleasure; for it is the very absoluteness of this absolute refusal which opens up a chink of utopian possibility, the purely negative hope of a transcendence in the form of a happiness in which desire and gratification would no longer be alienated.

The suspicion of pleasure and the segregation of pleasure from value which are to be found in Richards, Adorno and Horkheimer undergo some interesting mutations in some more recent critical accounts. Laura Mulvey has perhaps been the most radical antagonist of pleasure in recent years. In her influential 'Visual Pleasure and Narrative Cinema', Mulvey argues that it is the job of theory and feminist theory in particular to resist the 'skilled and satisfying manipulation of visual pleasure' in Hollywood cinema. For that visual pleasure is primarily the pleasure of the male viewer, or the female viewer constituted as the male viewer, and the object of that pleasure (and so its objectified victim) is primarily the woman. Most of the work that has flowed from this article has emphasized the structure of power relations between the male gaze and the female object of that gaze; but the force of Mulvey's argument lies in her rejection of the pleasure involved in this relation:

> It is said that analysing pleasure, or beauty, destroys it. That is the intention of this article. The satisfaction and reinforcement of the ego that represent the high point of film history must be attacked. Not in favour of a reconstructed new pleasure, which cannot exist in the abstract, nor of intellectualised unpleasure, but to make for a total negation of the ease and plenitude of the narrative fiction film.
>
> (1975: 87)

But the austere call for a 'total negation' of pleasure is instantly qualified by an assertion of the value of such a negation in terms of a distinctly pleasurable transgression. 'The alternative', writes Mulvey, 'is the thrill that comes from leaving the past behind without rejecting it, transcending outworn or oppressive forms, or daring to break with normal pleasurable expectations in order to conceive a new language of desire' (1975: 87). So what is being abandoned here is not pleasure *per se*, but a certain assimilative model of pleasure, pleasure as the profit of the ego. The affective language switches from terms that suggest inertia to terms suggesting dynamism, from 'ease' and 'plenitude' to 'thrill' and 'daring', in a way that appears to reinstate something like the vitalism of Richards's model, where the rejection of pleasure in the interests of value or ethics becomes a promotion of certain ethical pleasures which promise life rather than death, novelty rather than the recursion to the same and risk to the self rather than its reinforcement.

Desublimation: pleasure against value

This reconfiguration of pleasure is to be found elsewhere in contemporary theory, and perhaps most notably and in-fluentially in Jacques Lacan's promotion of the principle of *jouissance*. Lacan reacts against the Freudian pleasure principle on the grounds of its conservatism and homeostatic inertia, and finds a true 'beyond' of the pleasure principle not in death (for the drive of pleasure to keep the level of tension in the organism as low as possible is itself a kind of death instinct) but in *jouissance* or desire, which tends insatiably towards unattainable limits:

> Pleasure limits the scope of human possibility – the pleasure principle is a principle of homeostasis. Desire on the other hand finds its boundary, its strict relation, its limit, and it is in relation to this limit that it is sustained as such, crossing the threshold imposed by the pleasure principle.
>
> (1979: 31)

Lacan's distinction between pleasure and *jouissance* is taken over and given a particularly aesthetic resonance in Roland Barthes' *The Pleasure of the Text*. Barthes suggests, like Lacan, that there are in fact two kinds of pleasure and two kinds of text to go with them, the text of pleasure and the text of bliss. Plainly, the text of pleasure is rooted in the conservative, homeostatic pleasure principle as defined by Lacan, for it is 'the text that contents, fills, grants euphoria; the text that comes from culture and does not break with it, is linked to a comfortable practice of reading'. The text of bliss (Barthes uses the same word *jouissance* in the original) is 'the text that imposes a state of loss, the text that discomforts (perhaps to the point of a certain boredom), unsettles the reader's historical, cultural, psychological assumptions, the consistency of his tastes, values, memories, brings to a crisis his relation with language' (Barthes 1990: 14). Like Lacan's *jouissance*, Barthes' text of bliss is orientated towards extremity rather than contain-ment, but it is a paradoxical, nonteleological extremity, an extremity of nonfinality. As opposed to the centred, genital finality of texts governed by the pleasure principle and the sense of an ending, the text of bliss perversely resists or turns aside from centred pleasure. But this is not enough; for Barthes, even perversion can settle into a ploddingly predictable curriculum of pleasures, and so the text of bliss must be polymorphously, unpredictably, *perversely* perverse:

> . . . such texts are perverse in that they are outside any imaginable finality – *even that of pleasure* (bliss does not constrain to pleasure: it can even apparently inflict boredom). No alibi stands up, nothing is reconstituted, nothing recuperated. The text of bliss is absolutely intransitive. However perversion does not suffice to define bliss; it is the extreme of perversion which defines it: an extreme constantly shifted, an empty, mobile, unpredictable extreme. The extreme guarantees bliss: an average perversion quickly loads itself up with a play of subordinate finalities: prestige, ostentation, rivalry, lecturing, self-serving, etc.
>
> (Barthes 1990: 51–2)

Obviously, this is a claim for the absolute value of bliss over mere pleasure. The problem with all such assertions of absolute value, of course, is that they continuously require the structures of exchange they attempt to transcend; the demonstration of their absolute status requires paradoxically that they be estimated relative to other forms of profit or advantageous outcome. This is true even and especially of Barthes' own text, which constitutes such a relative evaluation in the very fact of offering a theory or thesis about the bliss that is unrecuperable for the pleasurable coherence of theory. This theory must therefore repudiate its own status as theory, remaining content merely to gesture at its own unsatisfactoriness (its failure to give pleasure) in this respect: 'No "thesis" on the pleasure of the text is possible; barely an inspection (an introspection) that falls short' (Barthes 1990: 34). In order to promote or make visible the absolute value of the text of bliss, it is better to resist assigning it any value in particular, 'better to renounce the passage from *value*, the basis of the assertion, to *values*, which are the effects of culture' (Barthes 1990: 34). And this means in turn that, in order to preserve the exchange value of his own demonstration of the value of bliss, Barthes must withhold it from exchange, refusing to allow it the standing of a model or exemplar.

Thus, as in the more austere account of valuable pleasure offered by Adorno and Horkheimer, the extreme pleasure offered by bliss can take the form of a frustration of pleasure, of the closed, homeostatic gratifications to which the ego is so addicted. This is a version of the aesthetics of the sublime as they are to be found in Kant, especially as interpreted recently by Jean-François Lyotard. The pleasure of the sublime is an anxious mingling of pleasure and unpleasure, a thrilling apprehension of some awesome largeness or grandeur which nevertheless frustrates all our attempts to conceive it, to draw it together in the form of a concept. Kant distinguishes between an aesthetic of beauty and an aesthetic of the sublime in terms of the different kinds of pleasure they invoke, the one a pleasure of conformity between the stimulus and human capacities, the other an anxious pleasure in the disruption of that conformity:

> Whereas natural beauty . . . conveys a finality in its form making the object appear, as it were preadapted to our power of judgement . . . that which . . . excites the feelings of the sublime, may appear, indeed, in point of form to contravene the ends of our power of judgement, to be ill-adapted to our faculty of presentation, and to be, as it were, an outrage on the imagination.
>
> (1952: 91)

This is why, for Lyotard, the postmodern aesthetics of the sublime are to be distinguished in a certain refusal of simply ego-based pleasure, the 'solace of good forms, the consensus of a taste which would make it possible to share collectively the nostalgia for the unattainable' (1984: 81), and why, indeed, the sublime might just as well be thought of in terms of melancholy and despair rather than in terms of pleasure: for Kant and Burke, Lyotard points out,

> sorrow (*der Kummer*) also counts among the 'vigorous emotions,' if it is grounded in moral Ideas. The despair of never being able to present something within reality on the scale of the Idea then overrides the joy of being nonetheless called upon to do so.
>
> (1988: 179)

The sublime in this account is always liminal, neither entirely above nor entirely below the threshold of human capacities. Indeed, the word 'sublime' illustrates in its history the crossing of the threshold it designates; the word sublime derives apparently from Latin *sublimis*, that is, *sub*, 'up to' and *limen*, 'the lintel'. The notion, perhaps originally architectural, that height may be measured in terms of an approach or approximation to a boundary, the point of division between upper and lower, becomes simplified in the use of 'sublime' to mean simply high or elevated. Usage therefore pushes the idea of going *up to* the lintel over the edge into pure transcendence, so that 'the sublime' comes to mean that which goes beyond the threshold. But for Burke, Kant and, recently, for Lyotard, the sublime always opens up or inhabits a gap between experience on the one hand and consciousness/conceptuality on the other. The sublime names neither the experience, lying *above* or *beyond* the capacities of the mind, nor the conceptualization, lying *beneath* the intensities of the experience, but the (incomplete) relation and movement between them. It is therefore not surprising that the Latin *root sublimis* also puts forth in 1824 the word 'subliminal' to represent psychological states or sensations which are *below* the threshold of conscious experience. (The *OED* gives J.G. Herbart's *Psychologie als Wissenschaft* as the first appearance of this word to denote that which remains 'unter der Schwelle des Bewußtseins'.) Here the idea of ultimate pleasure as an impingement upon a limit and the idea of ultimate pleasure as a transgression of that limit combine and alternate. The effort to imagine this ultimate pleasure is an anxiety of loss (the desolate *fort* of Freud's *fort/da* game) which can always yield pleasure in being mastered or bound by the concept of the sublime itself, a concept which simultaneously lets itself go into otherness and, in naming that process, gathers itself back to itself.

This is why Barthes' bliss is not simply a heightened pleasure. Bliss does not lie beyond the pleasure principle, but, as it were, on the very boundary between the pleasure principle and its beyond. In *The Pleasure of the Text*, bliss is promoted, not so much as the pure value of a transcendence of mere pleasure, but as the state between pleasure and its transcendence (in anxiety or death), between the consolidation of the ego and its dissolution:

> Whence, perhaps, a means of evaluating the works of our modernity: their value would proceed from their duplicity. By which it must be understood that they always have two edges. The subversive edge may seem privileged because it is the edge of violence; but it is not violence which affects

pleasure, nor is it destruction which interests it; what pleasure wants is the site of a loss, the seam, the cut, the deflation, the dissolve which seizes the subject in the midst of bliss. Culture thus recurs as an edge: in no matter what form.

(Barthes 1990: 7)

Whether applauded or decried, as liberating or repressive desublimation, Barthes' *Pleasure of the Text* is usually taken to be a hedonist text, a text which identifies value with pleasure rather than separating them. Oddly, despite the structure of the sublime that is enacted in the text, Barthes' hedonism may be said to be desublimating in effect; that is to say, it resists the attempt to elevate, educate or otherwise transform pleasure into value, in the manner specified in Freud's account of sublimation. In this, it joins with some other influential writing, including that of Pierre Bourdieu and Jean-François Lyotard, in the effort to oppose sublimation, whether in culture generally or in cultural theory, and to affirm the value of unsublimated pleasures. This effort is nowhere more visible than in the study of popular culture, where the influence of the rather aristocratic writing of Barthes has been if anything stronger than in the cultural mainstream from which his work emanates. Cultural studies have tended to take the negative definitions of mass culture offered by modernism and reverse its valencies; if mass culture is characterized by the formless intensities of its pleasures, an unmasterable energy of particularity which refuses the centring, channelling force of sublimation, then this may be affirmed as its value. Such accounts may draw energy equally from Mikhail Bakhtin's idea of carnival, in which categories slide, high and low interchange, energy overflows structure and desire masters law. In its opposition to theory, to the capturing force of conceptuality, and, above all, in the fact that it constitutes, not an inversion, the world turned merely upside down, but a topographic disruption, a dissolution of the threshold between high and low, Bakhtin's carnival is surely a kind of 'sublimity from below', and therefore potentially a populist, democratic version of the textual erotics evoked by Barthes.

Accounts of the value of such 'sublimity from below', must struggle with the same problem that Barthes does. This is the problem of maintaining the force of pleasure's pure unruliness without either abstracting it into a principle or, on the other hand, surrendering its political value as exemplary resistance. To maintain its pure value, in other words, pleasure must be kept separate from value; hedonism must protect itself from becoming a moralism.

Fredric Jameson confronts just this problem in his discusssion of Barthes' *The Pleasure of the Text* in 'Pleasure: A Political Issue' (1983). Jameson characteristically attempts to hold together without prematurely resolving the two terms of the antinomy set up by Barthes' essay, the hedonism of *jouissance* – 'the consent of life in the body' – with the moralism of political commitment – 'that very different relationship between myself or my body and other people – or in other words, with History, with the political in the stricter sense' (1983: 10, 11). The resolution of this antinomy is in terms of Jameson's argument in *The Political Unconscious* (1981), that a purely sensuous pleasure, a pleasure of extreme and autonomous physicality, is always political, even and especially in its apparent refusal or liquidation of the political realm. It is for this reason that Jameson can perceive that

> the immense merit of Barthes' essay is to restore a certain politically symbolic value to the experience of jouissance, and to make it impossible to read the latter except as a response to a political and historical dilemma, whatever position one chooses (puritanism/hedonism) to take about that response itself.
>
> (1983: 9)

If Barthes' pure pleasure is alienated from the political world, then that alienation must be read symptomatically, as a critical gesture pointing away from itself and back to the very political dimension that is absent from it.

Jameson achieves this conciliation of pleasure and the political via a characterization of Barthes' pleasure as sublime, not in the Kantian sense, but in the sense of the term offered by Edmund Burke's *Philosophical Inquiry into the Origins of Our Ideas of the Sublime and the Beautiful*. Jameson argues that the particular mixture of pleasure and unpleasure, rapture and fear, which constitute the experience of the sublime for Burke is founded on 'the apprehension through a given aesthetic object of what in its awesome magnitude shrinks, threatens, diminishes, rebukes individual human life' (1983: 12). If the threatened object is the individual body for Burke, it is the fragile bourgeois ego for Barthes. In both cases, the fear is provoked by a sense of what lies beyond, what painfully transcends the capacities of the human. As we have seen, this last crucially includes the capacity to *represent* the experience of the sublime. For this reason, Jameson calls the experience of the sublime an 'allegorical' one, in that the sublime as represented must always point beyond itself to some absent never-to-be-named referent, that 'sheer unfigurable force itself, sheer power . . . [which] stuns the imagination in the most literal sense' (1983: 12–13). But Jameson is perfectly confident that he can give a name to that repressed referent of Barthesian pleasure. Here it is:

> The immense culture of the simulacrum whose experience, whether we like it or not, constitutes a whole series of daily ecstasies and punctual fits of *jouissance* or schizophrenic dissolutions . . . may appropriately, one would think, be interpreted as so many unconscious points of contact with that equally unfigurable and unimaginable thing, the multinational apparatus, the great suprapersonal *system* of a late capitalist 'technology'.
>
> (Jameson 1983: 13)

So if the missing referent of the Burkean sublime is 'God', the missing referent or political unconscious of Barthesian pleasure is late capitalism. But there is something very odd here. For Jameson is designating as allegorical an experience which is the very frustration or untenability of allegory – that is, if we take allegory in the traditional sense of an embodiment of hidden rather than inaccessible meaning, of reference deferred rather than simply denied. Even if it is true that the sublime can never in fact achieve the immaculately self-refuting status that it seems to claim, in that it must always in some wise make representable and conceivable what it suggests is beyond the power of human beings to represent and conceive, nevertheless, the sublime can only be allegorical in a very specialized sense, as the allegory of the nonallegoricality of its experience, as the very figure of nonfigurability. Indeed, Jameson's identification of late capitalism as the missing referent of Barthesian pleasure is itself really only a repetition or *mis en abîme* of the problematic of the sublime, since the figured object here functions in a sense as a kind of unfigurablity, as a thing that can no longer be easily conceived or constituted as an object by theory. Nevertheless, by insisting that what assails the defenceless ego in the experience of the sublime is something hidden or repressed, rather than something permanently unnamable and unrepresentable, Jameson is in fact maintaining the dominion of the pleasure principle in the narrow sense decried by Barthes, that principle that gathers in and puts to its own service the experience of self-abandonment or dissolution. Jameson is completing the circuit of the *fort:da* of the pleasure principle, reclaiming for the pleasure of theory the unpleasure of bliss.

Where others might wish to maintain the sublime resistance to the sublimation of pleasure on its own terms, either by the hypertheorization of pleasure evidenced in Barthes' *Pleasure of the Text*, or by a kind of cultivated and strategic empiricism, a refusal to allow the unlegislatable energy and particularity of pleasure to be swallowed up by political theory and strategy, Jameson attempts the virtuoso feat of sublimating the very desublimating energy of pleasure, deriving a political value from its very refusal of sublimated value:

> . . . the thematizing of a particular 'pleasure' as a political issue . . . must always involve a dual focus, in which the local issue is meaningful and desirable in and of itself, but is also at one and the same time taken as the figure for Utopia in general, and for the systemic revolutionary transformation of society as a whole.
>
> (1983: 13)

This is an impossible and self-contradictory project in precisely the same way as Barthes' theoretical refusal to totalize pleasure in theory; for, in both cases, the hedonist and the moralist positions imply and inhabit each other. To assert the value of pleasure in itself, which seems the only way in which it can be rescued from the false sublimation of bourgeois aesthetics, is always to moralize, to make a principle of its unprincipled refusal of sublimation. The hedonist position that pleasure is value always becomes a version of the moralist position that pleasure only conceals, implies or figures a value, which must, by some exterior or supplementary operation of theory, be spelled out of it. It might seem as though things were simpler for the moralist critic of pleasure, as Jameson is in the end. But such a critic must always encounter sooner or later the objection of the hedonist that abstract systems of moral value can apparently always be desublimated, which is to say unmasked as forms of pleasure or gratification, as in the critique of a Freud or a Bourdieu.

These contradictions work against every attempt to hypostatize pleasure, whether in the good form of pleasure valued positively by the hedonist, or the bad form of pleasure suspected and rejected by the moralist. Pleasure resists this hypostatization, refusing to lie unambiguously either on the side of value or against value. A politics of pleasure must accordingly resist both the hedonist and the moralist temptations insofar as they rely on or tend towards notions of 'pure' (unsublimated) pleasure and 'pure' (sublimated) value. This will involve paying close attention to the complex instabilities of pleasure, aesthetic and otherwise, and the complex exchanges between pleasure and value. More than this, a politics of pleasure must also aim to participate in this dynamic process whereby pleasure and value endlessly produce and reproduce each other. The experience of pleasure in art and culture may be a useful place to start, not because art and culture offer access to any kind of pure or disinterested pleasure, but precisely because of the uncertain and impure nature of pleasure in these areas, poised between the interested and the disinterested, between use value and exchange value, between homeostatic ego-gratification and the indefiniteness of sublime pleasure. If the aesthetic has hitherto been constituted as a conceptual mechanism for separating pleasure and value out from each other, and for fixing their differential values, then it is conceivable that the aesthetic, in the enlarged form of a politics of culture, may yet become a realm in which the pleasurable renegotiation of the political value of pleasure may take place.

References

Adorno, Theodor and Horkheimer, Max. (1986). *Dialectic of Enlightenment*, trans. John Cumming. London, Verso.

Barthes, Roland. (1990). *The Pleasure of the Text*, trans. Richard Miller. Oxford, Basil Blackwell.

Bourdieu, Pierre. (1984). *Distinction: A Social Critique of the Judgement of Taste* (1979), trans. Richard Nice. London, Routledge and Kegan Paul.

Eagleton, Terry. (1990). *The Ideology of the Aesthetic*. Oxford, Basil Blackwell.

Fry, Roger. (1982). 'An Essay in Aesthetics', in Frascina, Francis and Harrison, Charles (eds) *Modern Art and Modernism: A Critical Anthology*. London, Harper and Row.

Jameson, Fredric. (1981). *The Political Unconscious: Narrative as a Socially Symbolic Act*. London and New York, Methuen.

—— (1983). 'Pleasure: A Political Issue', in Tony Bennett *et al.*, *Formations of Pleasure*. London, Routledge and Kegan Paul.

Kant, Immanuel. (1952). *The Critique of Judgement*, trans. James Creed Meredith. Oxford, Clarendon Press.

Lacan, Jacques. (1979). 'On the Subject of Certainty', *The Four Fundamental Concepts of Psycho-Analysis*, trans. Alan Sheridan. Harmondsworth, Penguin.

Lyotard, Jean-François. (1984). 'Answering the Question: What is Postmodernism?' in *The Postmodern Condition: A Report on Knowledge*, trans. Geoff Bennington and Brian Massumi. Manchester, Manchester University Press.

—— (1988). *The Differend: Phrases in Dispute*, trans. Georges Van Den Abbeele. Manchester, Manchester University Press.

Meyer, Leonard B. (1980). 'Some Remarks on Value and Greatness in Music', in Philipson, Morris and Gudel, Paul J. (eds) *Aesthetics Today*. New York and Scarborough, Ont., Meridian.

Mulvey, Laura. (1975). 'Visual Pleasure and Narrative Cinema', *Screen*, 16.

Richards, I.A. (1983). *Principles of Literary Criticism*. London, Routledge and Kegan Paul.

Index